Music Education for the New Millennium

Theory and Practice Futures for Music Teaching and Learning

Edited by
David K. Lines

First published as a special issue of *Educational Philosophy and Theory*, 2005, except for 'Improvisation and Cultural Work in Music and Music Education.'

BLACKWELL PUBLISHING
350 Main Street, Malden, MA 02148-5020, USA
9600 Garsington Road, Oxford OX4 2DQ, UK
550 Swanston Street, Carlton, Victoria 3053, Australia

First published 2005 by Blackwell Publishing Ltd

Library of Congress Cataloging-in-Publication Data has been applied for

ISBN 1-4051-3658-8 (paperback)

A catalogue record for this title is available from the British Library.

Set by Graphicraft Limited, Hong Kong
Printed in India
By Replika Press Pvt, Kundli

The Publisher's policy is to use permanent paper from mills that operate a sustainable forestry policy, and which has been manufactured from pulp processed using acid-free and elementary chlorine-free practices. Furthermore, the publisher ensures that the text paper and cover board used have met acceptable environmental accreditation standards.

For further information on Blackwell Publishing, visit our website:
www.blackwellpublishing.com

Contents

Notes on Contributors

Wayne Bowman is Professor of Music and Music Education at Brandon University, in Manitoba, Canada. Author of numerous journal articles, book chapters, and of the book *Philosophical Perspectives on Music* (Oxford University Press, 1998), his primary areas of scholarly interest coalesce around theories and philosophical problems in music and music education.

Robert A. Davis is Head of Department of Religious Education in the University of Glasgow. As well as teaching across a broad range of courses in teacher education, he has published widely in areas such as literature and religion, the cultural history of childhood and issues in Citizenship Education. He is currently examining the place of myth in contemporary arts education.

David J. Elliott is Professor of Music and Director of Music Education at New York University. He is the author of *Music Matters: A new philosophy of music education* (Oxford University Press, 1995). He is also an award-winning composer.

Lucy Green is Reader of Music Education at the Institute of Education, London University, UK. She is the author of *Music on Deaf Ears: Musical meaning, ideology and education* (Manchester University Press, 1988), *Music, Gender, Education* (Cambridge University Press, 1997), *and How Popular Musicians Learn: A way ahead for music education* (Ashgate Press, 2001). She has lectured in Europe, the Americas and Asia, and contributed articles on music education and the sociology of music to a number of journals and books. Her current research is on the incorporation of informal popular music learning practices into school classrooms.

Constantijn Koopman is a postdoctoral researcher and teacher at the Radboud University of Nijmegen and the Royal Conservatory of The Hague. His main research interests include philosophy of music, philosophy of music education, aesthetic education, and spiritual education. He has published in various international journals including The Journal of Aesthetics and Art Criticism, The Journal of Aesthetic Education, The Oxford Review of Education and the Archiv für Musikwissenschaft.

David Lines is Associate Head of Music (Research) at the University of Auckland, New Zealand. His research interests include the philosophy of music education, curriculum studies, jazz education and artistic research methodologies and inquiry. In the past few years he has been actively involved in music curriculum development and implementation in New Zealand schools. A recent recipient of the Early Career Research Excellence Award at his university, David is currently preparing a publication based on his doctorate in the philosophy of music education. David is also an active performer and composer of contemporary jazz fusion music.

Janet Mansfield is an art and music practitioner and educator with experience in primary and tertiary education. She has lectured at Auckland College of Education, the University of Auckland and Auckland University of Technology where she has developed courses at Bachelor and Masters levels. Her research interests are in music and art education, cultural studies and cultural policy issues in education and feminist research. She has co-edited a book with Elizabeth Grierson entitled *The Arts in Education: Critical perspectives from Aotearoa New Zealand* (Dunmore Press, 2003) and has recently completed a large research project entitled *Researching Women at Auckland University of Technology.*

Ros McMillan is Senior Lecturer in Music Education at the University of Melbourne, Australia. Ros is a member of the ISME directorate and her research interests include composition, performance and music teacher education.

Alastair D. McPhee is Senior Lecturer in Educational Studies Department, University of Glasgow, Scotland. Alastair is the Education Studies Co-ordinator of the BEd Music degree programme there. His research interests include music education, teacher education, teacher professionalism and comparative education.

Thomas A. Regelski is Distinguished Professor of Music (Emeritus), State University of New York at Fredonia NY. He has taught at Aichi University in Nagoya Japan, the Sibelius Academy in Helsinki, Finland and Helsinki University, and was a research fellow at the Philosophy of Education Research Center at Harvard University. A leader in music education, he is the co-founder of the MayDay Group, an international/interdisciplinary society of scholars interested in music, music education, and cultural studies. He is presently a Docent at Helsinki University, teaching courses in research writing to graduate students in the Faculty of Education.

Peter Stollery is Senior Lecturer and Programme Director BEd (Music)/BMus (Education) in the School of Education at the University of Aberdeen, Scotland. His research interests are principally in the field of electroacoustic composition, but also include music education, musical intelligence and musical ability.

1

INTRODUCTION

Music Education in Contemporary Culture

DAVID K. LINES
University of Auckland

What are the challenges for music education in contemporary culture? Clearly the world we know as 'music' is undergoing rapid technological, expressive and conceptual change. The world is a different place than it was a few generations ago. Many of Lyotard's (1984) predictions in *The Postmodern Condition* made over a quarter a century ago about the changing state of knowledge, have been realised. Our music has not been divorced from this change; in fact, new technologies, commercialism and changing forms of knowledge have had a major impact on music production, reception and dissemination. Today's music worlds bring together a fusion of performative functions, commodification, film and multimedia, technological change, diverse socio-cultural meanings, stylistic expressions, ethnic identity, competing discourses and the like.

Television and radio broadcasting systems have disseminated commercially appropriated music material to large audiences. By means of one-way broadcasts, the commodified music packages of these communication systems have had an impact on the orientations of music cultures and the receptive capacities of mass audiences. More recently, the Internet, with its web-matrix-like structure and possibilities of multiple communication points has raised the suggestion that the way is now open for more democratic, decentred music practices to unfold in virtual communities of mutual interest. Internet use has now become extremely popular, not just for economic gain, but as Poster (2001) notes, as a tool to open communication possibilities for citizens in all walks of life. Its tendency to promote a radical democracy, however, has had contradictory manifestations—such as the recent examples of music file sharing software that has not economically compensated artists and music corporations. Poster is also cautious of political and commercial appropriations of the Internet, particularly the threat of increased surveillance practices and big brother tactics on an unassuming public.

Babich (2001, p. 5) observes (as did Adorno) that the invention of recording was a 'necessary coincidence' with the advent of modernism in music a la Schoenberg and the atonal movement. Clearly, the entombment of music in electronic reproduction has been a major facet of 20th century culture and recorded music has had a profound impact on our relationship with music *per se*. The invasion of recorded music via multiple technological means in everyday lives and contexts has provided a new environment of musical dispersion. Barthes (1977) has also identified this, and noted a transformation of musical engagement from performing to widespread 'listening' following the pervasive use of recording technologies. Di Scipio (2002) holds a pessimistic view, calling the new music environment 'global diffusion' and 'deaf consumerism', noting similarities between these phenomena and the 'devastation of the natural environment' (e.g. deforestation, pollution). Is music becoming too controlled and driven by other means? Deleuze and Guattari (1987) write of 'machinic' cultural assemblages and their power to order cultural change; they see culture as being driven, in part, by technological systems. Commercial technologies have the potential to control the way we approach music production. New keyboard technologies, for instance, endorse fixed determinations of chromatic intervals, time sequenced rhythms (i.e. rhythm viewed as meter), chordal hierarchies, and preset timbres.

Lyotard's (1984, p. xxiv) concept of the postmodern as 'incredulity toward metanarratives', provides us with a frame of reference for how we might investigate and critique dominant and hegemonic power relations in the field of music education. Metanarratives or grand themes have held firm in music education despite changes in the contemporary music environment. Western schools and universities have perpetuated traditional systems of music learning by means of strictly controlled pedagogical systems and ordered curricula. Other ways and means of music education have remained dominant for decades including: the lauding of the elite, talented musician; the preservation of the Western European music canon; the transmission of ordered tonal and rhythmic ways of knowing[1]; and the rise of technicism in systems, methods and teleological curricula. Institutional music educators have used these and other metanarratives to legitimate their practices and maintain 'standards' in learning environments that have become increasingly economically determined. The hierarchical ordering of modernist music education has excluded 'other' music practices and community participation from the sphere of music learning—thus implicitly denying their value and existence. Those excluded in past decades have been ethnic musics, community musics, dance music, pop, and rock styles. Further, the image of the elite performer has been enhanced by commercial forces that have aligned capital gain with the concept of the music 'star'. While a few young musicians 'make it' and have lucrative performing careers in music, many become disillusioned with the system. Among the many graduates of music schools, only a few become commercially or artistically 'successful' in the sense of becoming widely known or recognised as musicians. The majority of music graduates leave their studies having to theorise their demoted condition without necessarily having acquired the conceptual tools to do so. Despite the startling contradictions and concerns found in institutional music education, the contemporary condition of music in general practice has remained under-theorised and obscured, notwithstanding clear warning signs of change.

This collection of essays brings together a number of theorists and thinkers in music education in order to explore contemporary issues impacting on the field. The collection provides a rich tapestry of themes and issues for the reader to ponder, not only from the perspective of music study, but for educational theory and practice in general. The investigation of music in education brings forth a number of interesting perspectives that the broader realm of education would do well to consider. Music provides education with a particular qualitative experience; one that combines humanly generated sonic expression with social and communicative significance. The perspectives and explorations of music education suggest broader questions of education, for the music experience engages learning in diverse, creative and multidimensional ways.

Our music-sound worlds appear to be in perpetual conversation with living global and cultural changes that we experience on a daily basis. Yet are we suitably equipped as music teachers to meaningfully respond to such change? Music educators require the conceptual tools to understand their working environments so they can make appropriate and effective teacher decisions for the benefit of their students. As such, a key aim of this volume is to stimulate thinking in music education—ways of thinking that take into account not only the immediate classroom or studio environments that music teachers work in, but also the broader knowledge of the discourses that impact on music in education and music in society at large.

In the first article Thomas Regelski takes the pragmatic view that value and meaning can be found in the actual 'difference' made whenever something is put to use. He relates this idea to historical problems inherent in the aesthetic tradition of music and the way music education has appropriated ineffective and confusing views of aesthetic 'contemplation' and 'connoisseurship'. In contrast to these historical orientations, Regelski argues for a more pragmatic stance on music education to be taken, one that focuses on 'praxis'—on the 'doing' of music that 'makes a difference' for the people concerned. Regleski is concerned with affirming music in everyday life; in the use of music by humans and the diverse points of difference and richness such use makes to everyday activity and learning.

In the next paper, 'Music Education in Nihilistic Times', Wayne Bowman suggests that our systems of teaching are concerned with 'inherent, intrinsic and given values' perpetuated by both instrumentalism and technical rationalism. Using a Nietzschean derived analysis of the concept and condition of 'nihilism' in modern society, Bowman proceeds to describe how music education pursuits have tended to take on increasingly value-less and purpose-less orientations. For Bowman, the distinctive characteristics of 'negative', 'reactive' and 'passive' nihilisms pervade music education teaching and research to the degree that a sense of exhaustion and inaction often accompanies attempts at political advocacy and revitalisation. Bowman's exegesis of music education is not all-despairing. He takes a pragmatic stance by emphasising the possibilities of life-affirming action in music education and he calls for the restoration of the social construction of value. He suggests that music educators would do well to think more critically and clearly about what 'valuing' entails and seek to restore the question of value in the becoming of music.

Robert Davis explores key themes in the interlinking fields of music, education and cultural identity. In his essay, Davis situates music education in the region of changing cultural identity and difference where meaningful expressions are communicated and different perspectives negotiated. He locates at least three important themes in the regeneration of music education and cultural identity: The *Kulturkritik* movement which he traces back to Herder; the Interculturalist movements of the post-imperial period; and more recently, the emphasis on economic instrumentalism and performative estimations of educational value. In his search to understand identity formation Davis explores the role of musical sound in the development of the foetus and early language acquisition. He finds a close connection between musical emergence and the formation of parental, and thus local and other identities. This is encapsulated in the musical lullaby which cannot be easily separated from the circumstances of its constitution and internality. Despite music's close proximity with primal learning and identity formation, the location of a musical imaginary, Davis notes, can become ethically vulnerable as was the case in the Nazi appropriation of musical beliefs and their accompanying music education manifestations

Davis finds that expressions of cultural identity can become normalised and lost in the 'totalising discourse of Classical and Romantic stylistic repertoires'. Such problems have re-emerged in the contemporary conditions of music education including the normalisation and mutation of ethnic musics, world musics and music for children (e.g. the lullaby) by means of dominating music education regimes. Davis suggests some respite and promise may be found where music education is located in an environment that fosters 'exchange, composition, improvisation, interrogation of received traditions and unpredictable creativity'. Further, Davis thinks that the resilience of local, vernacular musics may be underestimated by theorists. Music educators would do well to focus on music's dialogical nature and situate music education as 'a move within cultural identity'. In doing so, the restoration of the energy of desire and the sensuous in music could be a focus or aim that helps to re-engage the musical past and present.

In my own article I discuss music improvisation and the educational insights and possibilities such activity can provide. Improvisation favours the momentary nature of the musical experience and helps us enter into musical cultures in a direct and pertinent way. Despite this, the practice of improvisation has not been favoured in music teaching programmes. I suggest that a closer experience of the musical event demands an awareness of the cultural work present in the moment—work that shifts and changes in intensity and character. The dialogical and interactive character of the musical moment, I maintain, is an important feature for musicians and music educators to come to terms with. The synchronic character of music engages us in both the texts and contexts of music. Understanding this feature, which is often notable in improvisation settings, is an important educative principle, and one that could help music students explore musicality and musical expression as ways of 'becoming'.

In the next article, 'Musical Experience and Social Reproduction: A case for retrieving autonomy', Lucy Green looks to move beyond recent debates focussed on the relative significance of music as either 'text' of 'context'. To achieve this, she proposes a theory that considers and helps explain the dialectical relationship between musical text and context. She argues that both 'inherent' and 'delineated' meanings play a necessary part in the senses of celebration, alienation or ambiguity perceived in music and that this reconstructed picture of things helps explain patterns of social reproduction observed in traditional music education. Following on from her recent research in gender and music, Green takes care to point out the role of school music in the reproduction of gender identities. Green's essay, however, concludes with an even more challenging notion: She argues for the reinstatement of musical autonomy in our theoretical conceptualisation of the musical experience. While inherent and delineated meanings enter into an inevitable dialectical relationship, Green maintains that inherent meanings are indeed autonomous in the sense that they are 'logically separable' from the possible diverse delineations that may occur as a result of their presencing.

David Elliott's article, 'Musical Understanding, Musical Works, and Emotional Expression: Implications for education', suggests a conceptual framework to aid the teaching of musical expressions of emotion. Elliott expands contemporary music philosophers' ideas about musical emotions by emphasising the multidimensional aspect of the music-emotion field. He suggests that music's emotions are entwined with not only sonic and design dimensions, as commonly believed, but also with cultural, emotionally expressive, historical, stylistic and ideological dimensions. He notes that teachers 'seldom teach students how to hear, interpret, and create musical works in relation to expressional musical meanings and the role of such meanings in our enjoyment of music'. He sets out to restore this problem by redefining and articulating the multidimensional fields of music works, listening and music making and by suggesting how musical expressions of emotions relate to these dimensions. Elliott reminds us that contemporary theories of human consciousness and brain research also support the notion of inter-relational dimensions in music expression. 'Our synapses are plastic: they are open to modification by selection and/or instruction and construction'. Multiple brain networks suggest that there are many relationships between musical formal structures and the affective lives they relate to. Elliott's philosophical and psychological considerations suggest that music teachers can be confident that diverse methods of teaching emotional expression in music will enhance the musicianship and learning of their students.

Alistair McPhee, Peter Stollery and Ros McMillan challenge pervading 'myths' in music education about innate musical talent. In their study based on comparative research, they examine environmental and cultural factors influencing the musical development of student music teachers in their respective countries: Scotland and Australia. Their work raises some interesting issues, most importantly that we need to consider environmental factors in musical development more seriously in teaching and learning programmes. The authors maintain that teaching and culture-specific factors may positively or negatively impact on musical development, an observation made even more graphic by comparing student responses across both countries.

Constantijn Koopman examines two postmodern phenomena impacting on music education today: performativity and aestheticization. Koopman maintains that performativity—the instrumental drive for efficiency in contemporary society—has a negative impact on artistic developments in music education. He warns music educators not to submit to the rhetoric of efficiency in their attempts at advocacy and discipline justification. Koopman points out that it is music's life fulfilling and enriching role, not performativity and its related characteristics, that should be at the forefront of music education rationales, for this role better exemplifies the 'here and now' experience that music especially provides.

Drawing from the ideas of the contemporary German philosopher, Wolfgang Welsch, Koopman also finds that aestheticization—the increasingly aesthetic constitution of reality and experience—is a predominant force in today's society. Koopman observes that aestheticization processes threaten the arts in education for they water down the special significance of the arts by attributing an aesthetic flavour to all aspects of society. He takes care, however, to note a distinction between aestheticization and the kind of aesthetic sensibility that education in the arts offers. He concludes by noting that aestheticization is linked to performativity and music education can offer a viable qualitative learning alternative to overtly performative ends-driven educational experiences.

Janet Mansfield considers the need to 'protect' musicality—'being musical'—in a contemporary global music education climate that finds itself subjected to dominating technological and commodifying discourses. She seeks to deconstruct the idea of an unquestioned technological, musical subject that, she argues, now infiltrates curriculum policy and the globalizing processes affecting music. Mansfield uses Heidegger's theory of modern technology to question and challenge the technological, musical subject. She is concerned that music education's uncritical embracing of technology neglects the 'essential unfolding' of musicality that a 'hands-on' experience of music establishes and affirms.

This set of excellent essays provides the reader with much to consider about the way ahead for music teaching and learning. Music practitioners are noted for their work in the field—'doing music'. Music practice, however, can only be enhanced by considered explorations of pertinent forces acting on such work and changes in the work-contexts themselves. It is hoped that the themes addressed here will continue to stimulate thinking and research in contemporary music education and other artistic education endeavours.

Note

1. For an interesting discussion on how Western tonality and harmony is viewed ethnocentrically see Christopher Small's (1996) Music, Society, Education.

References

Babich, B. (2001) Postmodern Musicology, in: V. Taylor & C. Winquist (eds), *Encyclopaedia of Postmodernism* (New York, Routledge), pp. 255–259.

Barthes, R. (1977) Musica Practica, in: *Image, Music, Text* (London, Fontana). pp. 149–154.

Deleuze, G. & Guattari, F. (1987) *A Thousand Plateaus: Capitalism and schizophrenia*, trans. B. Massumi, (London, University of Minneapolis Press).

Di Scipio, A. (2002) *The Question Concerning Music Technology*, Cited on the www on 8/1/03 at http://switch.sjsu.edu/switch/sound/articles/discipio_intro.html

Lyotard, J. F. (1984) *The Postmodern Condition: A report on knowledge* (Manchester, Manchester University Press).

Poster, M. (2001) *The Information Subject* (Amsterdam, G and B Arts International).

2

Music and Music Education: Theory and praxis for 'making a difference'

THOMAS A. REGELSKI
SUNY Fredonia & University of Helsinki

Making a Difference

Basic to the idea of pragmatism is that value and meaning are seen in the actual (or at least potential) difference made when whatever is at stake is actually put to use—for example, a thing, idea, theory, hypothesis, claim, or supposition. Without results that 'make a difference', so to speak, the issue remains at best ambiguous; and where actual results are not as claimed or are negative, then the alleged value and meaning can be doubted or challenged. This pragmatic criterion has become almost a matter of 'common sense' in its customary application to social institutions and practices, especially those involving public circumstances where people expect to 'get their money's worth' at the personal or societal level.

This seemingly basic fact of life is among the leading causes for the critical attention most people pay to the praxis of *schooling*—especially compulsory or comprehensive schools.[1] While much of this concern may deal with whether schools are seen as producing good citizens and promoting a beneficial social order, doubting the relevance of certain school subjects is far from uncommon because many average people, as former average students, cannot confirm that certain studies 'made a difference' in their own lives that is lasting and therefore valuable to them. For example, when their child struggles with higher math studies, the parent may well reflect, 'Well, that's OK; I wasn't very good at math either—and look how I turned out!'.

The Value of Music Education

Music teachers are fond of advocating the relevance of musical study, on one hand, by the rationale that 'music is special' or different in some way from most other subjects. And, indeed it is! How and why *music education* should also be special, however, is typically taken for granted. Thus the special kind of positive difference that could or should be made by musical studies is also disregarded—as is the question of whether such studies actually make a special or any consequential *musical* difference in the lives of students while they are students and after graduation.

On the other hand, the slogan 'music is basic' is also commonly offered to legitimate the study of music as part of 'basic' or *general education*. On this ground, music teachers advocate that the study of music is 'basic' to being generally well educated. Precedents for this claim can be traced, of course, back to the ancient Greeks. But changes in schools and society have only added confusion concerning what, overall, being generally well educated might mean in actual practice for the typical citizen. Consequently, it is not surprising that the specific and special role claimed for music in general education is especially ambiguous.

The situation for music education is further complicated by the ideal of *universal schooling*. This embraces reaching each and every child with a basic and general formal education. As the industrialization of modernism proceeded, schools became more factory-like in serving this ideal. In the early twentieth century in the USA, so-called 'scientific management' techniques for improving efficiency and productivity in factories were widely applied to schools, with important and enduring consequences (deMarrais & LeCompte, 1998, pp. 74–87)—including serving as models for other countries. One consequence has been a certain uniformity of curriculum, methods, even teacher certification—a one-size fits all approach that has led increasingly to national curricula or specific 'standards' of various kinds, and thus to standardized results and students (*cf.*, Popkewitz & Gustafson, 2002). Even in this milieu, however, music teachers are often granted an autonomy that can often allow great idiosyncrasy concerning curriculum and pedagogy, at least in comparison to teachers of most other subjects. Nonetheless, music teachers widely share certain taken-for-granted assumptions concerning music and musical value, and these uncritical dispositions lead to an underlying similarity of results that often belies differences in instruction.

First of all, unlike teachers of most other subjects, music teachers tend to be *practitioners*. The 'subject' they teach is, outside of school, a widespread *praxis* that is an important part of popular culture and of culture as understood by anthropologists, ethnologists and ethnomusicologists, but at the same time is connected with class-based ideas of High Culture and of being 'cultured'.[2] To become qualified to teach, music teachers are thus expected to become musicians and musical studies consume the preponderance of their teacher preparation. These studies typically take place in a university setting dedicated to producing professional musicians and scholars. While musics other than Classical may sometimes be addressed, such studies and their influence are still minor in comparison to the conservatory model that dominates studio and ensemble instruction. Furthermore, acceptance to university studies and, thus, to music education programs usually depends on prior Classical music studies. Even where other options for admission exist, the pre-service teacher is still expected to become broadly competent in the Classical music tradition.

When music teachers, thus enculturated in Classical music, find themselves in compulsory and comprehensive schools, they are confronted by an institution having an entirely different social agenda—namely the already mentioned agenda of general education for all students, not professional preparation for a select few. A second problem arises from the obvious fact that society nourishes a wide variety of musics, not just the western Classics that have been the core of a teacher's preparation and traditionally at the heart of curriculum practices of schools.[3] Furthermore, the intimate relation of adolescents to music—their deep familiarity and association with popular musics outside of school, and their very specific use of music in ways that go well beyond or even contravene traditional assumptions of musical value—complicates the teaching of it in ways that is not the case for most other subjects, except possibly sex education!

So-called 'general music' classes evolved to serve the ideals of general education and universal schooling. This type of class originally gets its name and function from the institutional mission of promoting 'music in *general education*' (Regelski, 1984). However, in practice, most general music classes only address a sampling from music theory, history, and the like that teachers hypothesize promote the kind of general understanding and background needed to properly 'appreciate' music—i.e., music *in general*. In some countries, particularly North America, comprehensive schools also provide options for specialized ensembles, such as bands, choruses and orchestras, that tend to perform Classical literature or quasi-Classical arrangements of other musics. When the Classical background and assumptions of most teachers and the traditional role of such music in school curricula are considered in comparison to the ubiquity and plurality of musics outside of school, and taking into account the divergent convictions of music teachers that music is basic yet special, it becomes apparent that music educators should not take the value and meaning of music education for granted. The ways in which music is both basic and special, therefore, must be made explicit, critically examined, and used as a basis for a thorough reconsideration of why and how music education should 'make a difference' for typical students served.

The Problem and its Sources

I

Given the many difficulties and inconsistent variables sketched above, it is evident that present theory and practice in music education have not 'made a difference' (e.g., Ståhlhammer, 2000). The aphorism, 'If you don't know where you're going, you're likely to end up somewhere else!' clearly applies to music education. As a rule, the 'somewhere' in question 'makes a difference' only on rare and random occasions, while the 'somewhere else' either fails to make any difference, or actually makes a negative difference; for example, in alienating students. The philosophical rationale upon which traditional curricular theory is usually predicated has made a variety of dignified and weighty sounding claims for the supposed *aesthetic* value of music and thus of music education. Yet, for individuals and society, the long-term pragmatic benefits of study predicated on such claims have been so vague or varied that they are either viewed as inconsequential (e.g., the common 'Its nice if you can afford it but ...' and the 'icing on the cake' assessments of music education's value), or such benefits are not noted or valued by the public at all! Either consequence has led to the widespread marginalization of music in school schedules, budgets, etc.,[4] and thus in lieu of 'making a difference' musically that is widely recognized and esteemed by society, music educators engage increasingly in the politics of 'advocacy'.

This marginalization is a result of the kind of 'legitimation crisis' analyzed by Habermas (1975). Crises arise in social institutions and systems when internal contradictions and other basic weaknesses result in the failure of the institution to make the differences it claims to be its benefit to society. This becomes apparent under conditions of 'immanent critique' where the benefits *claimed* are used as *criteria* for judging the actual value added to society. When success is wanting or when negative problems typically result, the institution faces a crisis and typically resorts to *legitimation*, i.e., various ways of either 'rationalizing' its putative benefits or of restating those benefits in language that is generous enough to accommodate its infirmities in more positive sounding terms. Legitimation also has the reassuring effect of 'protecting' the institution's 'integrity' from what 'insiders' see as 'illegitimate' criticism by 'know-nothings' (*viz.*, 'outsiders') and, thus, of preserving the institution in as close to its present form as possible. In music education, for example, the postmodern spirit of pluralism and multiculturalism did lead to an inconsequential insertion of 'world musics' in the school and university curriculum, but this has clearly amounted more to lip service than a groundswell of curricular change or innovation.

II

The *politics of advocacy* in music education today is a compelling indication that music educators themselves recognize and are on the defensive against the progressive marginalization of music education in the schools.[5] Related to these verbal attempts to convince people[6] of the legitimacy of school music is the constellation of assumptions and practices that arise from the uncritically accepted rationale mentioned earlier that music's special nature and value is *aesthetic* and, thus, that music education is 'aesthetic education' and meets a widespread 'need' for, or otherwise importantly cultivates so-called aesthetic sensibility, responsiveness, or experiences.[7] Unfortunately, the various claims made on behalf of these assumptions amount in effect to the fallacy of *obscurum per obscurius*, the logical error of accounting for something that requires explanation because it is exceptionally vague and ambiguous to begin with, but doing so in terms and conditions which are themselves unobservable and that thus contribute further to the enigma that was supposed to be clarified. Although a full-scale critique cannot be undertaken here, the most consequential issues concerning this aesthetic rationale can be summarized.

To begin with, contrasting uses of the very term 'aesthetic' need to be addressed because inattention to these differences and their implications is submitted as a leading source of the legitimation crisis facing music education. Most musicians, and thus most music teachers, do not typically study aesthetics as part of their formal preparation. Nonetheless, the 'hidden curriculum' (deMarrais & LeCompte, 1998, pp. 13–14, 242–247) and ideological assumptions of the university music school do socialize them into certain uncritical assumptions and thus language concerning music as necessarily being in some way aesthetic. Referring to music as aesthetic stems from Aristotle's idea of *aisthesis*,[8] which recognized a kind or quality of knowledge and judgement that is rooted in the senses, independently of the faculty of reason, but that is not simply equated with hedonism and sensory excess. This notion of *aisthesis* served as the source of what was to become, after Kant, aesthetic philosophy *per se*. But the term 'aesthetic' is frequently used loosely or non-technically in the original sense of *aisthesis* to refer to the attractive or pleasing sensibility (Williams, 1983, pp. 31–33) involved not only with the arts but also in familiar expressions such as the 'aesthetics of sport' or 'aesthetic surgery'.[9] This informal use might be innocent enough elsewhere, but in music education it is easily confused with more technical uses of the term,[10] of which there are at least two that are in direct opposition (see Määttänen, 2002).[11]

John Dewey's pragmatist conception of aesthetic experience is part of a comprehensive and naturalist (see, e.g., Popp, 1998) rather than transcendental theory of experience. For him, aesthetic experience is a qualitative, affective sense of unity that pervades 'an experience', as opposed to being 'in' art 'works'. 'To experience' something is different than 'an experience', for Dewey; the former amounts to just 'undergoing' the experience, while the latter involves a tangible, unresolved 'situation' or problem that reaches fulfillment or solution through the mindful actions of the individual. Such situations are, for Dewey, not detached from practical matters; in fact, Dewey's entire theory of art seeks to promote an heightened sensibility in connection with all experience, ordinary as well as extraordinary, that is more richly 'felt'. For Dewey, and as later confirmed by Wittgenstein, meaning is in use, and 'the meanings attached to an aesthetic experience as a perceptual experience are basically habits of action, use. The interpretation takes place in a framework of the practical social world because that's where meanings reside' (Määttänen, 2002, p. 2).

Aesthetic theories in the neo-Kantian tradition are completely at odds with Dewey's theory (Määttänen, 2002).[12] Notably, there are an infinite number of theories of this kind because they depend on the different metaphysical speculations of each aesthetician.[13] The very proliferation of such theories and the often contradictory stances they argue simply add to the lack of clarity concerning the details of what aesthetic meaning, quality, essence, experience might actually be. In fact, since its inception, the very idea of aesthetic experience as advanced by formal aesthetic theories has been the source of considerable disagreement in the history of philosophy (e.g., Rancière, 2000; Williams, 1983), and aesthetic theory in general is often criticized by philosophers themselves for its failure to illuminate rather than obfuscate (e.g., Urmson, 1989; Proudfoot, 1988). However, certain general outlines can be isolated for present purposes.

First, and perhaps most important, aesthetic experience is said to be 'disinterested'. This 'purposiveness without purpose' inherited from Kant means that an 'aesthetic distance' is to exist between art and practical matters of the kind that concerned Dewey and that are featured in, as we shall see, praxial accounts of music. Conjectured, then, are criteria and conditions of pure, ideal, 'free' beauty that *transcend* particulars of time, place and person.[14] Such aesthetic theories of 'free' beauty typically reject 'dependent' or 'pragmatic' beauty that is, so to speak, good or beautiful of its kind, even though the latter was acknowledged by Kant[15] and figures centrally in ideas of music that are socially grounded, such as concerning musics other than Classical music and, in general, in current sociology of music.

From the 'disinterested' posture of orthodox aesthetic theory arise two further but related ideas; that music exists to be *contemplated*, and that 'works' of music exist *autonomously*, as self-sufficient entities that are valued 'for their own sake'—i.e., in 'strictly musical' terms that thus, and again, disconnects them from practical situations and uses. This putative autonomy creates a distinction between Fine and 'applied' or 'practical' arts (or crafts) and further separates music from life and leads to what Bourdieu called the 'sacralization' (1993, p. 236; see also Schaeffer, 2000, p. 6) that reserves music to quasi-sacred locations such as concert halls.[16]

With the idea of music as an aesthetic Fine Art also comes the idea of refinement—of cultivated 'taste' (Williams, 1983) that depends on a certain *connoisseurship* of knowledge and experience. Correspondingly, esoteric music becomes by implication if not by explicit admission superior, more (aesthetically or ecstatically) valuable than exoteric and profane music (Schaeffer, 2000, p. 6): The less accessible the music, the more aesthetically valuable it is, thus necessitating the 'cultivation' of special knowledge and understanding. The strong idealist and rationalist influence on orthodox aesthetic theory reinforce this latter assumption; mind and body are thus separated and reason and intellectual apprehension are favored, while visceral responses and related emotional states are correspondingly deprecated.[17] In being aestheticized, emotions are thereby *an*esthetized (Williams, 1983) and supposedly universalized and are to be more 'known' or 'understood' than 'felt' for their affective *qualia*.

The complexities of such distinctions, claims and arguments go on and on. Thus a separate literature has arisen in order to elucidate the many contradictions and confusions of aesthetic philosophy (e.g., Cooper, 1992; Gaut & Lopes, 2001). This meta-commentary does not, however, add any clarity or resolution that could serve as an actual basis for musical experience, even that of accomplished musicians. For example, Christopher Small observes of a book on aesthetics he was asked to review,

> The trouble was that most it *bore very little relation to anything I recognized in my own musical experience*, as listener, or as performer, or as a composer. In the first place, all the writers deal exclusively with what we today would call the western high classical tradition. ... And in the second place, the theories they developed were all terribly abstract and complicated. ... I could not make myself believe that so universal, and so concrete a human practice as music should need such complicated and abstract explanations. (Small, 1991, p. 1; italics added)

For the same reasons, philosopher Michael Proudfoot writes,

> *aesthetic theory often seems false to our experience of art* ... Recently, such inadequacy to our experience of art has been evident; a result, I believe, partly of aestheticians' preoccupation with what it is to treat something 'aesthetically', and partly from a concentration on works of art in isolation from the circumstances in which they are actually created or appreciated. (Proudfoot, 1988, p. 850; italics added)[18]

It seems that accomplished musicians, too, would find the puzzling complexities of aesthetic theory to be false to their own experience of music if they were familiar with that literature. The fact that most are not, however, itself suggests either that aesthetic theory is neither necessary nor helpful to competent musical experience, or that certain vague or casual aesthetic assumptions of the kind mentioned above in connection with *aisthesis* are simply taken for granted by most musicians—at least to the degree that many, among them music teachers, feel validated and legitimated by the noble, important-sounding, even spiritual claims made for music. This succor may be needed because musical performance in the university is often seen as an 'odd bedfellow' by intellectuals and scholars who regard it as more a 'professional' trade, as mere craftsmanship, or even as a kind of musical 'athleticism' in comparison to the liberal arts or even to the study of music theory and history. These latter, in fact, are often more highly esteemed for their contribution to 'liberal' education precisely because their 'scholasticism' (see Bourdieu, 1998) fits the contemplation and connoisseurship assumptions of aesthetic philosophy.

III

The falseness to actual musical experience of aesthetic philosophies demonstrates their weakness as a rationale in support of music education in schools. Furthermore, the complexities and contradictions of these competing theories are largely lost on most music teachers. As a result, any agreement predicating instruction on such bases is extremely unlikely, even for faculty in the same school, and curricular integrity is thereby lost. However, several other problems also contraindicate aesthetic premises for music education that seeks to 'make a difference'.

First, circumstances in schools are rarely conducive to the 'disinterested' and other conditions set forth for aesthetic responding. Secondly, and more problematic, because aesthetic experience is covert by definition and prerequisite,[19] there is simply no reasonable way to observe whether or to what degree 'it' has occurred, or whether or to what degree 'it' was educated, improved, cultivated, etc. Without overt indications of some kind, learning is not guaranteed and instruction is not accountable! To the counter-claim that the learning will be evidenced 'someday' or 'somehow' in later life, precisely the lack of such tangible evidence of eventual relevance is clearly the source of the legitimation crisis facing music education.

Furthermore, students know whether or to what degree their classroom experiences result in any kind of useful or relevant learning along such lines. And the fact is clear that, for most, instruction predicated on assumptions of *music-appreciation-as-connoisseurship* (MAAC) falls on deaf ears (Green, 1988). In fact, it also fails when rock, rap, reggae, and other such musics are taught according to the MAAC paradigm—with, that is, instruction that features history, theory, 'classic' examples, etc., as though such music is autonomous, exists for contemplation for its own sake, and that *knowing more 'about' it* contributes to actively 'understanding' and thus 'appreciating' it, rather than simply passively 'receiving' it. However, young people's musical lives outside of school sharply conflict with the MAAC model and their ways of musicking are neither passive nor lacking intensity (Ståhlhammer, 2000). As a result, 'school music' and what for students is 'real music' exist at some considerable remove. This disjunction results too often in attitudes that are either openly dismissive of 'school music' or a begrudging admission that it might have value for some people, but not for them personally. This, alone, counts heavily in attitudes towards music education once such young people are adults, parents, political and educational leaders, and taxpayers.

IV

Nonetheless, music teachers in schools persist, whether with Classical music or other musics, in what may be called an attempt at 'converting' students to the MAAC paradigm as a kind of 'salvation theme' (Popkewitz, 2001)—an attempt at redemption where students can be restored to musical virtue. Judging by direct observation, methods texts, and instructional materials, this conversion is most often attempted by teaching music as a 'discipline'. Curriculum theorists have noted how 'subjects' get transformed, neutralized, and even negated when they are addressed in schools (see, e.g., Popkewitz & Gustafson, 2002). Most 'disciplines' of study have grown around 'fields' of *praxis*, such as the sciences, mathematics, and the like. Some, such as language study, are predicated on eventual use. More typical, however, is teaching the discipline for its own sake, thus leading to widespread complaints that much of schooling is 'merely academic'.[20] This is problematic enough concerning the usual subjects of instruction, but given the important *praxial role* of music in students' lives outside of school—especially as they approach adolescence—the structure-of-the-discipline approach to curriculum becomes a sure-fire recipe not just for failure to promote relevant learning, but also for promoting alienation. The praxis of music, otherwise so relevant to their existential Being, gets reduced to a mere 'academic subject'!

As mentioned above, the structure-of-the-discipline curriculum consists largely of information 'about' music history and theory. Following a long rationalist prejudice in intellectual history, 'understanding' and 'appreciation' are taken for granted as being synonyms[21] and any enjoyment that does not involve studied understanding is considered lesser or lower; for example food, even *haute cuisine* (Korsmeyer, 1999). With the so-called Discipline-Based Music Education method in the USA, aesthetics, history, theory, and criticism dominate study. Far more common there and elsewhere is teaching the 'elements of music',—*viz.*, melody, harmony, rhythm, form, timbre—and other musical terminology through 'activities' and 'experiences' that putatively result in 'concepts' students then supposedly use as listeners.[22]

Indeed, listening is the main emphasis of MAAC; even performance in class is regarded as an active and thus more attractive way of instantiating abstract concepts—rather than as promoting skills that could actually be used in life! However, most concepts—particularly the abstract categories named by the so-called 'elements'—are, first of all, open-ended in that there is no ultimate 'essence' of the concept. Secondly, in approaching concepts one at a time, students are subjected to a jumble of lessons focused on teaching labels and other isolated abstractions. Consequently, they learn few if any skills or anything lasting that could serve much beyond the duration of the class period or term.

In recognition of the resistance of students to this kind of instruction and thus its futility, more teachers in classrooms today address popular musics. Already mentioned, however, are the problems created when the MAAC model for 'appreciating' Classical music is applied in teaching other musics. Some teachers go beyond MAAC and also attempt to *perform* such music, be it by creating a number of, say, 'rock bands' within the class or by engaging the whole class in, say, some kind of traditional drumming, etc. These attempts, however, also typically fall short of making any lasting impact—though they may be welcomed by students in comparison to traditional alternatives—simply because *independent musicianship* (Regelski, 1969) sufficient to at least a beginning and personally satisfying level of participation fails to develop under such conditions. An enormous amount of time thus goes into rote instruction where students may develop only the 'proficiency' sufficient to 'get through' one or only a few pieces. Or skills are learned that have little or no direct application to 'real' praxis outside of school, however appealing classes may have been.

V

A final problem concerns what I have elsewhere called 'methodolatry' (Regelski, 2002b). This amounts to a 'how to', *technicism* of teaching. Such a pedagogy of recipes, formulae, and prescriptions has ill-served music education over the years. While, in general music classes, at least, MAAC is often assumed and the focus is on teaching 'elements' and 'concepts', in fact it is the 'method' *per se* that is the 'curriculum'; the simple act or fact of employing the teaching method becomes the focus of the teacher's planning. A lesson is evaluated as 'good' if it was 'delivered' according to the traditions and procedures associated with the methods and materials in question, not according to whether it produced results that 'make a difference'.

For instrumental lessons, the methodolatry is often built-in the 'methods books' used. Lesson after lesson is slavishly undertaken in the expectation that the result will be some kind of musicianship and technical ability sufficient to musical independence. This is most usually not the case, if only because the 'literature' in question often has little relevance beyond 'school music' (or the duration of parentally enforced 'music lessons') and because the focus is too often on technique for its own sake. Because the goal is to teach the *instrument* as such, not *music*, the 'discipline' involved amounts to compliant practicing in the service of a progressive acquisition of technique. Quite rarely, in any case, is literature selected for its relevance to lifelong learning (in particular as listeners), and asking many music teachers about the difference between, say, a *trumpet* lesson and a *music* lesson via the trumpet leaves them scratching their heads in bewilderment. Finally and most typically, learning to improvise and play by ear too often falls by the wayside in the excessive preoccupation with instrumental technique and music reading.

Music as Praxis

I

The hegemony of accounts of music and music education based on aesthetics-premised connoisseurship models is being increasingly challenged by *praxial theories* from both social theory and the philosophy of music.[23] Approaching music and music education as *praxis*, then, offers alternatives that can 'make a difference', especially because, by definition, praxis involves tangible 'doing' that 'makes a difference' of some kind for the individuals or groups served. A full account of the idea of praxis is not possible here (see Dunne, 1993; Regelski, 2003; 2002a; 1998), but important features can be outlined.

The idea of praxis is first featured in the ethics of Aristotle who distinguished three types of knowing. *Theoria* was knowledge created and contemplated for its own sake. Following Plato's lead, Aristotle privileged the 'faculty' of reason as the essence of being human and thus as the source of the good life. This bias for rationalism has dominated philosophy ever since.[24] In consequence, the rationalizing and aestheticization of *aisthesis* has led, as we have seen, to the prejudice of aesthetic theory for rational contemplation of music and its supposed universal meaning, and against the particulars and *qualia* experienced through the senses.

Techne was associated with *poiesis*, the making of things. Such practiced skill and craft operate in the service of uncontroversial and thus taken-for-granted ends, such as making certain useful objects or playing an instrument. *Techne* becomes problematic, however, to the degree that musical technique (i.e., virtuosity) becomes an end in itself, and in relation to claims that only technical expertise can properly realize the full aesthetic or artistic integrity of the music performed.

Praxis, however, involved not the making of things but 'doings' of various kinds that concern people. As such, praxis is governed by an ethical dimension (called *phronesis*) where 'right results' are judged specifically in terms of the people served or affected. The 'rightness' of results thus varies according to the situated needs in question. The praxis of medicine is an apt example; there, where 'making a difference' in the direction of improved health is at stake, the 'rightness' of results depends on the presenting patient's symptoms and needs. Standards of care are involved, not standardized care or results. Thus, 'right results' are not interpreted in absolute or singular terms; rather, 'good health' is an *action ideal* that is met according to the particular situation of each patient.

II

Aristotle's distinctions have important implications for music and music education. First, when music is considered as praxis, the 'goodness' or 'rightness' of musical experiences vary according to the individuals or groups in question. Music thus serves a variety of 'goods' that are as diverse as the people who avail themselves of it. Also, echoing Dewey's theory, musical meaning is socially saturated and situated. Particular social variables govern important aspects of the musical meaning afforded. A composition with sacred text has one meaning for churchgoers engaged in worship and another meaning for most in the audience at a secular concert; and concert music used in film is similarly transformed, often dramatically. Likewise, music is judged not according to the *a priori* and rational standards hypothesized by aesthetic theory, but according to the difference it makes, the values it adds to the occasion and for the people involved. As a result, music for worship is not relegated to the lowest regions of the putative aesthetic pecking order, and music for dance, ceremony, celebration, etc., is not regarded as lacking important musical value.

Concert listening (or listening to recordings at home) is not a matter of aesthetic qualities purported to be 'in' the music that are then attended to cerebrally and for their own sake, but for the sake of the listener. These benefits can range from the analytical or intellectual reflection of performing musicians and musical cognoscenti, to the affective delights typically mentioned by most audience members. Viewed praxially, the quasi-sacredness of the 'work' is demystified from being timeless, placeless, and faceless in its meaning. People listen according to differences in their life-worlds, interests, values, backgrounds, and present intentions and needs. The latter also differ for the same individuals at different times and this temporal factor is always central in the musical meaning of the moment.

III

In this understanding, music does not exist just for or solely in the 'terms' of musicians, nor does it exist to be appropriated according to any 'exclusive' model of aesthetic or 'strictly musical' meaning that limits 'appreciation' to a privileged few cognoscenti. To begin with, music is never 'strictly musical' since, as a social praxis, it is always imbued with sociality (Shepherd, 1991; Shepherd & Wicke, 1997). Aesthetic traditions promote focusing only on the 'sounds' of the moment, thus ignoring the background of sociality from which music arises and the conditions in and for which it is 'appreciated'.[25] Ethnomusicologists have researched the complex holism of sounds and sociality in indigenous societies, and sociologists of music also find such holism to be equally implicated in the music of our more complex society. Music as a nexus of sociality may be less *obvious* in the Western concert paradigm, but is no less *central* to musical meaning. Small (1998), for example, has analyzed social variables and conditions that, while not part of the 'sounds' of the moment, are inescapably part of the audience's experience of music and thus are not 'un-musical' or even 'extra-musical' as aesthetic theories speculate.

Of course the 'sounds' of music are to begin with saturated with social import. Sounds available for music are determined by social variables that range from what geography provides indigenous peoples, to the technological options of modern societies. Secondly, the criteria governing when 'sound' is considered 'music' is entirely a matter of a society's *generative idea* of 'music'—what sociologist Emile Durkheim called a socially created 'category of cognition'.[26] Thus, what is considered 'music' in a particular society is a 'status function' added to sounds according to the socially governed goods they serve as praxis.[27]

In complex societies, where many goods and goals are at stake, a plurality of musics arises. Each is governed by both the society's general idea of music and the particular social good or goal served; every musical praxis thus has its own conditions, criteria, and unique contributions. Each exists as its own 'field' within the larger 'music world'[28] where it 'positions' itself for advantage among other musics—sometimes with controversy as to whether a certain praxis *is* 'music'. Each field will have some homogeneity based on its 'common practice', but blending and crossing-over of fields, at least at their peripheries, occurs frequently—increasingly so with modern technology. As a result of the inherent sociality and pluralism of musics, and the complex interaction between them, the idea of a single model of 'music appreciation' is simply out of the question, as is the sacralization of music.

IV

In this praxial account, 'good music' is first a matter of what it is 'good for'[29] and subsequent considerations of quality involve how well a good in question is served. Thus, even distinctions of quality are made in the field of Classical music. Furthermore, the standard repertory is not, as aesthetic theory claims, the paragon of quality for all music, but one type of music—a particular praxis valued by a small fraction of people. Music, then, is 'good' relative to its kind, each of which is considered on a lateral continuum, not on a hierarchy according to putative aesthetic virtue—usually with chamber music and symphonies (i.e., 'pure' music) at the top, and a descending order of other musics ranked according to the fancy of the authority. Some aesthetes deny aesthetic virtue to exoteric musics altogether by labeling them as 'popular', 'folk', 'ethnic' or 'practical' (e.g., church hymns, etc.), thus denying them a place in the aesthetic hierarchy to begin with.

It is predictable for aesthetes to decry the situatedness of the 'social construction of musical meaning' that is the central finding of contemporary sociology of music (Martin, 1995) as 'mere relativism'. However, they fail to understand or accept that the *universalism* of unconditional values they promote *is itself culturally relative* to the social differences and conditions by and into which they were socialized, either by primary socialization in the home or by secondary and tertiary socialization in school and university.[30] The situatedness and social construction of music meaning does not amount to 'anything goes' or mere self-indulgence. The social conditions and conventions that account for different musics guide the musicianship demands of each and serve as the criteria by which 'goodness' is evaluated in each case. Furthermore, viewed from the perspective of the sociology of music, while any music does provide certain 'objective' *affordances*, how these are appropriated[31] or selectively 'taken' or attended to varies according to important differences between people, their interests, backgrounds, needs, intentions, habits, all as conditioned by the specific occasion (DeNora, 2000).

Education as and for Praxis

I

From such considerations of the philosophical and social conditions and criteria of music as praxis emerge a picture of musical meaning and value that decidedly contradicts and challenges the aesthetic premises and music-appreciation-as-contemplation model of connoisseurship that have served, explicitly or tacitly, as the traditional rationale of music education.[32] Throughout society, in social fact, music is valued according to the purposes and criteria of its use! This 'use' encompasses a wide range of decidedly down to earth roles for music in everyday life (DeNora, 2000) in addition to its more rarefied or specialized roles. The 'music' in *music* education, then, should not be premised on a narrow or limiting view of praxis that excludes or alienates students from meaningful and relevant musical learning; instead, it needs to be expanded, not just to include a broader range of musics, but to the idea of enabling students to appropriate musical meanings and values in ways or to a degree that 'makes a difference' as a direct result of their schooling.

This need to 'make a difference', in turn, requires that music education itself should aspire to the conditions of praxis and thus needs to approximate more of the criteria of a true *profession* (see Regelski, 2002b). So-called professional *practice* in, say, law or medicine, is in fact a matter of professional *praxis*.[33] Professions are guided, then, by a professional ethic for 'right results' and with ethical criteria such as 'to do no harm'. Results are judged in terms of the beneficial difference made for those served, not in abstract *a priori*, metaphysical, or strictly technical terms. Praxis of any kind arises on the bases of the contribution made to individuals or society; thus, any *professional* praxis is valued by society to the degree it 'makes a difference'. Looked at from the perspective of the crises facing Classical music and music education, the music-appreciation-as-connoisseurship model 'makes a difference' for far too few people, and then not necessarily on the aesthetic terms claimed.[34]

Viewed in terms of praxis, what is called 'appreciation' is seen in the use(s) made of music; i.e., its 'doing', and the *value added* to life as a result. Understood in praxial terms, connoisseurship thus becomes a matter of *habits of active use*[35]—actions that Small (1998) has dubbed 'musicking' and Elliott (1995) 'musicing'. Such habits can be informed by formal study and dedicated practice; but 'informal study' and even just habitual involvement in a praxis also lead to a certain kind of 'appreciation' that is not less, just different from that arising from studied expertise. In fact, most 'music lovers' are not highly expert in the ways that characterize 'musicians'. Amateur performers 'practice' their connoisseurship and evidence their appreciation by learning new literature, and often gain expertise as a result. Audiophiles similarly 'cultivate' their praxis by acquiring recordings of different literature and performances. The formal study of musicians can often be as narrow as it is deep; for example, it is often confined to a particular instrument and to a limited literature. Performers might well benefit from composition studies and composers might well benefit from playing all the instruments for which they compose, but these conditions are not typical and performers often enjoy musics for which they have no special expertise. For the same reasons, listeners—even 'professional listeners' such as critics—may well benefit from performing or composing studies, but listening is clearly a practice of its own, with its own conditions, criteria, purposes and benefits, and can thus be 'practiced' on its own terms.

II

Music education as and for praxis should, in the view submitted here, focus on 'study' that 'makes a difference' in the lives of students, now and in the future. Such 'study' must, therefore, take the form of 'doing', of praxis, not academic study 'about' music of the kind that has characterized aesthetics-based premises of connoisseurship and contemplation. Such study amounts to *curriculum-as-practicum*, as Elliott has described (1995). Moreover, despite the low status associated with amateurism as a result of the assumption that only advanced virtuosity serves music's aesthetic or artistic values, music education as and for praxis should promote the dedicated *amateuring* described by Booth (1999) where the sheer love of music and sharing it with like-minded others is a principal value in the life well-lived. A practicum that promotes amateuring—and the shift from the noun amateur to the gerund points to the active habit and its processual criteria and benefits—need not apply only to performing, but to listening, composing, and other pursuits as well, e.g., audiophile's interests in music criticism, audio reviews, etc. It also need not apply only to Classical music; in fact, offering options in addition to, not instead of the Classics should also be a major focus of any praxis-based curriculum for young people—in schools or individual lessons.

Such a curriculum of and for musicking will benefit from taking into consideration how, why, and when music is used in society. Here, options provided by the *local music world* should especially be taken into account. Folk, ethnic, and other musics can be included based on local availability; but the desirability of advancing musicianship of a general nature that can be applied to other musics should always be kept in mind. Curriculum should also consider how conveniently certain musics and musicking 'fit' into the busy schedules of modern citizens.[36] While large ensembles offer much of musical interest and value, amateur groups of this size are difficult to schedule. Chamber music (not just Classical but, for example, jazz, folk, rock duos and trios), in contrast, is much more suitable in this respect and thus more people can continue to perform. However, the literature, musicianship, and habit or taste for such musicking should be developed *while students are still in school*. For example, developing the habit of using computerized 'accompaniments' for solo instruments can benefit a lifetime of solo performance at home—as can learning MIDI-instruments that can be played without bothering the neighbors.

Recreational, folk, and social instruments (i.e., those not usually associated with the standard repertory of Classical music) should also be featured. They provide, to begin with, a functional way of teaching music reading; but instruction should also seek to initiate the interest and habit of home and community (or church) based performing, and as a potential source of listening enjoyment (e.g., collecting recordings, attending concerts). In like manner, 'everyday music' should receive due consideration; thus thoughtfulness and options concerning music for aerobics, 'occasional music' (e.g., dinners, parties, ceremonies, celebrations, weddings, etc.), religion, and the like can benefit students in tangible and lasting ways. Film and TV music also deserve emphasis, particularly in general music classes. And composition/arranging skills and applications (including computer-based) should not be ignored, such as creating accompaniments for one's own performance, for recreational groups, for home videos and video-based photography shows, etc.

III

In all of this a balance of 'depth versus breadth' needs to be achieved if instruction is to result in more than a superficial sampling of music. Focus, then, should be on what might be called *general musicianship*; that is, on knowledge and skills that are broadly applicable to more than the specific practices they are first developed in connection with. General musicianship thus involves fundamental knowledge and skills shared by *several* of the musics generally available within a particular music world. Such musicianship encompasses wide-ranging 'basics' that allow musicians to operate in more than one type of music—'basics' that get 'specialized' or fine-tuned, however, by the criteria of a particular praxis to which they can be applied.[37] Also, keeping in mind that listening, performing, and composing/arranging are themselves unique practices, general musicianship developed through, say, composing or performing should, as a focus of curriculum, also be 'generalized' in application to listening. The range of musical fields involved—i.e., particular genres or types of music included—should be predicated, then, on the likelihood of promoting general musicianship and its potential for so-called 'transfer of learning' to other situated conditions—in this case, to other musical practices and, of course, generally to the future. However, and again, general musicianship should be developed via the 'doing' of selected musical practices and it should at least serve as the bases for continuing experience and, thus, further or more specialized musicianship in those practices.[38]

Conclusion

Speculation about music's aesthetic nobility, profundity, and spirituality is not needed to legitimate its special status in society. Whatever experiences people have in connection with its use, *that they use it shows they value those experiences.* Thus the wide use of music shows clearly that it is already 'special'. For ethnologist Ellen Dissanayake (1991; 1992), 'making special' is a function art and music contribute to social practices in every culture. And, music in particular makes a special contribution to individual and social life in comparison to most other school subjects. I submit that it is particularly this ubiquity of music in society that creates the specific need for music education to 'make a difference'. Students come to school each day already enculturated into a deep appreciation of music as praxis. Some may be the beneficiaries of a socioeconomic life-world that has advanced their dispositions towards Classical music, or opera, or jazz; others will grow up in other musical environments and be thus predisposed to those musical directions.

In either case, all students will have developed some musical skills, attitudes, and habits of appreciation prior to and outside of school. Given the conditions of universal schooling and general education, then, music educators must think in terms of a *value added* approach where students are *newly or better able to 'do' music* as a result of instruction. Even students engaged in voluntary music education (i.e., extracurricular participation, studies in community music schools, or taking private lessons, etc.) will be benefited by such a value added approach to instruction. This approach implies, then, building on the music backgrounds students bring with them to school, not 'redeeming' them from their existing musical dispositions and practices by 'converting' them to models of connoisseurship that are so alien as to be alienating.[39] In addition, new musicianship (e.g., learning new musics, composition/arranging skills, etc.) developed as a practicum that serves praxial ends will

enrich students' musical options and thus enhance the likelihood that music will 'make a difference' in their lives and in society.

Music appreciated is music used! A life of so-called 'music appreciation' is a life in which music 'makes a difference'. An effective music education, then, advances not some speculative theory of appreciation based on connoisseurship as aesthetic or otherwise disinterested contemplation for its own sake; instead, it directly promotes musicking that adds value to individual lives and enlivens society. The kind of praxis-based approach to music and music education described here sets out to 'make a difference' in the musical lives of students and society by increasing the wealth of skills and options for musicking. Its success amounts to the kind of value added that is not just noticeable but notable. And with such notability, music education as a field will be acknowledged as promoting values that are both *basic* to life and *special* in their unique contribution to the good life.

Notes

1. Much of the analysis and argument presented herein also applies to 'voluntary' studies involving what are variously called municipal, community, or private 'music schools', and even individual studio instruction, such as piano lessons.
2. The 'cultivation' needed for the social 'refinement' associated with the Fine Arts motivates many parents to support their children's musical study on the assumption of the cultural status supposedly gained—although most such study falls far short of the 'classy' pretensions associated with being musically 'cultured' and, as analyzed by Bourdieu (1984), such 'distinction' is more typically an accident of birth or other enculturation than a result of formal schooling.
3. See in connection with the USA, for instance, McCarthy, 1997.
4. Music education is an instance of what Bourdieu describes as a 'social field' (e.g., 1990, pp. 67–68). Like the playing field of sports, such a field is an arena where various interests and power groups 'position' themselves for social advantage with a larger 'world'. Any musical praxis, then, is a field within a larger 'music world', and music education is a field within its 'world' of praxis called 'schooling'. Progressive marginalization of music within that world means a weakening of its position or power with regard to a reasonable share of resources, etc.; and music educators widely acknowledge this marginalization and bemoan their loss of status in the school and society. For details, see Regelski, 2003.
5. See in particular the advocacy section of the International Society for Music Education Website (http://www.ISME.org).
6. An important source of societal attitudes toward and valuing of music and music education is that most people experienced 'school music' during their school years, and now have musical lives quite at odds with what was offered as part of those studies.
7. More or less necessarily and automatically; e.g., the belief is that listening, singing, or performing somehow routinely increase aesthetic responsiveness and inevitably promote an aesthetic education.
8. Plato, on the other hand, did not recognize *aisthesis* as a 'judgement of sense' in the way Aristotle did (Summers, 1987) and was convinced that the arts risked the debasement of reason by the senses.
9. Equally non-technical references have been made, for instance, to the 'African aesthetic', where everyday music is decidedly *praxial*, and 'Nazi aesthetics', in reference to the Nazi's sociopolitical *uses* of music. After a while, such uses of the term can become unfortunately circular, or even clichés (Edstrom, 2002).

10. Symbolist poet Paul Valéry (1945) coined the neologism 'esthesic' to distinguish such contemporary reference to *aisthesis* in the arts from the language and implications of aesthetic philosophy generally rejected by the avant-garde outside of the music world. Williams' (1976) précis stresses the controversy surrounding the term and the dangers of its loose use, and concludes that it has become 'an element in the divided modern consciousness of *art* and *society*: a reference beyond social use and social valuation which, like the one special meaning of *culture*, is intended to express a human dimension which the dominant version of society appears to exclude. The emphasis is understandable but the isolation can be damaging, for there is something irresistibly displaced and marginal about the now common and limiting phrase "aesthetic considerations", especially when contrasted with practical or UTILITARIAN (q.v.) considerations, which are elements of the same basic division' (p. 32).
11. Phenomenological aesthetic theories tend to form a category of their own, but generally confirm the situatedness of Dewey's theory and its emphasis on the unique and unifying *qualia* of artistic experiences.
12. For a contemporary application of Dewey, see Shusterman, 2000.
13. Schaeffer (2000) describes a 'speculative theory of Art' that is '*speculative* because in the diverse forms it assumes in the course of time, it is always deduced from a general metaphysics ... that provides its legitimation'. According to Schaeffer's analysis, 'what this amounts to is the claim that the arts and art works have to legitimate themselves philosophically. They can do so, however, only when they are in conformity with their postulated philosophical "essences"', thus creating circular reasoning where in effect 'the search for the essence is in fact a search for philosophical legitimacy' (p. 7).
14. Idealist aesthetic theories are also 'transcendental' because they include putative 'faculties', functions, and structures of reason and understanding held to be *a priori* bases for experiencing both the world and art.
15. For an incisive critique of the distortion of Kantian theory of taste into a theory of art, see Carroll, 1998, pp. 89–109, and *passim*.
16. Nonetheless, orthodox aesthetic theory is very ambivalent about sacred music since, to begin with, it has words and is thus not 'free' or 'pure' of conceptual meaning; and, secondly, because its use as worship violates the criterion of disinterestedness (see Kivy, 1990 on 'strictly musical' experience and Wolterstorff, 1980 for a defense of religious music).
17. As a result of this bias against the body, very little of aesthetic theory concerns itself with the performer. However, the professionalization of performance has discouraged amateur performance (see Levine, 1988, pp. 139–40) because anything less than virtuosity falls short of realizing properly aesthetic instantiations of 'works'. This assumption also calls into question the aesthetic status of student ensembles and student performance in general, since, by definition, such performance fails to reach appropriate aesthetic heights. For the same reasons, recorded music and a focus on listening rather than performing are often advanced for music education on the premise that the recordings provide appropriate heights of artistry.
18. The alternative to treating 'works' of music 'aesthetically' and thus as autonomous of the 'circumstances in which they are actually created or appreciated' is discussed in more detail below concerning music as praxis.
19. That is, it is cerebral; any bodily urges, such as foot tapping or conducting along while listening, are expressly discouraged.
20. This oft-heard expression stems from references to the Academy, the building in which Plato taught. Plato's idealism treated ideas, theories and the like as more real or reliable than the empirical world; and to the degree that this is the case in schools, the charge of academism rings true. On the 'scholastic fallacy' see Bourdieu, 1998.
21. They are not; the historical usage connected with the word 'appreciation' stems from the Latin word for 'value' (as in to 'appraise') or 'esteem' and thus to 'prize' something

in the sense that it is experienced as providing a 'reward' or 'benefit'; also, then, use refers to an increase in value, as money in a bank 'appreciates' due to interest paid. 'Understanding', used as 'grasping meaning', 'technical acquaintance' or 'studied familiarity' is not synonymous with 'appreciation' as valuing or prizing an experience. Perhaps for this reason, Dewey, in *Art as Experience*, often speaks of 'prizing' (i.e., 'using') art rather than referring to 'appreciating' it. Thus, we appreciate much that we have no studied understanding of and understand much that we do not appreciate—sometimes as a result of that understanding.

22. What graduates of 'school music' listen to, or whether 'concept teaching' facilitates or improves listening are never determined.
23. Aesthetic theory and the philosophy of music have separate histories; see Bowman, 1998, p. 6; for a praxial philosophy of music education, see Elliott, 1995.
24. The scientific empiricism and philosophical rationalism of the Enlightenment were, from the first, largely antithetical and the resulting 'modernism' was erected on an unstable foundation. Aesthetic theory exposes the resulting 'fault lines' as the superstructure of modernism slowly erodes.
25. See Proudfoot 1988, p. 850 and Williams, 1983, both quoted earlier.
26. For Durkheim, 'not only the contents of knowledge but even the forms of cognition are socially constituted. The categories of space and time, power and causality, the person and the species, he claims, are all derived from social circumstances and are the model for perceiving and knowing the world as a whole' (Joas, 1993, p. 62).
27. The assigning of a 'status function' to what are otherwise simply physical properties of things, including nature, is the central premise of John Searle's 'construction of social reality' (Searle, 1995; 1998). For a more detailed application of this idea to music, see Regelski, 2000a, and Regelski, 2003.
28. On 'fields' within a larger art or music world, see Bourdieu, 1993; for other sources, and details on the interaction of fields within the music world, see Regelski, 2003.
29. E.g., concert listening, 'occasional music', worship, ceremony, celebration, dance, recreation, and 'good time' as time meaningfully 'spent', etc.; on 'good time', see Regelski, 1997; on 'spending' time well, see Lakoff & Johnson, 1999, 161–65.
30. As Bourdieu (1984) shows, aesthetes regularly fail to see or acknowledge the social conditions and relativism of their own self-'distinction', and the class-based (and biased) issues involved..In general, ideas and values are always those of a historical time, situated conditions, or person (who is always in situated in time and place). Thus, even the *hypothesis* of universal and absolute ideas and values is relative to its own originating conditions.
31. 'Affordances' are empirical qualities that are 'out there' to be perceived by all present. These affordances, however, are attended to, or 'appropriated' differently according to the 'selective attention' of each person or of the same person at different times. Thus the physical properties of a stimulus object can be seen as 'good for' and thus 'appropriated' for different goods or goals. A 'tennis ball' can become a 'dog toy', a 'rock' can become a 'hammer', and a 'lake' affords fishing, swimming, boating, etc., each according to situated circumstances that include differences between individuals. DeNora (2000) provides extended ethnographic evidence of this idea for music.
32. See, as concerns the USA, McCarthy, 1997. Ample evidence exists of similar assumptions in many other nations.
33. On the nature of a profession, see DeMarris & LeCompte, 1998, pp. 149–54.
34. That is to say, repeated reference to 'aesthetic' experience by people is not sufficient to confirm the actual existence of the speculative values and meanings alleged by orthodox aesthetic theory. No one knows what another person's experience of, say, color is actually like but color terms at least have social consequences as bases for their inter-subjective reliability; i.e., agreement concerning differences between a red or green traffic light. In contrast, the subjective experience some label 'aesthetic' has no

unequivocal basis for comparison to experiences similarly labeled by others. Without any inter-subjective reliability, the label others use (especially 'significant others') to refer to pleasures and 'appreciations' connected with music and art is uncritically adopted on the basis of tradition as the preferred term to refer to the uniqueness of experiences of art and music (just as 'spiritual' get used just as variably in regard to experiences connected with worship). Thus, whatever the 'aesthetics of rock' might be, adolescents inevitably use other terms to describe their experience of that music. Much mischief and grief arises when certain words (i.e., concepts) refer to experiences that are supposedly shared—such as experiences of 'being in love'—but where inter-subjective agreement is actually lacking.

35. For pragmatism, such 'habits' are not mindless routines, but mindfully reflective in their concern for 'making a difference'.
36. Cost, availability, handling, maintenance of instruments and equipment can also be considered—both in terms of school resources, and as criteria for the likelihood of personal acquisition by students and adults.
37. Thus, for example, triads learned in connection with folk guitar serve as the bases for jazz harmonies; simple strums are the bases for rock figurations; keeping a steady beat, playing in tune, etc., are also 'basics' that can serve many different musics, and that figure, as well, in listening judgements and pleasures. In similar manner, blues improvisations can be expanded to rock and jazz, and aspects of drumming skills learned in one tradition can be employed in other styles, or can generally inform listening.
38. Thus the beginning folk guitarist, for example, can extend musicianship and enjoyments within that praxis.
39. Musical dispositions, like religious commitments, are highly resistant to overt conversion strategies, especially if such attempts are viewed as ideological manipulations. Unlike the situation with other subjects, the strongly held attitudes of adolescents towards, habits regarding, and uses of 'their' music leads them to reject musical instruction they sense to be conversion attempts.

References

Carroll, N. (1998) *A Philosophy of Mass Art* (Oxford, Oxford University/Clarendon Press).

Cooper, D., (ed.) (1992) *A Companion to Aesthetics* (Oxford, Blackwell).

Booth, W. C. (1999) *For the Love of It: Amateuring and its rivals* (Chicago, University of Chicago Press).

Bowman, W. D. (1998) *Philosophical Perspectives on Music* (New York, Oxford University Press).

Bourdieu, P. (1998) *Practical Reason: On the theory of action* (Stanford, Stanford University Press).

Bourdieu, P. (1993) *The Field of Cultural Production*, R. Johnson (ed.) (New York, Columbia University Press).

Bourdieu, P. (1984) *Distinction: A social critique of the judgement of taste*, trans. R. Nice (Cambridge, Harvard University Press).

DeMarrais, K. B. & M. D. LeCompte (1998) *The Way Schools Work: A sociological analysis of education*, 3rd edn. (New York, Longman).

DeNora, Tia (2000) *Music in Everyday Life* (Cambridge, Cambridge University Press).

Dissanayake, E. (1992) *Homo Aestheticus: Where art comes from and why*? (New York, Free Press).

Dissanayake, E. (1991) *What Is Art For*? (Seattle, University of Washington Press).

Dunne, J. (1993) *Back to the Rough Ground: Phronesis and techne in modern philosophy and Aristotle* (Notre Dame, Notre Dame University Press).

Edstrom, O. (2002) *En Annan berättelse om den västerländska musikhisotiren och det estetiska projektet* [*A Different Story of the History of Western Music and the Aesthetic Project*] (Göteborg, Sweden, Göteborgs Universitet).

Elliott, D. (1995) *Music Matters: A new philosophy of music education* (New York, Oxford University Press).

Gaut, B. & D. McIver Lopes, (eds) (2001) *The Routledge Companion to Aesthetics* (London, Routledge).

Green, L. (1988) *Music on Deaf Ears: Musical meaning, ideology and education* (Manchester, Manchester University Press).

Habermas, J. (1975) *Legitimation Crisis*, trans. T. McCarthy (Boston, Beacon Press).

Joas, H. (1993) *Pragmatism and Social Theory* (Chicago, University of Chicago Press).

Kivy, P. (1990) *Music Alone: Philosophical reflections on the purely musical experience* (Ithaca, Cornell University Press).

Korsmeyer, C. (1999) *Making Sense of Taste: Food and philosophy* (Ithaca, Cornell University Press).

Lakoff, G. & Johnson, M. (1999) *Philosophy in the Flesh* (New York, Basic Books).

Määttänen, P. (2002) Aesthetic Experience: A problem in praxialism, *Action, Criticism, and Theory for Music Education*, 1:1, (April), http:// http://www.Maydaygroup.org/ACT.

Martin, P. J. (1995) *Sounds and Society: Themes in the sociology of music* (Manchester, Manchester University Press).

McCarthy, M. (1997) The Foundations of Sociology in American Music Education (1900–1935), in: R. Rideout (ed.) *On the Sociology of Music Education*, pp. 71–80. (Norman Oklahoma, University of Oklahoma School of Music).

Popkewitz, T. (2001) Pacts/Partnerships, and Governing the Parent and Child, *Current Issues in Comparative Education*, 3:2 (May), http://www.tc.columbia.edu/CICE.

Popkewitz, T. & Gustafson, R. (2002) Standards of Music Education and the Easily Administered Child/Citizen: The alchemy of pedagogy and social inclusion/exclusion, *Philosophy of Music Education Review*, 10:2, (Fall), pp. 80–91.

Popp, J. A. (1998) *Naturalizing Philosophy of Education: John Dewey in the postanalytic period* (Edwardsville, Southern Illinois University Press).

Proudfoot, M. (1988) Aesthetics, in: G. H. R. Parkinson (ed.) *The Handbook of Western Philosophy* (New York, MacMillan).

Rancière, J. (2000) What Aesthetics Can Mean, in: P. Osborne (ed.), *From an Aesthetic Point of View*, pp. 13–34 (London, Serpent's Tail Books).

Regelski, T. A. (2004) Social Theory, and Music and Music Education as Praxis, *Action, Criticism, and Theory for Music Education*, (December), http:// http://www.Maydaygroup.org/ACT.

Regelski, T. A. (2002a) Musical Values and the Value of Music Education, *Philosophy of Music Education Review*, 10:1 (Spring), pp. 49–55.

Regelski, T. A. (2002b) On 'Methodolatry' and Music Teaching as Critical and Reflective Praxis, *Philosophy of Music Education Review*, 10:2 (Fall), pp. 102–123.

Regelski, T. A. (1998) The Aristotelian Bases of Music and Music Education, *Philosophy of Music Education Review*, 6:1 (Spring), pp. 22–59.

Regelski, T. A. (1997) A Prolegomenon to a Praxial Theory of Music and Music Education, *Canadian Music Educator*, 38:3 (Spring), pp. 43–51.

Regelski, T. A. (1984) To Be or Not To Be ... General?, *Soundings* [Journal of the Society for General Music, Music Educators National Conference], 1:3 (Spring), unpaged insert.

Regelski, T. A. (1969) Toward Musical Independence, *Music Educators Journal*, 55:7, (March), pp. 77–83.

Searle, J. (1995) *The Construction of Social Reality* (New York, Free Press).

Searle, J. (1998) *Mind, Language and Society: Philosophy in the real world* (New York, Basic Books).

Schaeffer, J-M. (2000) *Art of the Modern Age: Philosophy of art from Kant to Heidegger* (Princeton, Princeton University Press).

Shepherd, J. (1991) *Music as Social Text* (Cambridge, Polity Press).

Shepherd, J. & Wicke, P. (1997) *Music and Cultural Theory* (Cambridge, Polity Press/Blackwell).

Shusterman, R. (2000) *Pragmatist Aesthetics: Living beauty, rethinking art, 2nd edn.* (Oxford, Rowman & Littlefield Publishers, Inc.).

Small, C. (1997) Musicking: A Ritual in Social Space, in: R. Rideout (ed.) *On the Sociology of Music Education*, pp. 1–12 (Norman Oklahoma, University of Oklahoma School of Music).

Small, C. (1998) *Musicking: The meanings of performing and listening* (Hanover, New Hampshire, Wesleyan University Press).

Ståhlhammer, B. (2000) The Space of Music and its Foundation of Values—Music Teaching and Young People's Own Music Experience, *International Journal of Music Education* (Journal of the International Society for Music Education), 36, pp. 35–45.

Summers, D. (1987) *The Judgement of Sense: Renaissance naturalism and the rise of aesthetics* (Cambridge, Cambridge University Press).

Urmson, J. O. (1989) Aesthetics, in: J. O. Urnson & J. Rèe (eds), *The Concise Encyclopedia of Western Philosophy, Revised Ed.* (London, Unwin Hyman).

Valéry, P. (1945) Leçon inaugurale du cours de poétique au Collège de France, *Variétiés*, V, pp. 297–322 (Paris, Gallimard).

Williams, R. (1983) *Keywords: A vocabulary of culture and society, Revised Edition* (London, Oxford University Press).

Wolterstorff, N. (1980) *Art in Action* (Grand Rapids, MI, Eerdmans).

3
Music Education in Nihilistic Times

WAYNE BOWMAN
Brandon University, Canada

> The highest values have devalued themselves. There is no goal. There is no answer to the question, 'why'?
>
> —Nietzsche, *The Will to Power*

In *Art as Experience*, Dewey writes, 'The conception that objects have fixed and unalterable values is precisely the prejudice from which art emancipates us' (Dewey, 1934/1980, p. 95).[1] But does it? Has it? In music education our pedagogical practices, our curricula, our research agendas, and the way we prepare prospective teachers—all betray an orientation quite different from the one Dewey suggests we might realistically expect of undertakings like music. In many of our practices, the notion of 'fixed and unalterable value' figures quite centrally: music's value is inherent, intrinsic, given; and our professional undertakings as music educators are self-evidently those necessary for revelation, transmission, and proper appreciation of such value(s). In such a system, musical instruction consists of the means to ends that are beyond scrutiny; and accordingly, our paramount professional concerns have to do with how to fine tune these means, making them ever more 'efficient' and 'effective'. Music education's overriding concern has become how to do more efficiently what we already do: not the intent with which we do it; not the ends to which such doings lead; not the kind of responsive resourcefulness that creatively transforms practice; and not, I submit, the nurturance of life affirming musical value.

The point I will pursue in this essay is that the instrumentalism or technical rationalism that has come to predominate music education (in North America, at any rate) warrants, from the perspective of value and values education, a much more apt and disturbing label: nihilism.[2] Our seduction by the positivistic air of our times; our seeming determination to render systematically transparent the murkiness and messiness of musical value; our newfound obsession with musical standards; our apparent inability to conceive of curricular alternatives to conventional practice: these are powerful evidence of just how far we have drifted from the kind of potential Dewey imputes (rightly, I think) to endeavors like music. The all-too-common product of such drift among the students who are its beneficiaries: indifference; disengagement; mechanistic enactment rather than creative exploration; music-like gestures deprived of the vividness and intensity essential for values that are durable and resilient. To put the matter bluntly, music education might reasonably be expected to function as an antidote to nihilism; instead, the institution is becoming an unwitting source.

I propose to explore, through Deleuze's interpretation of Nietzsche (Deleuze, 1983),[3] three kinds or manifestations of nihilism: negative nihilism, reactive nihilism, and passive nihilism. I want to sketch in a preliminary manner various ways the assumptions, beliefs, and practices of music educators might reflect these nihilistic orientations, and to offer some speculations on how music education might be re-construed as value exploration and affirmation. At the heart of my argument will lie a performative understanding of musical engagement, one in which music-making is conceived of and approached as an active process of sense-making—an act that foregrounds musical agency, the creation of narrative, and the social construction of value.

1. Introduction

The music education profession finds itself in the throes of a legitimation crisis, a crisis that, while not entirely of its own creation, is at least one in which it has played (and continues to play) a substantial role. Although this crisis manifests itself in a number of ways, its upshot is that claims to musical value have deteriorated into mere arbitrary preferences, habitual conventions, or worse. On this view, value assertions are manifestations of political power and influence, products of socialization, and to that extent, baseless. Value is little more than, in Nietzsche's vivid phrase, 'the opposite of its opposite'—a totally circular affair, a matter of infinitely ungrounded referral. The fact Nietzsche raised this issue many years ago is evidence that this is not exactly a recent development; nor is its contemporary prevalence particularly surprising in light of globalized trade, the free market economy, and late capitalism. What is both surprising and disturbing, however, is music education's complicity: the extent to which the beliefs and practices of the profession have accepted and incorporated uncritically the rhetoric and strategies of this nihilistic age.[4]

The symptoms of this radical failure, this collapse of value, are widespread in music education. One of its more striking manifestations can be seen, I believe, in curricula designed to prepare music teachers, where training has long since replaced genuine education.[5] Music teacher curricula are overwhelmingly 'practical,' devoid of things like theory, complexity, and controversy—prime ingredients, one would think, in the crucible where independent thought and informed creative practice should be forged. But this is only one example in a list that is potentially vast. Consider:

a) Where the existence of music education's crisis is sensed or acknowledged, its strategic response is advocacy. Advocacy efforts are generally construed as rhetorical programs of political persuasion, designed to convince others of the shortsightedness of their skepticism about the worth of music education. Rather than interrogating current practice, advocacy is designed to protect it—both from criticism and from the kind of critical scrutiny that might identify needs for substantive change. Advocacy typically 'promises the world',[6] without asking about the circumstances under which its promises might be realized, or acknowledging their contingency. It invests all its energies and resources rhetorically and politically, treating musical value as self-evident.

b) Scientism and positivism have become ideological touchstones for a profession anxious to substantiate its dignity and credibility among the behavioral sciences. Since, from these perspectives, to be substantive is to be scientific and to be scientific is to be concerned with matters of fact rather than of value, value-theoretic concerns are regarded as dispensable, as embarrassments, as passé. To be an 'advanced music educator' is to be armed with an arsenal of scientifically-proven, irrefutable 'facts' about music and music education—and not to be distracted or diverted from those facts by reflective or self-critical inquiry.

c) Curricula at all levels are increasingly designed to eliminate the possibility of failure through prediction, control, and precision. The possibility that the world loses its depth along with its recalcitrance is not seen as a serious consideration, nor is the deprofessionalization of teaching that generally accompanies it.

d) There is a rush to improve music education by ever more effective centralized and efficiently managed systems and tidily-packaged instruction: technology, multiple 'levels' of Orff or Kodaly studies, the summer conducting institute, Gordon's musical learning theory—any and all, available for efficient consumption in a three week package, or 'on line'. Sustained engagement with challenging problems is anathema to such tidily-bundled courses and the programs they in turn comprise.

e) The metaphor best descriptive of music education's aspirations is, in short, the smoothly running machine—to which obdurate things like values relate, if at all, as ghosts. The source of inspiration for music education curricula, the overwhelming preoccupation of music educators, is 'what works,' 'the practical'. This kind of technical rationalism has as its exclusive focus the refinement and increased efficiency of instructional means, to the widespread neglect of questions and deliberations about instructional ends. What counts is the development and refinement of skills—doing 'better' what we are already doing—not whether we are doing the right things (at the right time, with the right intent, to the right ends, and so on).[7]

The effect with which these various concerns and considerations come together, however unintentionally, is as prescriptions for decisions and behavior, as formulas for action, as substitutes rather than incentives for thought. Ease of curricular passage is assured by close attention to sequence and the systematic elimination of ambiguity or contradiction. In all these ways, students are protected from the challenges associated with authentic personal growth, and the profession, in turn, from creative self-transformation. We in music education may talk values; but we teach techniques and technical rationality.

The role typically played by philosophy or theory in music curricula (when and where such content is even addressed) is similarly technical: devoted to providing predetermined answers, distinguishing music's absolute ('objective', 'inherent') values from mere subjective or associative ones, and assuring appropriate deference to facts and truths. The low priority accorded scholarly work in such theoretical areas is reflected in its near absence from research journals, the paucity of teaching positions stressing philosophical expertise, and by the cursory 'coverage' given to philosophical considerations in music teacher education. 'Philosophy', where taught, is dispensed technically, as a body of truths to which students are expected to subscribe. In each of these ways philosophical/theoretical inquiry differs only marginally from the technical, value free modus operandi that prevails elsewhere in the curriculum. Values, we teach implicitly, are mere conventions: abstract positions articulated by others for our optional consumption.

Clearly I have in mind a particular understanding of the term 'value': after all, it might be argued, conventional or abstract values are values nonetheless; and indeed, even 'technical rationalism' designates something that might be described in some sense as a value orientation. I acknowledge at the outset, then, that when I speak of nihilism in what follows, I refer (with justification, I believe) to the absence of values *of a particular kind*—the kind that people use to forge and re-forge coherent sense in their lives, the kind that help transform mere existence into lives worth living. The alternative to nihilism as I use the term here is creative, present tense life affirmation. My point of departure is a strong conviction that meaning is not just out-there, something arbitrary and optional one may choose to endorse or not. Rather, meaning is created through, and resides in, *use*: forged in and through human *action*. Music and music education are, on this view, meaningful only to the extent they become use-full and 'part of the action'—integral to people's identities and their ways of being in the world. Agency and meaning arise in and are sustained by action—action that is always situated, embodied, and social. Thus, meaning that is authentically musical is never just out there for the taking, nor does it occur simply in virtue of having gone through the appropriate motions or having engaged in activities that are deemed musical institutionally.

Nor does music 'add' value to experience. Rather, musical experience becomes valued and valuable through a constructive act in which it becomes woven into a coherent and goal-oriented personal narrative.[8] Resistance and personal challenge are crucial ingredients in this process, I believe; and attempts to circumvent these elements in pursuit of efficiency are predestined to failure. The realm of value is not a realm rendered more easily accessible by technique or more tidily manageable by reason. Its concern is, as I have argued elsewhere, ethical (Bowman, 2001): tightly bound up in choices as to how to act rightly, in pursuit of ends that are unpredictable, changeable, and never fully knowable.

In advocating an ethical basis for educational practice in music, I am advocating a return to Wittgenstein's 'rougher ground,' an acceptance of respons/ability (Bowman, 2002) grounded in action and pursued without the false comfort of certainty (Bowman, 2003). The positive side of this coin is, I believe, creative freedom, self-determination, and genuine engagement.

2. Negative Nihilism

I do not intend to develop a thoroughly or comprehensively Nietzschean framework here, only to adapt several of Nietzsche's claims about nihilism for the purposes to which I have alluded above. What Nietzsche has to say about nihilism is neither tidy nor entirely consistent, and as a result many of the nihilistic convictions commonly attributed to him are in fact views that he opposed quite strenuously.

Two key points frame his stance on nihilism. First, he maintains that nihilism is a necessary and unavoidable consequence of the Western philosophical tradition. Second, and as a result, nihilism will remain a central part of Western intellectual and cultural heritage for centuries to come. All thoughtful people, then—thoughtful in the ways we have been taught to think by our philosophical predecessors—must be nihilists. However, neither of these assertions means that Nietzsche himself espouses nihilism, at least not nihilism as we commonly understand that term: a debased, pessimistic state characterized by the utter absence of value and meaning. On the contrary, Nietzsche is highly critical of such dispositions and devotes considerable effort to correcting them.

Nietzsche gives us not one kind of nihilism, but several—most of which are neither justified nor defensible in his view. The orientation he calls 'religious' nihilism is typified by its efforts to explain, justify, and impute some kind of ultimate purpose to the given world. Ironically, though, this preoccupation with justification—with finding some higher (or deeper) purpose in the world as lived and experienced—amounts to a rejection of the real world. The pursuit of transcendent meaning, in other words, betrays the unconscious conviction that the world lacks sufficient value in and of itself, and thus needs to be shored up in some way. Western philosophy's efforts to identify for the world and our place in it some kind of ultimate purpose, some sense of higher worth, proceeds from the unwarranted assumption that the world is deficient in purpose and worth. Since they stem from failure to find value in 'what is', and to that extent *negate* the here-and-now, appeals to higher value and purpose amount to what Deleuze designates 'negative nihilism'.

Negative nihilists, then, are those who seek to ground the value of the world in some transcendental realm outside it, substituting a kind of fetishized abstract value for real value. This apparently fulfills a significant psychological need, making the flux, contingency, and unpredictability of life more tolerable—just as the idea of an omniscient, benevolent God serves to impute meaning and purpose to what might otherwise be random, horrifying events. Negative nihilism thus stems from the widespread need for order and the sense that all is well, from attempts to dispel the riskiness of everyday life by resort to belief systems grounded in such things as necessity and atemporal stability—or, in more Nietzschean terms: ultimate purpose, underlying unity, and transcendental truth. These belief systems on which negative nihilism is founded are, however, fabrications. As affirmations of another world, they are unwitting negations or denials of this one. In place of value that is immanently constructed or created by human agents, 'value' atrophies into a hollow, idealized abstraction–out there, disembodied, immaterial.

Again, it is not my intent here to develop a definitively Nietzschean account. The spirit of his observations about well-intended belief implicating unwitting negations, however, strikes me as potentially fruitful. The notion that practices and beliefs espousing significant concern for values in an abstract sense may actually compromise the ranges of values with which music educators should properly concern themselves is one we should take quite seriously. Here I have in mind a long history in music philosophy that seeks to construe music as a purveyor of ineffable insights, or as a symbol that somehow mediates perception of the otherwise unknowable realm of human feeling, or quite an extensive list of similar claims—each of which imputes to music some transcendental, abstract, universal purpose. What each of these does, however inadvertently, is suggest that music as heard, as experienced, as enacted, or as collectively undertaken, is somehow in need of further justification. The doing or making of music is of value only to the extent it partakes of some further, more lofty purpose. This view not only undercuts but negates the value of musical experience and musical action.

Lest we music educators be tempted to deny our complicity in such nihilistic systems of thought, we need to consider the extent to which we have attempted to justify and ground our educational practices in such abstract systems. The notion that music education is musically substantive only to the extent it is conceived of and pursued as a form of 'aesthetic education' is surely a case in point. And most if not all the advocacy arguments to which the profession is drawn—whether the development of aesthetic sensitivity or of spatial reasoning—betray a similar conviction that musical action and agency are not sufficient in themselves to substantiate a claim to genuine value. In much the same way, our inclination to speak of 'the' nature and 'the' value of music and music education reveals an aversion to acknowledging the contingency, plurality, and fluidity of these values—an aversion rooted in the unspoken assumption that such states of affairs are somehow deficient or undeserving of the name 'value'.

We need not develop an exhaustive inventory here, only to sketch some of parameters that may enable others to take up the task. Our appeals to abstractions and universals, our failure to acknowledge the contingency of musical value, our inclination to treat musical value as something inherent, objective, and absolute—each of these reveals our predilection for treating values as conventional, settled, and yes, stale. We endorse canonization and teach deference to works of genius rather than attempting to generate and ground value in active, creative risk-taking. Our advocacy consists largely of doctrinal justification and appeals to 'intrinsic' or 'inherent' worth—things that are unconditional and ostensibly follow automatically rather than contingently from our musical activities and instructional interventions.

In each of these ways and many more the music education profession engages in and purveys a kind of negative nihilism, saying 'nay' to the potency of musical action—its multivalence, corporeality, transience, and unpredictability.

3. Reactive Nihilism

The second manifestation of nihilism identified in Nietzsche's work is what Deleuze describes as 'reactive'. In contrast to the naïve optimism of negative nihilism, reactive nihilism is characterized by a sense of loss. The power or persuasiveness of the 'highest ideals' at the core of negative nihilism deteriorates, and leaves in its wake a kind of vacuum, a despair, or emptiness. The need for the reassurance formerly provided by universal and transcendent beliefs remains, but can no longer be filled by beliefs of that kind. The reactive nihilist's nihilism is thus conscious, and to some degree at least, pessimistically nostalgic. My interpretation of this state of affairs is that people seek other, more mundane sources of meaning to fill the void—but the void remains, and indeed, constitutes both the backdrop and the motivation for ways of proceeding. To this extent it still entails an effort to repudiate presumed emptiness, and it still constitutes a fundamental denial of authentic meaning in the world-as-given.

Put differently, reactive nihilism still represents a failing—a failure to renounce the need for such things as ultimate unity and underlying purpose—and a corresponding failure to direct its attention to life-affirmation, to creative action, and the kind of things I will discuss under the heading of 'completed nihilism'. Since it continues, in White's words, 'to judge the world by traditional categories of value', (White, 1990, p. 17) it harbors a kind of inverse belief: a generalized belief in the arbitrariness or the meaningless of human strivings. One way of characterizing this would be 'existential despair', but I do not want to make so extreme a claim when it comes to music education. Instead, I want to suggest that many of our current preoccupations can be seen to stem from the loss of belief in 'higher values' while we continue to cling to the idea that this represents an actual loss, and, as a result, scramble for ways to legitimate and sustain our endeavors—to show that what we do is justified in ways that are unified and purposeful. The system and its maintenance become their own points.

From my perspective, there is a tremendously long list of indicators of such a stance in music education at present, each of which amounts in one way or another to an attempt to compensate for a demise in the security formerly afforded by the highest ideals. In the opening paragraphs of this essay I characterized these as a 'what works' mentality. It is markedly technical and means-driven, with remarkably little attention to or concern for ends served.[9] Our preoccupation with what Regelski (2002) aptly calls methodolatry provides a vivid example. From this stance, (a) what counts instructionally is adherence to a preordained structure and sequence; (b) what counts as evidence of effectiveness is the development of preordained skill levels (attainment, that is, of 'standards'); (c) what matters most is knowledge (and still further knowledge) of 'how-to', with little if any concern for such matters as 'whether to' or 'under what circumstances' or 'to what ends'; and (d) what counts as teaching is the efficient transmission of content or development of predetermined skills. Educating gives way to what is more accurately described as training, and eventually, to mere management. And the avoidance of failure eventually replaces the idea of success.

Such instrumentalism, with its pride in 'being practical', keeps both teachers and students active and occupied. But mere activity and occupation do not assure, nor are they concerned with, the construction of personal and collective meaning, the provision of opportunities for sense-making, or the development of coherent narratives in which musical choices and embodied actions figure vividly. As a result, little if anything in the lives of students stems from or depends upon their musical involvements. Nor, unfortunately, is there much room for creativity, divergence, or the pursuit of unforeseen meanings of the kind that make and keep life vital.

Although, as has been indicated, this gives music students lots to learn (and both music teachers and teacher educators lots to teach), much of what is involved is a kind of mimesis, of going through the motions. The focus on values, to the extent there is one, is purely conventional. To the extent that appropriate instructional actions and sequences are given at the outset, teaching is deprofessionalized. Ironically, although there is more to do than ever, there seems to be less and less point in doing it. It is but a short step, I submit, from this to the kind of abject nihilism Nietzsche calls 'passive'.

4. Passive Nihilism

In 'passive' nihilism, nostalgia fades and resistance finally withers: the absence of worth—the utter negation of all values—is accepted with resignation. Gone is the 'active' response, the sense of loss characteristic of the reactive nihilist. Instead, 'what is' just is: *whatever*. This is the overt sense of nihilism most of us have come to associate with the term: the kind of postmodern, anything-goes frame of mind in which all claims to value are reduced to politically-motivated power moves.

This is also the kind of nihilism commonly but wrongly attributed to Nietzsche, who saw it as a kind of dead-end for the weak of spirit—a state of utter incapacity for valuing represented vividly in *Thus Spake Zarathustra* through his characterizations of the 'last man'. Nietzsche's last man is weak-willed, resigned, and tired. He takes no risks, seeking only comfort and security. He is last because his passivity has rendered him incapable of dreaming or doing anything decisive. He is also last because this is the state of mind toward which Nietzsche thinks Western civilization has been moving inexorably, through its negative and reactive phases. What began as an idealistic[10] quest for security and refuge from complexity and change, and what eventually gave way to the disillusioned quest for something to replace it, comes to fruition in people who are no longer capable of saying 'no' (let alone 'yes') to life. Ease, contentment, avoidance of burden: these define the last man's existence.[11]

The last man cannot take a committed stand on anything. Success is no more than the absence of failure. 'What is love?' asks the last man. 'What is creation? What is longing? What is a star?' Such things lie so far outside his experience that he cannot respond, only blink, absently. He has 'left the regions where it is hardest to live', seeking only warmth and comfort, thus making 'everything small'. 'No shepherd, and one herd! Everyone wants the same; everyone is equal ... "We have discovered happiness"—say the last people, and blink thereby' (Nietzsche, 1993).[12]

If negative nihilism is ends-driven, and reactive nihilism means-driven, passive nihilism is not driven at all. The world of passive nihilism is a world of mindless tolerance and acceptance, of unbounded, unrestricted cultural pluralism—a world in which anything and everything goes, and in which minds have become so 'open' brains appear to have fallen out.[13] The world of passive nihilism is characterized by uncritical, indifferent activity in the service of ends that no longer really matter[14] and that can no longer sustain claims to be unique or distinctive in any way. This is the world of McDonaldization. It is also a world in which responsibility and commitment are scarcely discernible. Tasks are reduced to mundane sequences of activities, purged of real challenge, resistance, difficulty, risk, and therefore, meaningful effort. The challenge of acting meaningfully or choosing the best from among desirable courses of action is replaced by the conventional, the habitual, the easy.

As Blake puts it, 'This is a leveled world ... where the will of the people is so enfeebled that it is directed only towards a life of ease and freedom from discomfort' (Blake, 2000, p. 56).

It would be both unfair and inaccurate to characterize contemporary music education as passively nihilistic. Yet, the profession needs to acknowledge the existence and influence of such forces—to think carefully and critically about its potential for unwitting complicity in such circumstances, and the subtlety of the erosive process that culminates in such a value vacuum. What are the socio-cultural forces that lead to passive nihilism? How do they influence music education? And what can be done to resist such influence? My concern is that the music education profession's comfortable slide from idealism into technicism (where to be an advanced music educator means to have a large arsenal of techniques at one's disposal and to deploy them efficiently) has delivered us precipitously close to this stage of utter passivity. We have not seen it coming, but in retrospect the path from negative to reactive to passive nihilism is easily enough discerned. At its end point, the effort to show that we are actually accomplishing something and to legitimate what we are doing have become over-riding concerns—made manifest in a 'standards' and 'advocacy' frenzy. However, standards and advocacy initiatives address symptoms rather than causes—they are rear-guard strategies designed primarily to defend and preserve the status quo.

This is a point of crucial importance, because in addressing symptoms rather than causes, we contribute to the perpetuation rather than the resolution of the problem. Rather than asking how we might revise practice so as to eliminate the need for standards, standardization, and political persuasion, we embrace these latter—accepting the nihilistic frames of reference from which they have emerged and in which they remain ensconced. We have endorsed multiculturalism, for instance, but failed to take seriously the ways cultures are created and sustained—the ways they become momentous and vital, and the ways people learn to 'live into' them.[15] As a result, many of us (and many more of our students) have come to regard values as arbitrary or political matters—as perspectives whose claims to our allegiance are largely casual and inconsequential.

This kind of non-conviction is at the heart of Nietzsche's passive nihilism. If all perspectives are equally non-binding, then determining which should take precedence (such choices, note, being central concerns of curriculum development) is little more than an act of arrogance and power. As nihilism becomes increasingly banal[16] and our acceptance of it increasingly blasé, value is simply replaced with power: the claim 'This is good' amounts to nothing more than a subjective assertion whose validity is a function of the authority or force behind it.

Detachment, diffidence, indifference: these are the 'values' that typify passive nihilism. And they are the logical outcomes of instruction which focuses on means (efficiency, expediency, and 'what works') or ends (the intrinsically or inherently good), one to the exclusion of the other. The challenge facing us, then, is to reconceptualize our instructional efforts in ways that demand investment, engagement, responsibility and attachment—ways that weave means and ends together in fabric that is rich, engaging, and vital.

5. Nihilism 'Completed': Present-tense, Creative Action

Although the progression (or is it, rather, a regression?) from negative to reactive to passive nihilism is empirically prevalent, it is by no means inevitable. Indeed, this was the point Nietzsche was at pains to make. His attitude toward the various nihilistic stances we have been tracing here was largely contemptuous. He renounced the dualistic, life-denying assumptions at the core of Western philosophical traditions, and urged the assumption of a courageous, affirmative stance toward the world and life in it. I do not intend to follow the particulars of Nietzsche's move here, but its general strategy is, I think, both instructive and positive.

According to philosopher Alan White (1990), Nietzsche's discussions of nihilism actually make use of a fourth category of nihilism,[17] one that inverts negative nihilism's irony by appearing to be nihilistic, while it is not.[18] 'Complete' nihilism is the state of one who has *worked through* nihilism, one who, like Nietzsche, has moved beyond negation and reaction, and whose stance amounts therefore to a 'Dionysian affirmation of the world as it is' (White, 1990, p. 19).[19] This stance may appear nihilistic from the perspective of those who still cling nostalgically to the positions we have called negative and reactive—because it emphatically rejects the value assumptions and aspirations of both those perspectives. The 'complete' nihilist has abandoned the quest for meaning and value in otherworldly claims, and has equally little use for reactive attempts to replace these with systems and prescriptions. However, and quite unlike the passive nihilist, the nihilist Nietzsche calls 'complete' has lived through nihilism to its exhaustion or termination. Complete nihilism is 'the logic of our great values and ideals, thought through to its end' (White, 1990, p. 21)—and the complete nihilist, therefore, is one has learned to live life outside 'logic' of that sort. This complete nihilist, concludes White, is one who has 'completed nihilism, thereby ceasing to be a nihilist' (White, 1990, p. 22)—and has become, somewhat ironically, an anti-nihilist. In short, the 'complete nihilist' returns to the position that was lost in negative nihilism's initial endorsement of transcendence and its rejection of the lived world. Nietzsche's 'complete' nihilist is one who 'deifies becoming and the apparent world as the only world, and calls them good' (White, 1990, p. 22).

From this perspective, argues White, religious (or as I have been calling it here, negative) nihilism is the 'immediate and necessary precursor' of reactive nihilism. And the historical successor to reactive nihilism, according to Nietzsche—the one that is emerging or has emerged as prevalent—is the pathetic ('last man') state here called passive nihilism. However, the crucial point to be made is that this historical result does not obtain necessarily or follow inevitably. One can reject *both* 'the highest values' *and* the framework within which such values are held to be desirable. This does not leave one destitute of all values; rather, it disavows the need for values beyond those that inhere in the world and life as they are. This position, then, is one that affirms life and the world *as they are in themselves*—without recourse to such things as ultimate purpose, underlying unity, or absolute truth. 'One who is left with nothing in this manner', explains White, 'has gained rather than lost: in denying that the world requires "purpose", "unity", or "truth" of the sort posited by [negative] nihilists and despaired of by [reactive] nihilists, one may regain the world of becoming in its original innocence' (White, 1990, p. 21).[20]

To repeat, the position I am advancing here is not Nietzchean in its particulars. Nor do I advocate that the music education profession take up a position that can be characterized as nihilistic in any legitimate sense. I do want to urge, however, that we take seriously Nietzsche's distinction between apparent and actual nihilism, that we ask carefully after the ranges of values our actions and convictions seem to entail, and indeed, that we ask more critically what 'valuing' entails. What Nietzsche shows is that the nihilistic failure to endow the world with value can occur in various ways, including, and in particular, sincere efforts to 'add' value to our world of becoming.[21] The world, Nietzsche tells us, does not require such additions, improvements, or justifications. The world is not the kind of thing that needs shoring up by values, nor can the mere 'addition' of values compensate for a mistake of the magnitude of the one that presumes the world requires such improvement in the first place.

These points should be, I believe, of paramount concern to us as music educators in a nihilistic world that is, in part, our own creation. For not only is it possible to create and sustain value without resort to other-worldly ideals (teleological determinism) or the false security of rational prescriptions for action (mechanistic determinism), these are conditions that *actually negate values*. We need, I submit instead, to accept and embrace what Hans Joas calls 'the risk-and responsibility-laden nature of present action' (Joas, 1996, p. 250).[22]

Risk, responsibility, presence, and action. These, I submit, constitute the core of a *pragmatic* stance,[23] one that accepts things like temporal change, and the fluidity and alterability (and indeed, the fragility!) of value—the things to which Dewey alludes in the statement with which I began this essay. This stance is also pragmatic in its emphasis on the fundamental creativity of action, the social construction of value, and the equation of meaning with use. For the pragmatist, values are always relational, never absolute; always work in progress, never wholly resolved; always contingent in some respect, never beyond potential dispute. I have already offered repeated suggestions as to ways commitments like these might reorient and transform music education, suggestions further amplified, I hope, by the various contrasts and comparisons advanced in the following table.[24]

Pragmatist convictions maintain that human action is the source of meaning and value; and given the creativity of action and the ever changing contexts (natural and social) in which it occurs, meaning and value can never be the kinds of things that are simply given—objectively, static, uniform, and predictable. From this perspective, music takes whatever meanings it may have from its use—present tense, here and now. And the concern of musical instruction, therefore, is neither 'the good' nor 'what works', but what musical endeavors are 'good for'[25] in the real world—in full recognition that such goods are radically diverse, exceedingly fragile, and potentially as numerous as the people who find good in such actions. This flies in the face of standardization and uniform instructional method (grounded as they are in nihilistic notions of fixity and uniformity, and in nostalgic yearning for

	NEGATIVE (Unwittingly nihilistic)	**REACTIVE** (Void left by loss of transcendent value)	**PASSIVE** ('Tired,' will depleted: *Last Man*)	**'COMPLETED'** (Worked-through, life-affirming)
Epistemological orientation	Intuitive, spiritual, abstract, 'what's good'	Instrumental, technical 'what works'	Arbitrary 'whatever'	Action/praxis, 'good for …'
Impetus	Ends driven (teleological determinism)	Means driven (mechanistic determinism)	None apparent	Action driven (the present, here-and-now)
Philosophical orientation	Idealism, rationalism (naïve optimism)	Technicism, instrumentalism, positivism	None: only politics	Pragmatic, practice-driven
Meaning	Given, absolute	Beside the point, a byproduct	Absent, or merely serendipitous	Arising from use: performative, embodied, relational
Values	Ideal, abstract, other-worldly	Conventional, 'objective,' instrumental, ease	A passé notion (replaced by mere preferences)	Narrative, construction, complexity
Student expectations	Appreciation, connoisseurship	Skills, mimesis	Motions only	Action, narrative, identity, becoming
Student experience	Developing good taste	Jump through hoops	Apathy, disengagement, motions only	Making, doing, absorption, narrative construction
Experiential Characteristics	Idealized coherence (rational), aesthetic reverence	Sequential structure (tidiness, neatness, ease), efficiency	Eclectic structure, random sequence	Narrative unity, embodiment
Instructional orientation	Revelation	Neutral transmission, socialization	Time-filling, busy-ness	Personal development, grounded value
Focus of teacher education	Inspirational rhetoric, 'good taste,' appreciation	Technicism, 'methodolatry,' replication of status quo	'Management' skills, activities, advocacy, Mc-Donaldization	Sense-making, action, plurality, locally embedded
Point of pride	'Philosophical,' rational/logical	'Practical'	Occupied, busy	Intensity, engagement, groundedness
Curricular focus	Canon, the good or great, truth	Means, 'how-to,' 'what works,' skill development	Vacuous plurality & eclecticism	Sense-making, creative variation, right action
Curriculum standards	Universal, doctrinal, fixed	Technical, 'means'-focus, crisis-aversion	Irrelevant, trivial, banal	'of care'; agency-focus, local, use
Criteria	Inspiration	Efficiency	Attendance	Agency, engagement, sense-making

certainty). It suggests strongly the kind of educational praxis that abjures the security and comfort of the tried and true, choosing instead to work without a safety net—on grounds that the loss of creativity, responsibility, and value is simply too great a cost to pay for predictability and security.

From this perspective, the focus of musical learning extends well beyond developing appropriate deference to 'greatness', and well beyond the refinement of skills to preordained standards.[26] Becoming musically educated extends to who and what one is: to one's character or identity. Its key is learning to act meaningfully, a process of active sense-making in which what one does gets its particular sense from the place it occupies in the narrative structure of one's life. It is marked, therefore, not by detached deliberation and execution, but by the intensity and absorption that always attend life-shaping choices. Its enemies are the very ease and effortless systematicity[27] that have become hallmarks of music education.

From this perspective, music education should be concerned with the process of narrative sense-making, of weaving meaningful and coherent personal (and interpersonal) stories from musical actions. It should be concerned with the development and nurturance of lived commitments, attachments, and engagement in the process of living. What it teaches, beyond musical skills, concepts, and understandings, is the authenticity of human action and the non-arbitrary nature of value. And music, always and unavoidably a bodily event, offers to teach such lessons with a vividness and durability that eludes most other instruction.[28]

Finally (although the idea of 'finality' needs to be taken provisionally here), one of the value-related insights that should attend a musical education from the pragmatic perspective being discussed here is the non-threatening nature of change. As Dewey's observations suggest, the insight that values are malleable and constructed rather than fixed and unalterable is among the most important things a musical education should deliver. If music teaching and learning place genuine problems and the improvisatory pursuit of solutions at the creative center of music-making, then of equal importance to what music education teaches us about music is what it teaches us about life and living, both individually and socially: and a central part of that lesson, one should think, is that successful action is a function of agility, and ever light on its feet.

6. Beyond Nihilism: Action, Affirmation, Narrative, and Value

In other essays I have written recently I have urged the ethical basis of educational practice in music, advocating a return to what I have variously described as the rougher ground, a space-between, *praxis* guided by *phronesis*, and respons/ability grounded in musical agency and musical action.[29] I have argued for an explicitly educational commitment, in contrast to the training with which we have become increasingly content: instruction reduced to methods, formulas, prescriptions, and preoccupied with what Regelski calls 'the pet and the pat'. I have advocated a focus on character, values, the kind of people we tend to become while being instructed 'in' or 'about' music, on grounds these are always important parts of what music is and what it means.

Here I have attempted to approach these arguments in slightly different ways, suggesting that without difficulty and resistance we create conditions of uncritical and indifferent activity—not the kinds of engagement and sense-making that people can subsequently drape their lives around. Our curricula, our instructional methods, and the reductive standards by which we are inclined to gauge their worth reveal our complicity in a Faustian exchange of depth for systematicity—one that stems from failure to think seriously about the deeper significance of these undertakings. And if we don't 'get it' ourselves, we can scarcely expect more of others. We have failed to assure that the musical experiences in which we engage our students have the kind of vividness and richness that demand nothing less than total personal investment. These are failings that cannot be fixed by mandating standards or by mounting advocacy arguments intended to convince people of the extent and sincerity of our hard work, or to persuade them that what we are currently doing deserves more respect.

What I urge us to consider is that music education properly considered should be emancipatory in nature—an endeavor that frees people from the debilitating notions that values come ready-made; that value-based choices reduce to arbitrary assertions of personal preference; that what most 'counts' about music is the ability to execute it with a minimum of errors; or that what 'counts' as being musically educated is some kind of standardized knowledge or uniform proficiency. In society at large, values are increasingly viewed like brands of goods: options whose claims to our allegiance are largely functions of product placement, concerned with nothing more meaningful or substantial than market share. Value? Whatever. The term rings hollow.

Music education's response to this deplorable state of affairs has been twofold. On the one hand, we have treated values as incontrovertibly factual: musical value is inherent, intrinsic, absolute, objective—'there' to be appreciated, quite apart from what anyone may perceive or experience. The concern of instruction is thus to assure appreciation for 'what's good'. On the other hand, and a corollary of this presumption of the utter facticity of musical value, we focus our efforts and attention on instructional means: the efficiency or effectiveness with which we are able to attain standardized behavioral outcomes. The instructional concern is with 'what works'.

These 'what's-good' and 'what-works' orientations have several things in common: (a) a complacent presumption that musical (and by extension, educational) value is simply given and therefore largely beside the point when it comes to teaching and learning; (b) their primary interest in maintaining the trappings believed to deliver or transmit musical value, so-construed, efficiently and effectively; (c) their pathetic failure to engage students in the active construction of meaning; and (d) their resultant inability to deliver on the deeper aims of value education. Rather than engaging students in the kind of musical sense-making that is gripping, momentous, compelling, and tightly bound to character (inseparable, that is to say, from one's identity); and rather than encouraging the pursuit of creative engagements that can take root and flourish outside the confines of the institutions in which we work; we have been content to cultivate appreciation of others' efforts and to mimic the external trappings of music making. What's good. What works. Whatever.

It makes a difference, and a profound one, how we envision and approach the processes of music making, music teaching, and music learning. They may be liberating and educational in the broadest sense. But they are more often, it has been argued here, part of the machinery that perpetuates the debilitating beliefs that consciousness rather than action is the foundation of human thought;[30] that the validity of values is a function of refinements afforded by rational deliberation; that values are mere commodities, and meaning a mere acquisition; and that values are, beneath it all, arbitrary conventions. We can help students learn to cherish the risk-and-responsibility-laden world of creative action, or leave it the mysterious domain of geniuses. The choice is ours: a choice, I submit, between engagement and apathy, between agency and passivity, between affirmation and nihilism.

Notes

1. Dewey goes on to state that the removal of conventional associations allows 'the intrinsic qualities of things' to emerge more fully, a claim that seems to beg the question of whether there can be such things as intrinsic qualities. My reservations about this point will be made clearer below.
2. This essay is indebted in many ways to the insightful work of Nigel Blake, Paul Smeyers, Richard Smith, and Paul Standish (in Blake, 2000).
3. I have also drawn heavily on chapter 2, 'Nihilism', in White (1990). See as well, 'Choice, Narrative, and Work', in Blake (2000) pp. 30–52.
4. Julia Koza's critiques of the MENC (Music Educators National Conference) and its corporate alliances are a case in point. See Koza (2003).
5. On this distinction between training and education, see Bowman (2002).
6. Constance Gee (Gee, 1996; 2002) aptly characterizes this approach with the phrase, 'For you, Dear, anything.'
7. This line of questioning is central to Aristotelian ethics. It's also central to successful action, with which, I will argue, music education should be more centrally concerned.
8. 'The trouble is that deep personal commitment to even a small portion of the world's musical heritage does not follow automatically from an appreciation of the vastness of the range from which it is drawn. Nor does mere awareness of the cultural value of music dispose one to the sense of personal commitment so essential to the preservation of music that is the best in its kind. We must accept the obligation to provide sufficiently rich experience in at least one musical world that it may take root and grow' (Bowman, 1991).
9. Blake observes, importantly, that 'what works' may be morally repugnant ... its very success as means to an end may encourage us not to consider whether the end is appropriate or desirable. It tells us what to do, and it saves us from thinking ... Being wholly a question about means, such talk forecloses on questions of the ends which are proposed' (Blake, 2000, p. *xiii*).
10. Here I refer to philosophical idealism, not the kind of optimistic frame of mind sometimes designated 'idealistic' in casual discourse.
11. Heidegger warns against slipping into 'a way of thinking that' carries an air of harmlessness and ease, which causes us to pass lightly over what really deserves to be questioned'. Heidegger (1968) p. 154, quoted in Blake (2000) p. 13.
12. Here I reference Common's translation because it is so widely available. Please note, however, that my translation here is not Common's. I have taken some liberty, in particular by using the phrase 'last people' instead of 'last man'. Quite a variety of interesting English translations for these passages from Prologue section 5 can be found on the Internet.

13. This is the kind of relativism Richard Rorty has called 'silly relativism'.
14. For a compelling treatment of these issues, see Sennett (1998).
15. The idea 'living into' music is advanced in Sparshott (1987).
16. See Carr (1992).
17. White's point is, more precisely, that Nietzsche uses the term nihilism in this *additional* way. The distinctions I have been drawing among various senses of the term nihilism are distinctions inferred from Nietzsche's usage of the single term 'nihilism,' not distinctions made explicit by Nietzsche himself.
18. Recall that negative nihilism presumes to be endorsing value in fact while rejecting it.
19. The quotations in this paragraph are from passages where White draws variously on Nietzsche's *Nachlass* and his *Will to Power*.
20. In this passage I have parenthetically replaced White's terms 'religious' and 'radical' with 'negative' and 'reactive,' respectively.
21. 'World of becoming' is a Nietzschean phrase that I use in contrast to the nihilistic notion that there is a way the world just 'is' or 'must be'.These latter are the kind of prejudices I think Dewey suggests art and music should help us 'get over.'
22. The terms 'teleological' and 'mechanistic' determinism come from Joas as well.
23. To be clear: I am not suggesting that Nietzsche is a pragmatist. I am saying that his 'take' on nihilism may be compatible with the pragmatist's rejection of these same stances. The pragmatist's solution to the 'problem' thus created is a great deal more nuanced, vital, and positive than Nietzsche's.
24. I stress the tentative and preliminary character of this Table. Like all diagrams, it is a simplification of something inherently more complex. I hope it clarifies more than it obfuscates, and that readers may find it a useful point of departure for further explorations.
25. This is the way Regelski puts it in numerous essays. To put the point another way, all values are necessarily grounded—never simply given, never intrinsic or inherent.
26. This is, in part, because from pragmatist perspective true learning manifests itself in an increased power to act successfully, 'successful' or 'right' action being both situation- and person-specific and therefore unsusceptible to standardization.
27. These verging closely on the 'slack' and 'humdrum' Dewey designates as enemies of 'experience' properly so-called (Dewey, 1980).
28. Bowman (2004).
29. Bowman (2000), Bowman (2001), Bowman (2002), Bowman (2003).
30. In Friedrich Hayek's words: 'The mind does not so much make rules as consist of rules of action'. And further, 'We can make use of so much experience, not because we possess that experience, but because, without knowing it, it has become incorporated into the schemata of thought which guide us'. Hayek (1973) pp. 18 and 30–31 respectively.

References

Blake, N., Smeyers, P., Smith, R. & Standish, P. (2000) *Education in an Age of Nihilism* (London, RoutledgeFalmer).

Bowman, W. (1991) A Plea for Pluralism: Variations on a theme by George McKay, in: R. Colwell (ed.), *Basic Concepts in Music Education, II* (Niwok, Colorado, The University Press of Colorado) pp. 94–110.

Bowman, W. (2000) Discernment, Respons/ability, and the Goods of Philosophical Praxis, *Finnish Journal of Music Education*, 5:1–2, pp. 96–119, (Reprinted in *Action, Criticism, Theory for Music Education*, 1:1). http://www.siue.edu/MUSIC/ACTPAPERS/ARCHIVE/BowmanPhronesis.pdf

Bowman, W. (2001) Music as Ethical Encounter, *Bulletin of the Council for Research in Music Education*, 151 (Winter, 2001), pp. 11–20.

Bowman, W. (2002) Educating Musically, in: R. Colwell & C. Richardson, (eds) *The New Handbook of Research on Music Teaching and Learning: A project of the Music Educators National Conference* (New York, Oxford University Press) pp. 63–84.

Bowman, W. (2003) Re-Tooling 'Foundations' to Address 21st Century Realities: Music Education amidst diversity, plurality, and change (The dream of certainty is a retreat from educational responsibility), *Action, Criticism, and Theory (ACT) for Change in Music Education*, 2:2, http://mas.siue.edu/MUSIC/ACTPAPERS/v2/Bowman03.pdf.

Bowman, W. (2004) Cognition and the Body: Perspectives from music education, in: L. Bresler (ed.), *Knowing Bodies, Feeling Minds: Embodied knowledge in arts education and schooling* (Dordrecht, Kluwer Academic Publishers) pp. 29–50.

Carr, K. (1992) *The Banalization of Nihilism: Twentieth century responses to meaninglessness* (Albany, State University of New York Press).

Deleuze, G. (1983) *Nietzsche and Philosophy*, trans. H. Tomlinson (New York, Columbia University Press).

Dewey, J. (1980) *Art as Experience* (New York, G. P. Putnam's Sons).

Gee, C. (1996) For You Dear—Anything! *Arts Education Policy Review*, 100:4 & 100:5, pp. 3–18 & 3–22 respectively.

Gee, C. (2002) The 'Use and Abuse' of Arts Advocacy and its Consequences for Music Education, in: R. Colwell & C. Richards (eds) *The New Handbook of Research on Music Teaching and Learning* (New York, Oxford University Press) pp. 941–61.

Heidegger, M. (1968) *What Is Called Thinking?* trans. J. G. Gray (New York, Harper & Row).

Hayek, F. (1973) *Law, Legislation and Liberty*, vol. 1, *Rules and Order* (London, Routledge & Kegan Paul).

Joas, H. (1996) *The Creativity of Action* (Chicago, University of Chicago Press).

Koza, J. (2003) *Stepping Across: Four interdisciplinary studies of education and cultural politics* (New York, Peter Lang Publishing).

Nietzsche, F. (1968) *The Will to Power*, trans. W. Kaufmann & R. J. Hollingdale (New York, Vintage Books).

Nietzsche, F. (1993) *Thus Spake Zarathustra*, trans. T. Common (Amherst, New York, Prometheus Books).

Regelski, T. (2002) On 'Methodolatry' and Music Teaching as Critical and Reflective Praxis, *Philosophy of Music Education Review*, 10:2, pp. 102–123.

Sennett, R. (1998) *The Corrosion of Character: The personal consequences of work in the new capitalism* (New York, Norton).

Sparshott, F. (1987) Aesthetics of Music: Limits and grounds, in: P. Alperson (ed.), *What is Music?* (New York, Haven Press).

White, A. (1990) *Within Nietzsche's Labyrinth* (New York, Routledge).

4

Music Education and Cultural Identity

Robert A. Davis
University of Glasgow

The links between music, education and the variegated discursive formations of cultural identity may appear to be unreflectively obvious, even intuitive, to the contemporary educator. Yet the easy conceptual identification of the relevant terms disguises deep fissures in the relationship between at least three mutually antagonistic perspectives on both the meaning of culture and the place of education in its ongoing legitimation. In the ideological struggle for control of the modern curriculum and its governing pedagogies, the expressive arts in general—and music in particular—have for the past fifty years been caught up in the rival claims of the nineteenth century *Kulturkritik* tradition, the Interculturalist movements of the post-imperial period (Bhabha, 1994, pp. 53–60) and the recent, aggressive, state-sponsored emphasis on economic instrumentalism and the performative calculation of educational value (Blake *et al.*, 2000, pp. 30–54).

Kulturkritik, in its classic European form, first arose in the later eighteenth century as a normative and effectively negative commentary on the emerging symbolic universe of capitalism, democracy and the embryonic institutions of mass industrial society, most especially education. Germany was the continental crucible of the *Kulturkritik* movement, with Herder the first public intellectual to call for the interrogation of *Zivilisation* by *Kultur* (Herder, 1774, pp. 179–224). England, Germany's major economic rival, swiftly became the second important centre, its efforts crystallized around the writings of the poet, critic and schools inspector Matthew Arnold. For Arnold, 'culture' held an intrinsically developmental moral interest and application. Directed towards the 'cultivation' of all that was distinctively human in humanity, education in 'culture' provided for the formation of the 'best self' that might qualify and overrule the 'ordinary selves' of everyday class and sectional loyalty in an increasingly stratified society (Williams, 1961). Replacing religion, culture, as promulgated by Arnold, constituted the spiritual infrastructure of a renovated civil order and the governing principle of a good society, as binding in its domain, and as potentially commanding, as the apparatus of the state itself (Arnold, 1869). Arnold's advocacy of this dogma became foundational in English-language educational thought in the early twentieth century and exercised a particular influence over the elaboration of the role of the expressive arts in the modern curriculum. The assumptions embedded in Arnold's manifesto, with their adherence to the view that the norms of culture were self-evidently those of a generalised humanity, departed sharply, however, from the European idealist

Kulturkritik traditions from which they originally derived. Despite a lingering Enlightenment attachment to the claims of *Humanitat* and its advancement, Herder's resolute defence of the mediating role of culture was always in reality avowedly plural and rigorously historicised. Cultures were, for Herder, the organic expressions of localised human communities, shaped in specific historical conjunctures and developing in response to the pressures of each unique environment and circumstance. The civilizing work of education could not ignore or smooth out such difference, but, instead, held forth the prospect of its institutional synthesis and affirmation in a higher form of celebratory organisation such as the tribe or nation: 'Human nature is not the vessel of an absolute, unchanging and independent happiness ... Even the image of happiness changes with each condition and climate ... each nation has its centre of gravity within itself ...' (Herder, 1774, pp. 185–6). Herder's romantic counter-Enlightenment emphasis on culture as communal property and as the organic virtue of a clearly-defined people redraws the boundaries of Arnold's essentialised humanism and in important respects anticipates the Intercultural aesthetics of the postcolonial period, providing them, indeed, with some of their important ethical and political bearings.

Music is central to Herder's valorisation of an anterior indigenous 'culture' on which the work of education can perform its humanising tasks (Norton, 1991). It is soon obvious that his interpretation of the actual dynamics of musical exchange in primitive societies has little to do with preliterate or oral civilizations in the scientific or anthropological senses of these terms (Zammito, 2001). It is, nevertheless, Herder's cultural imaginary, and the place of music within it, that exercises such a decisive influence over the critical history of music education in the nineteenth century and helps confirm the place of music in the curriculum of the post-Humboldtian schools and universities of Europe and, later, North America. Herder's aesthetics illustrate the often unrecognised, and sometimes troubling, continuities between the *Kulturkritik* traditions of twentieth century expressive arts education and the radical Interculturalism from which so much contemporary music education draws its present vitality and with which it tries (naïvely perhaps) to resist the homogenising encroachments of a globalised, technocratic world. In a series of seminal works—most especially his *Volkslieder* of 1778–9 and *Calligone* of 1800—Herder articulated a vision of the primordial musical experience in which 'living singers and hearers' (Herder, 1830, 25: 314) participate in the formative mystique of cultural identification mutually nurtured by the self-transcending solidarity of communal song. There is no mention in Herder's analysis of song of the noisy give and take of genuine preliterate cultural production; of precisely those vexatious features to which the structuring processes of music education are required to respond—the problems of memory and storage, the necessary redundancies, the laborious construction of a musical tradition. The voice of Herder's archetypal singer is no real voice burdened by limitations of volume and projection, and his listeners are no real bodily assembly, galvanized by physical proximity. Above all, there is no mention of the rigorous educational discipline, the mnemotechnics, the schooling of the voice, the training in set forms characteristic of the music of authentic oral cultures. Music is not, for Herder, a technology of voice and performance, but rather the absolute internality of attentive absorption in singing and listening in which the imagined collectivity, in the inwardness of its audition, hears and submits to the originary song of its cultural imprint: 'boundless and tireless, it flows in tender cascades, in repeating phrases and cadences, just as the ear of the people longed for' (Herder, 1830, 25: 315; Booth, 1981)

Two complimentary procedures sustain the operation of primordial music that Herder's thought endows with such overarching mythic dignity: the embodiment of the collectivity and the internalisation of musical sound. The group is unified as an individual subject absorbed in the phantasmatic effects of the voice that resonates within it, inscribing and reinforcing its interior life. The intimacy of the resultant emotional bond is captured in a powerful Herderian metaphor for the circuitry of voice and ear. The singing voice, 'at the end of every line, closes our eyes and lays our heads in sleep so that they might awaken to new visions' (Herder, 1830, 25: 315). The primitive rhapsode's atavistic song before his rapt assembly of listeners––which is for Herder the primal scene of cultural performance and initiation—becomes a lullaby sung to a child and the donation of cultural identity is seen to emanate from an inherently maternal source. The work of music as the bearer of culture reproduces the salience of the mother-child dyad and shapes the template for all subsequent musical learning, requiring music almost uniquely among the arts to be configured as a vehicle for the communication of care, sympathy, intimate feeling and the emotional grammar of the fully affective, inculturated self (Nisbet, 1985).

Discharging this responsibility became, of course, enormously problematic for the nineteenth century Western classical tradition, the consolidation of which was to parallel the rise of mass education. The imbrication of European art music in the various ethnic, racial and nationalist liberation movements of the high imperial period, publicly proclaimed in the works of canonical composers such as Listz, Smetana, Dvorak, Tchaikowski, Sibelius and—most notoriously—Richard Wagner, embroiled the processes of composition, performance and musical learning quite explicitly and irreversibly in the volatile politics of identity (Dahlhaus, 1998). The methodological backdrop to music education in both the metropolitan centres of European cultural production, such as the major conservatoires and music schools, and the provincial teaching academies came swiftly to embody post-Herderian idealist concepts of ethnic particularism and folk belonging. As a result, the practice of music instruction assumed a central role in the formation and intensification of local and national cultural allegiance, vigorously supporting in the tuition of children the appreciation and reproduction of supposedly indigenous and ancestral musical forms (Labuta & Smith, 1997, pp. 24–48). The nature of these forms reflected the pervasive Romantic nostalgia for the rural, the pastoral and the feudal as the defining sources of unitary and binding cultural authenticity. Nineteenth century European orchestral music abounds in motifs of the hunt at just the point at which the practice of hunting was shifting from subsistence economics to recreation and artifice. The widespread elevation of the music of an imagined agrarian past, especially in the instruction of the young, underlined a growing belief in music as the key to the recovery of lost cultural patrimonies malignly submerged by the combined effects of imperial oppression and the dislocating yet homogenising forces of industrialisation. This movement in the history of European musical thought was destined to culminate in the hypernationalist catastrophe of Nazi musicology, with its spuriously racialised contrast of the allegedly Dorian mode of 'Aryan' music with repellent and alien chromaticism of 'Jewish' music. Nazi intellectuals invoked as precedence for their views Book 3 of the *Republic*, in which Plato describes the musical education of the leaders of his ideal society: an education to be based upon the severity and virility of the Dorian diatonic scale (Riethmuller, 2002, pp. 183–85). Specious though this reading was, the racialisation of Plato's thought by Nazi musical eugenics, and the ease of its appropriation, revealed some of the contradictions and perils lying at the heart of the German idealist project and the ethical vulnerability of music and music education within it.

Recognising that the patterns of association linking together concepts of music, education and the possession of culture are invariably imaginary, interacting in complex forms with the material conditions of historical experience, goes some way towards releasing music education from the confines set by reified notions of identity and affiliation. Indeed, just such a process of emancipation has figured as an enabling ethic in many of the narratives of modern music education (Mark, 2002, pp. 287–291). The genealogy of the Western classical tradition and its complex relations with the teaching and learning of music continues to reveal, nonetheless, the enduring and perhaps insidious influence of representations routinely exposed as the discursive constructions of ideology and power. To this day, it remains unclear why the ancient Greeks labelled the various scales or melody-types with which they were familiar from tribal names (Dorian, Phrygian, Lydian etc). It is nevertheless apparent that these names were firmly associated by the Greeks with a series of supposed ethnic traits or dispositions of character believed to be embodied in the modes themselves ('excitable', 'vigorous', 'ordered' etc.) (West, 1992). This abiding association of musical forms with ethnicity may find a particularly elaborate formulation in the writings of Herder and his contemporaries, but the important strategic manoeuvre in both cases—and possibly recurring wherever Western musical thought has achieved dominance—is the rapid assimilation of seemingly Interculturalist attitudes to an uncompromisingly *Kulturkritik* educational agenda. In the nineteenth century, the revolutionary revaluation of the music of the folk prompted idealistic efforts across Europe to retrieve fading vernacular musical and folksong traditions in which it was hoped the signatures of marginalised peoples or nations might be rediscovered. The undertaking began—regardless of its naïve or defective methodology—as a sincerely high-minded intercultural endeavour, an important act of resistance and renewal, contesting the bourgeois cultural hegemony of the great empires. It was quickly domesticated, however, as simply another expression of that same post-Kantian cultural regime it originally wished to question, universalised through the rationalist criteria of 'taste' as merely another standard of judgement by which all musical merit and 'originality' were to be measured. Shedding its affinities with the local and the organic, losing its roughness and inconsistency, it assumed the status of a transcultural aesthetic on which formal education in music, its performance and its appreciation, was to be based. Cultural distinctiveness was either erased or exoticised in this process, as the plethora of indigenous European musics first championed by Herder and his contemporaries lost even their imagined histories and merged into the totalizing discourse of the Classical and Romantic stylistic repertoires. An intervention in the forms of musical life that began as an assertion of difference became party to the institutional effacement of difference by the twin recuperative forces of art and education (Kramer, 1990).

This integral and longstanding reciprocity between the *Kulturkritik* expectations of European art music and the progressive, even subversive, aspirations of musical Interculturalism complicates the seeming divergence of outlook and purpose of the two perspectives, while problematising still further the tasks of contemporary music education, which is heir to both. The nineteenth century moment of innovation and recuperation has been several times recapitulated in the recent history of music education, exposing the permeable boundaries of apparently fixed or irreconcilable views of cultural life in the activities of the educated polity. Current controversies surrounding the role of music education in the promotion or interrogation of cultural identity have witnessed a Herder-like return to the fundamentals of musical apprehension and cultural fidelity—with uncertain results. The pursuit of an incontrovertible basis for a culturally coherent yet liberally inclusive music education has been drawn recently to the frontiers of ethnomusicology and cognitive psychology for its intellectual validation, searching out in the primary domain of Herder's mother-child dyad a programmatic understanding of musical development that might ratify the claims of cultural specificity while avoiding rigidly hierarchical or dangerously essentialist correlations of musical awareness and ethnic or linguistic identity. Refuting the 'blank slate' social constructivism of the 1960s, psycholinguists have known for some time that every newborn human infant has a preference for the mother's voice over any other woman's voice, and equally over the father's voice. Accepting that babies generally have a preference for low-frequency sounds, it seems clear that the baby's exposure to the mother's voice *in utero* accords mothers an adaptive advantage for their subsequent vocal and intersubjective engagements with their neonates (Spelke, 1999). The apparatus of the cochlea and the transductive nerve cells of the sense of hearing become active in the foetus at about the seventh month, exposing the unborn child to a level of internal and environmental sound comparable to the acoustic envelope of an airfield. Recent research has shown that the conduction of the mother's voice down her back to the pelvic area not only leaves the fundamental vocal harmonics of her voice intact but also amplifies them into the human range of perception (DeCasper & Spence, 1986; Smith *et al.*, 2003). As the pregnancy nears term and the baby's head is finally engaged, the mother's pelvis, as a result of bone conduction, acts like a vibrating speaker resonating with the ivory-hard, crystalline structures of the baby's inner ear.

At birth, the baby's immediate auditory environment is much quieter than that of the womb. The low-frequency noises that dominate the womb have faded. At the same time, it is also evident that the hearing of newborns is significantly worse than that of adults. Owing to the immaturity of the outer ear and, particularly, the pre-pneumatised and subcalcified condition of the middle ear, babies have hearing thresholds that are of the order of 30 to 70 decibels higher than those of adults. Sounds therefore conduct to the nerve cells of the baby's inner ear far less efficiently than they do in an adult. In this partially deafened condition, newborn babies find themselves nonetheless suddenly exposed to a much wider range of frequencies than previously in their sensory experience. Non-nutritious suckling experiments have demonstrated that from as early as twelve hours after birth babies can differentiate their mother's voice from a stranger's voice (DeCasper & Fifer, 1980). Babies also have a preference for human voices over other sounds of a similar pitch and intensity and a bias towards generic sounds from within the human vocal range rather than those outside it (Eisenberg, 1975). Evidence for prenatal hearing is further manifest in infant crying. Analyses of the cries of babies born of English, Moroccan and Chinese mothers have shown that baby cries are ethnically and geographically specific, tuned as a result of *in utero* exposure to the intonations of their native languages (Moon *et al.*, 1993). These factors are of course crucial in subsequent language acquisition. The ability to hear differences between speech sounds appears to develop as early as the fourth day of life, by which time infants can differentiate the plosives *b*- and *p*-, the expressive registration of which is separated by one twenty-thousandth of a second. Comparisons of English and Chinese babies in the first month of life, exposed to the salient acoustic profiles of their native languages, show the babies able to detect semivowel sound-shifts from liquid *l*- to *r*-. By six months, the Chinese baby, immersed in Chinese home language, hears the two sounds as the same, while the English baby, for whom the difference is aurally contrastive and linguistically constitutive, hears them as distinct (Clarkson & Berg, 1983). The babies are already categorising sounds into the speech patterns they will have to learn as the building blocks of their, aptly named, mother tongues (Werker & Desjardins, 1995).

There is also now widespread acceptance that what are termed 'proto-musical' predispositions may help intensify the infant bond with both the biological mother and the native culture transmitted through the medium of her speaking and singing (Papousek, 1996). The acclaimed work of Sandra Trehub and her associates powerfully suggests that the human infant is hardwired not only for the experience of music itself, but for the intersubjective response to the indigenous music subtly interwoven with the fabric of the mother's prenatal and immediately postnatal communications (Trehub *et al.*, 1997). In a remarkable echo of Herder's cradle-song trope, Maya Gratier's study of immigrant mother-infant dyads has demonstrated that the properties of the proto-musical interactions between mother and baby—the patterns of which remain remarkably consistent across cultures—can be destabilised as a consequence of the 'identity confusion' that immigrant mothers experience when marooned in unfamiliar societies where their vocalisations to their infants may become disorientated (Gratier, 1999). It appears that the communication of cultural rootedness, or its lack, penetrates the psychoacoustic cocoon of the instinctual musical exchange between adult and child, reinforcing the bonds that tie music to the emergent phenomena of personal and cultural identity. Theorists of music education have seized on findings of this kind to argue that those children who capitalise on their proto-musical capacities and study music from an early age show greater psychological and cultural adaptability when compared to those who are left untrained (Imberty, 2000). Musically literate adults, it is claimed, have stronger and faster neurological responses to multilateral and linguistic tasks associated with complex cultural negotiation, and certain parts of their brains, related to synthetic judgement and language processing, may well be larger or more responsive in many different categories of cognitive competence (Flohr *et al.*, 1996; Schlaug *et al.*, 1995; Gembris, 2002). Moving beyond the reductionism of the so-called 'Mozart effect', the weight of educational research strongly suggests that, as Herder first indirectly proposed, early musical experiences etch themselves indelibly on the templates of subjectivity, signalling the potential for music to alter the ratios of culture and identity across a range of emotional indices, from the individual through the interpersonal to the social (Dissanayake, 2000).

The cultural politics supported by ethnomusicological interpellations of this kind in the philosophy of music education remains imprecise and ambiguous. Evidence indicating even a weak form of biologically deterministic relationship between music and culture can be used to defend minority or marginalised musics from the hegemony of dominant musical and aesthetic regimes. Equally, it can be employed in the erection of ethnocentric barriers to multicultural interaction, diasporic hybridity and difference. Bhabha warns that the 'problem of cultural interaction emerges only at the significatory boundaries of cultures, where meanings and values are (mis)read or signs are misappropriated.' (Bhabha, 1994, p. 121). Hybridisation unsettles univocal systems of authority, defamiliarising and disempowering the cultural centre by exposing its prior contamination by those forces of the periphery that it purposes either to subordinate or expel, and upon the exclusion of which its own coherence depends At the same time—and most especially in a world vacillating between globalising uniformity and a countervailing ethnic primordialism—hybridisation intensifies the threat of cultural dissipation: the disintegration of those fundamental properties by which an endangered culture defends itself from plunder and annihilation inflicted in the name of multicultural syncretism (Constantin & Rautz, 2003). In their important essay '1837: Of the Refrain' from *A Thousand Plateaus*, Deleuze and Guattari explain this function of music in protecting territory and group: 'Now we are at home. But home does not pre-exist: it was necessary to draw a circle around that uncertain and fragile center, to organize a limited space ... marking out a wall of sound, or at least a wall with some sonic bricks in it' (Deleuze & Guattari, 1988, p. 311). They go on to argue that chants, snatches of song, Muzak, humming, putting the radio on, serve to mark the boundaries of a coherent individual or collective presence. Like Trehub, they cite lullabies in their inventory, for these are often the first way the edges of the world are fuzzily defined for a newborn child by a mother or nurse, and they take their title 'Of the Refrain' from the premise that familiarity through repetition defines this terrain until it is learned by heart. The thread of a tune extends indefinitely, they argue, the secure interiority of the home, allowing the singer or listener to venture into the dark, chaotic world of the 'unhomely' in the confidence that the reassuringly validating conditions of home inhere in the transferable musical reiteration of remembered songs and cadences, and through the performance of which the unfamiliar is mastered and made safe.

As well as enhancing the claims of those excluded or minority musics now so often seen as morally central to the work of music education, the promotion of home risks courting an oversimplified, even dualistic, construction of the Other in the processes of musical recognition. Trehub's highly-prized lullabies encode this unsettling feature quite directly in their sometimes ominous demonization of the foreign and the unknown, where figures embodying outlandish exaggerations of racial or ethnic difference are represented as the central menace to the child who refuses to go to sleep (Warner, 1998, pp. 217–19). Far from facilitating uncomplicated initiation into the consoling verities of a unitary culture, such lullabies betray the frustrations associated with the diurnal work of parenting—which may itself be the 'universal' social attribute isolated in such music—and demystify by the light of everyday life the supposed certainties of every seemingly self-sufficient or idealised cultural inheritance (Bowman, 2002). Two conspicuous features impact directly on the music educator's perception of a genre such as the lullaby in the cultural curriculum of music education: the fact that any and every teaching of a lullaby must necessarily involve wresting the text from its original context of production and reception (babies are rarely admitted to the music room); and the fact that the fundamental purpose of the lullaby—to induce sleep—also scarcely impinges on either its educational use-value or its anthropological cachet. It is this inveterate deferral of home, this constant reminder, enclosed in the musical experience itself, that—in the words of Adam Phillips—'To be at home in the world, we need to keep it inhospitable', that restores the lullaby's uncanny sense of estrangement, even from those closest to it (Phillips, 1993, p. 19). When music education engages with a superficially fixed, culturally talismanic form such as the lullaby, the dialogic processes of education inevitably reconfigure the cultural meanings of the musical object, relocating it to a symbolic order of acquisition and performance where its underlying remoteness from the discursive systems of cultural initiation are paradoxically revealed. 'What makes the Other *other*', observes Santner,

> is not his or her spatial exteriority with respect to my being but the fact that he or she is *strange*, is a *stranger*, and not only to me but to him or herself, is the bearer of an internal alterity, and enigmatic density of desire calling for response beyond any rule-governed reciprocity; against this background, the very opposition between 'neighbour' and 'stranger' begins to lose its force. (Santner, 2001, p. 9)

The lullaby dramatises Santner's false dichotomy of neighbour and stranger. It presents itself as evidence for two rival and seemingly incompatible claims: a sociobiologically derived universal humanism, based on a naturalistic and normative reading of shared human destiny, and a cultural particularism in which ownership of specific musical and linguistic idioms delineates the parameters of ethnic identity. Each view proclaims itself the vehicle of a progressive cultural and educational politics. Deleuze and Guattari point out that the refrain is, in this respect, essentially territorial, repetitively recoding sound in order to constrain and regulate variation, subject to the fearful anxiety that only repetition, imitation and substitution materialise an otherwise elusive and endlessly deferred identity. In its realisation of polyvocality, by contrast, music deterritorializes the refrain: 'music uses anything and sweeps everything away ... Childhood scenes, children's games: the starting point is a childlike refrain, but the child has wings already, he becomes celestial ... Produce a deterritorialized refrain as the final end of music, release it in the Cosmos—that is more important than building a new system' (Deleuze & Guattari, 1988, pp. 349–50). Music education as a location for exchange, composition, improvisation, interrogation of received traditions and unpredictable creativity fosters healthy distrust of singularised concepts of cultural identity because it uses the resources of culture to foreground the *aporia* at the heart of all territorialized constructions of identity, most resolutely those with which it is itself directly implicated.

At stake here is not merely a debate between modes of musical signification, but rather the idea that there is such as thing as the transcendental signified of 'identity' in the citation of which music and music education play a part. The issue is not only a particular relationship between music and culture that education might be required to safeguard or indeed question, but also more dangerously and disturbingly the power of music as a signifying system to make realities, to conjure into presence things that might not exist apart from signification. Moving out from the primal scene of the lullaby and the mother-child dyad, music education's more general historic attachment to the teaching of singing continues to figure prominently in debates about the nature and promotion of 'ethnic' music. Reimund Kvideland has suggested that songs are the ideal type of cultural expression and that the observable and universal phenomenon of singing is a defining benchmark of cultural solidarity, the dialectics of performance creating the shared consciousness and transcendental mystiquc of belonging upon which the whole notion of culture depends (Kvideland, 1989). In his controversial concept of 'group song', Ernst Klusen has gone further, isolating what he interprets as two functions of song in the life of communities: participation and spectacle. Klusen argues that modern music education's elevation of a classical song repertoire as the standard of technical excellence, for both listening and performing, has colluded in the displacement of participation by spectacle, robbing song of its integral relationship with the forms of life out of which its musical and cultural meaning, and its claims on preservation, arise (Klusen, 1986, pp. 185–90). These and other perspectives of music educators championing minority or folk musics perhaps understandably protest the increasing intrusion of the US-controlled corporate entertainment industries, classical and commercial, on the worldwide production and consumption of indigenous song; its steady occlusion by the commodification of otherness and the flattening of a diverse international musical landscape. In heightening the prestige of song as a touchstone of cultural authenticity it also understates, however, the *resilience* of local, vernacular musics and their potential impact on the music education curriculum. Precisely because of the 'rootedness' of group and individual singing, and its organic involvement with the interwoven textures of lived cultural experience, popular song can be mobilised in the active negotiation of cultural resistance and change—factors that functional ethnographic accounts of indigenous song have historically underestimated (Merriam, 1964, pp. 303–19). Studies of children's singing in traditional African societies now frequently highlight the interactive character of the children's engagements with international pop music, folksong and the formal disciplines of practice and appreciation demanded in their music education. The school playground regularly functions as a locus for musical invention and synthesis, anchored not in some attenuated concept of children's 'play', but in the complex 'musicalisation' by the children of their tribal customs, their (often irreverent) relations with their social and natural environments, and their creative responses to the ongoing pattern of events in their lives (Dzansi, 2002; Rasolofondraosolo & Meinhof, 2003). Against Campbell's solemn insistence that the music teacher must operate as a custodian and transmitter of inherited song, it is possible to posit a pedagogical practice where the relations between children, their playground spaces and their classrooms are dynamic, imagining a community of learners united more by an awareness of cultural osmosis and evolution than by fixed axes of identity and territory (Campbell *et al.*, 1996).

Of course, the principle of permeability lends itself to appreciation of other important features of the globalised condition of the twentyfirst century that inevitably inform the search for a viable postcolonial music education. Far-reaching and historic geopolitical processes such as decolonisation, economic migration and the flight of refugee populations from a multitude of conflict zones have resulted in increased cultural diversity *within* established territories and nations leading, in turn, to significant numbers from minority ethnic and cultural groupings entering the institutions of Western education (Campbell, 2000). As well as altering the educational policies of these institutions, and challenging some of the supposed categories of fixed cultural identity on which their previous practices rested, the presence of students from non-mainstream cultural settings has enhanced the ethical and educational status of intercultural accommodation and encounter in its own right. The clearest manifestation of this in arts education has been the acceptance into the classroom of the phenomenon of 'World Music', in which is recognised the integrity and equality of clearly distinguished and living ethnic musical traditions with an appeal to highly differentiated international audiences. The rise of the World Music movement, with its close affinities to multicultural education, has been accompanied by a vigorous educational and moral polemic on behalf of its originators and consumers, insisting upon guarantees for its position in the curriculum and closely aligning its advocacy to initiatives in antiracism and positive discrimination (Kwami, 1996). The classroom appeal of World Music epitomises two contrasting influences in contemporary educational thought: the allure of ethnic identification and the global penetration of certain mass cultural styles of fashion, communications and entertainment into the common cultural vocabulary shared by the youth of many different ethnic groups, especially in the capitalist economies (Burgoyne, 2000).

The juxtaposition of these forces has encouraged networks of music educators in both the industrialised and the developing nations to press for the promotion of a radically redesigned music curriculum in which the multicultural eclecticism of World Music reflects the multidimensional identity of highly mobile and heterogeneous student populations (Thorsen, 2002). The arguments in favour of such innovation, in particular the calls for the decentring of Western art music from the music syllabus and the endorsement of popular, postmodern and avant-garde musics in the acquisition of musical literacy, represent, in important respects, a persuasive response to the quest for cultural capital in a globalised society. The educational and musical analyses offered in support of these views, however, often recuperate the hegemonic discourses and the older aesthetic categorisations they superficially purport to reject. Concepts of 'classic', 'serious', 'authentic', 'definitive', 'excellent' etc., strengthened by the regulatory hierarchies of cultural production, recapitulate the post-Kantian disciplinary rhetoric of art music ideology, cordoning the various 'musics' of World Music within strictly-bounded and ethnically pure 'traditions', policing their performance procedures and limiting the interactions between them. Ethnomusicological fieldwork from various areas of the globe has highlighted the potentially damaging effects of this approach to music education, drawing attention to its impaired understanding of cultural identity and its diminished appreciation of other factors such as the dynamics of teacher-pupil relationships in diverse contexts of musical learning and teaching (Barton, 2001). The advent of World Music in the environments of music education invites much closer inspection than has hitherto been common of the contrasting modes of learning and teaching associated with those musics—the nature of diverse instructional paradigms and contrasting concepts of the 'teacher'; the influence of wider cultural, artistic and even religious and spiritual factors on the pedagogical experience; the role of musical performance and appreciation in the shaping of social, cultural and personal identity. As Estelle Jorgensen comments, these processes are multidirectional. A culture does not simply determine and seamlessly transmit its music to its members, generation upon generation. Music is dialogically involved in the creation and renewal of culture:

> It is a commonplace that music ... is part of culture and profoundly influenced by the particular places and times in which it is created and performed ... What is less often stressed is that society is as much shaped by music as music is shaped by society. Through singing and playing musical instruments, people create a corporate sense of their identity. The texts their songs employ and the values their musics express reinforce their beliefs and practices and educate their young ... The ancients understood that music is interconnected with spiritual and political life. Not only did they teach their wisdom to their young through songs and rituals, but their ... singers, instrumentalists and dancers looked for inspiration to an imagined future as much to an imaginatively reconstructed past, thereby helping to subvert and transform society as they also conserved and transmitted traditional wisdom. (Jorgensen, 2003, p. 30)

Any reproach by ethnomusicology to the appropriation of World Music by schools and academies moulded in the Western image is really a criticism that they do not allow music to go far enough in the exploration of cultural identity. As an alternative to the conventional support of educational pluralism, and the submerged polarities on which it is often predicated, a radicalised concept of World Music that acknowledges the complex systems of feedback and hybridisation between and across globalised music communities offers music education unprecedented and potentially transformative access to indigenous musical ontologies (Bohlman, 1999). Replacing unitary musicological frameworks implicitly derived from Western metaphysics, even where such metaphysics are expressly disavowed, with multiple and fluid hermeneutics can open music education to experimental, heterenomous systems of organisation and practice grounded in the actual materialities of different cultures and societies. The heuristic value of this method can be discerned immediately in the interrogation it enables of core concepts immovably entrenched at the heart of Eurocentric constructions of both music *and* culture. Veit Erlmann has gone so far as to suggest that 'musicology could have only emerged in relation to colonial encounters' (Erlmann, 1999, p. 8), arguing that it is only ever against the Other that Western imperial society was historically able to define itself and its musical epistemology. If musicology is intrinsically a mode of knowledge about (primarily) Western musical models, then it necessarily defines itself in contradistinction to the study of the musical practices of pre-modern societies, muting or mythologising otherness and universalising its own culturally specific taxonomies (Huggan, 2001). 'Foreign' musical discourses become redefined, disembedded from indigenous social and political contexts and eventually resituated within the dominant cultural system, becoming, in Graham Harvey's words, 'hybrids of modernity' (Harvey, 1996). The music education emerging out of this ideological nexus of reproduction, tends, in even its most culturally enlightened forms, towards the reinforcement of oversimplified notions of ethnicity, superimposing on the predetermined categories of race, nation, language and culture the vocabulary of Western musical value, including its technical classifications and its criteria of judgement (Green, 2003).

The scope for innovative visions of music education remains considerable, even at those points where the discourse of Western musicology and aesthetics seems least negotiable. If the contours of Western history regulate musical texts and genres from across cultures and periods, then the role of World Music, in all of its diversity, becomes crucial in unsettling the presuppositions of musical knowledge. Anne McClintock has described an imperial geography of the Western sensibility that conflates temporality with global space. Western civilization is poised at the pinnacle of cultural development, situating other cultures at lower levels of progress. Time, in this metaphor, becomes a linear track moving from underdeveloped peoples towards civilization. McClintock cautions that this temporal construct authorises strategic modes of organising culture and structuring ethnic and national groups: 'Imperial progress across the space of empire is figured as a journey backward in time to an anachronistic moment of prehistory. Geographical difference across space is figured as historical difference across time' (McClintock, 1995, p. 40). The logic of this view nourishes current attitudes to economic and social progress, which are concentrated on a white, Euroethnic normative centre and which serve to exonerate commercial, cultural and even military domination of the 'developing' world by the 'post-historical' Western powers. Music in all its forms, from the cunning simplicities of the lullaby to the abstraction of the twelve-tone row, and forever classified as a cultural universal, occupies a nonraced and depoliticised space within this economy of human behaviour, masquerading as the innocent soundtrack to a progressive humanism ineluctably bound to the enlightened dissemination of Western liberal-democratic values. One of the central tasks of a 'postmodern' music education philosophy genuinely attuned to the transformative effects of revitalised Interculturalism is to undo the assumptions supporting this prejudice, re-establishing the radical credentials of music education as an experience dissatisfied with the performativity of cultural competence, no matter how broadly conceived, and unwilling to be a passive instrument for the mere reception or transmission of culture (Stock, 2003). Instead, by prizing the agency of the cultural actors to whom it is morally responsible, music education lays claim to a much more active and self-fashioning involvement in the making and breaking of culture. Elmann summarises this aspiration as the recovery by music of a 'global imagination', and urges educators to the view that:

> Unlike any other aspect of mass culture, music organizes social interaction in ways that that are no longer determined by the primacy of locally situated practice and collectively maintained memory. The new role of music in global culture is based on the fact that music no longer signifies something outside of itself, a reality, the truth. Instead, music becomes a medium that mediates, as it were, mediation. In other words, music in global culture, by dint of a number of significant shifts in production, circulation and consumption of musical sounds, functions as an interactive social context, a conduit for other forms of interaction, other socially mediated forms of appropriation of the world. (Erlmann, 1999, p. 6)

Music becomes a medium that mediates, as it were, mediation. There can be, if this analysis is correct, no single historicised discourse of music education. The relationship between music and identity becomes one of circulation, exchange and iterativity rather than jurisdiction or reflection. It is the responsibility of the music teacher to trace out the multiple and complexly contested identities that make up the cultures in which music is implanted. While the connections between music and materiality occur through representational encodings and refigurings of social energy and cultural imagery that are not reducible to the terms of ethnic determinism or naïve referential correspondences, they can nonetheless be seen as the symbolic reproduction and circulation of mimetic capital. A culture in part consists of the stockpile of accumulated meanings upon the repetition of which educators rely and which are germane to the constitution and materialisation of power within the culture. Music education is itself a mimetic relation of production in that it is intimately connected to status hierarchies, resistances, and conflicts elsewhere in the culture. If committed music educators indeed eschew the Western myth of an overarching historical or aesthetic metanarrative, they nevertheless also dispute the suspicious ideal of a purely local, discontinuous knowledge. Cultural identity, wherever it appears to be momentarily objectified, is nowhere an external referent of music education; instead music education is itself a move within cultural identity.

It is a precondition of this reinvigorated portrayal of the activities of music education that it does not stop with a benign approbation of the twentyfirst century world's instantaneous musical diversity and the complacent celebration of all young people as music makers. As Jorgensen hinted, the inner dynamic of music education emancipated from the disabling accountability to both *Kultur* and consumption radiates multilaterally, authorising an ongoing reappraisal and reimagining of the Western tradition, most acutely where the faultlines of that tradition open it out to its own suppressed histories. The encounter between the canonical art-music systems of classical music—which continue to play such an important part almost everywhere in the pedagogy and prestige of music education—and the 'musics' of a globalised world blur the long-established hierarchies and genre boundaries of the classic tradition itself. The orientalising axiology of Western thought, which in the past repeatedly thematised the music of peripheral cultures as a repository for those elements inadmissible in its own dualistic aesthetics, was all along looking in the mirror of its own 'surrogate and even underground self' (Walder, 1990, p. 236). In its construction of the Other, it evaded its own deepest investments in pleasure, desire, the dancing body, sexuality, moral ambiguity and the dispersed materials from which subjectivity itself is wrought. Kierkegaard came to see this process not simply as the hidden subtext of Western musical greatness, but also as its enabling condition: the occluded basis of its capacity to communicate. Gripped by the powers in Mozart's *Don Giovanni*—for the effects of which his conventional education, with its division of mind and body, spirit and flesh, had left him entirely unprepared—Kierkegaard attempted to isolate the source of the opera's canonical status and found it unexpectedly in its 'musical erotic' appeal—a quality for which the epistemology of classical appreciation afforded him no language:

> In *Don Giovanni* ... desire is absolutely qualified as desire ... absolutely genuine, victorious, triumphant, irresistible and demonic ... Don Juan ... is a downright seducer. His love is sensuous, not psychical, and, according to its concept, sensuous love is not faithful but totally faithless; it loves not one but all—that is, seduces all. It is indeed only in the moment, but ... that moment is the sum of moments, and so we have the seducer. ... But its faithlessness manifests itself in another way also: it continually becomes only a repetition. (Kierkegaard, 1843, pp. 84–85, 90)

Kierkegaard's intention is to reinstate the 'sensuous' at the centre of response to the classic work of art, but also to recognise that Mozart's opera itself is a cultural (indeed religious) artefact always already dramatising, exposing and endeavouring to assuage the 'psycho-sensuous' contradiction at the heart of the culture that has produced it. The educative goal of Kierkegaard's essay is to move beyond arbitration of the definitive musical interpretation of *Don Giovanni* and to accept, instead, its disclosure of vital elements whose presence in culture is either scarcely acknowledged or actively repressed. In one sense, this is the familiar Romantic view that *Don Giovanni* reveals the irrational smouldering behind the façade of civilized behaviour. In another it is an act of homage to Mozart for restoring to the proper appreciation of canonical music 'the energy of desire, the energy of the sensuous' that occupies its cultural unconscious all along (Kierkegaard, 1843, p. 119).

Kierkegaard's audacious rereading of Mozart is a reminder that any music education that allies itself to 'the energy of desire' and that sees individual and cultural identity permanently reinvented in the play of difference will esteem not only the otherness of unfamiliar musics, but will vouchsafe the underlying strangeness of the productions and practices that appear most central to the elite 'Western' musical tradition, problematising even its apparently sealed 'musical ontology'. Musical futures that include a reengagement with the past fuelled by the musical plenitude of the twentyfirst century present will encounter the uncanny familiarity of a living heritage, one heard anew in the sound of its fractures and splits, its joys and its obsessions, as if for the first time.

References

Arnold, M. (1869) *Culture and Anarchy*, J. Dover Wilson (ed.) (1932) (Cambridge, Cambridge University Press).

Barton, G. (2001) Music as a Reflection of Culture: Implications for music teaching and learning, *Queensland Journal of Music Education*, 8:1, pp. 71–75.

Bhaba, H. K. (1994) *The Location of Culture* (London, Routledge).

Blake, N., Smeyers, P., Smith, P. & Standish, P. (2000) *Education in an Age of Nihilism* (London, RoutledgeFalmer).

Bohlman, P. V. (1999) Ontologies of Music, in: N. Cook & M. Everist (eds) *Rethinking Music* (Oxford, Oxford University Press), pp. 17–34.

Booth, M. (1981) *The Experience of Songs* (New Haven, Yale University Press).

Bowman, W. (2002). Introduction to Symposium: Music's Significance in Everyday Life, *Action, Criticism, and Theory for Music Education*, 1:2, pp. 1–4, http://mas.siue.edu/ACT/vi/BowmanIntro.pdf.

Burgoyne, R. (2000) Ethnic Nationalism and Globalization, *Rethinking History*, 4:2, pp. 157–164.

Campbell, A. (2000) Cultural Identity as a Social Construct, *Intercultural Education*, 11:1, pp. 31–39.

Campbell, P., Williamson, S. & Perron P. (1996). *Traditional Songs of Singing Cultures: A world sampler.* (Los Angeles, Warner Bros Publications).

Clarkson, M. & Berg, K. (1983) Orienting and Vowel Discrimination in Newborns, *Child Development*, 54, pp. 164–171.

Dahlhaus, C. (1989) *Nineteenth-Century Music*, trans. J. Bradford Robinson (Berkeley, University of California Press).

Decasper, A. J. & Fifer, W. P. (1980) Of Human Bonding: Newborns prefer their mothers' voices, *Science*, 208, pp. 1174–76.

Decasper, A. J. & Spence, M. J. (1986) Prenatal Maternal Speech Influence On Newborns' Perception Of Sounds, *Infant Behaviour and Development*, 9, pp. 133–150.

Deleuze, G. & Guattari, F. (1988) *A Thousand Plateaus,* trans. B. Massumi (London, The Athlone Press).

Dissanayake, E. (2000) Antecedents Of The Temporal Arts In Early Mother-Infant Interaction, in: N. Wallin, B. Merker, & S. Brown (eds) *The Origins of Music* (Cambridge, MA, The MIT Press), pp. 389–410.

Dzansi, M. P. (2002) Some Manifestations of Ghanaian Indigenous Culture in Children's Singing Games, *International Journal Of Education and the Arts*, 3:7, http://ijea.asu.edu/v3n7.

Eisenberg, R. B. (1975). *Auditory Competence in Early Life: The roots of communicative behaviour*, (Baltimore, University Park Press).

Erlmann, V. (1999) *Music, Modernity and the Global Imagination: South Africa and the West* (New York and Oxford, Oxford University Press).

Flohr, J., Persellin, D. & Miller, D. (1996). Children's Electrophysical Responses To Music. Paper presented at the 22nd International Society for Music Education World Conference, Amsterdam, Netherlands. (ERIC Document PS025,654).

Gembris, H. (2002) The Development of Musical Abilities, in: R. Colwell & C. Richardson (eds) *The New Handbook of Research on Music Teaching and Learning* (New York, Oxford University Press), pp. 487–508.

Green, L. (2003) Music Education, Cultural Capital and Social Group Identity, in: M. Clayton, T. Herbert & R. Middleton (eds) *The Cultural Study of Music: A critical introduction* (New York and London, Routledge), pp. 263–274.

Gratier, M. (1999) Expressions of Belonging: The effect of acculturation on the rhythm and harmony of mother-infant interaction, *Musicae Scientiae* Special Issue, pp. 93–122.

Harvey, P. (1996) *Hybrids of Modernity: Anthropology, the nation state and the universal exhibition* (London, Routledge).

Herder, J. G. (1774) *Herder on Social and Political Culture*, F. M. Barnard (ed. and trans.), (1969) (Cambridge, Cambridge University Press).

Herder, J. G. (1830) *Sämmtliche Werke: Zur Religion und Theologie*, J. G. Muller (ed.) (Stuttgart and Tubingen, Cotta). Author's translation assisted by Dr. Jan Kalbheim, University of Munich.

Huggan, G. (2001) *The Post-colonial Exotic: Marketing the margins* (London, Routledge).

Imberty, M. (2000) The Question Of Innate Competencies in Musical Communication. in: N. Wallin, B. Merker & S. Brown (eds) *The Origins of Music* (Cambridge, MA: The MIT Press), pp. 449–462.

Jorgensen, E. R. (2003) *Transforming Music Education* (Bloomington, Indiana University Press).

Kierkegaard, S. (1843) Either/Or, Part I, in: H. V. Hong & E. H. Hong (ed. and trans.) (1987), *Kierkegaard's Writings*, III. (Princeton, NJ, Princeton University Press).

Klusen, E. (1986) The Group Song as Object, in: E. Klusen (ed.) *German 'Volkskunde'* (Bloomington, Indiana University Press), pp. 184–202.

Kramer, L. (1990) *Music as Cultural Practice, 1800–1900* (Berkeley, University of California Press).

Kvideland, R. (1989) Folk Ballads and Folk Song, in: R. Kvideland, H. K. Sehmsdorf & E. Simpson (eds) *Nordic Folklore: Recent studies* (Bloomington, Indiana University press), pp. 165–177.

Kwami, R. (1996) Music Education in and for a Multi-Cultural Society, in: C. Plummeridge (ed.), *Music Education: Trends and issues* (London, Institute of Education), pp. 59–77.

Labuta, J. A. & Smith, D. A. (1997) *Music Education: Historical contexts and perspectives* (Boston, Prentice Hall).

Mark, M. L. (ed.) (2002) *Music Education: Source readings from ancient Greece to today*, 2nd edn. (London, Routledge).

Mcclintock, A. (1995) *Imperial Leather: Race, gender and sexuality in the colonial contest* (New York, Routledge).

Merriam, A. P. (1964) *The Anthropology of Music* (Bloomington, Northwestern University Press).

Moon, C., Cooper, R. P. & Fifer, W. P. (1993) Two-Day Olds Prefer Their Native Language, *Infant Behaviour and Development*, 16, pp. 495–500.

Nisbet, H. B. (ed.) (1985) *German Aesthetic and Literary Criticism: Winckelmann, Lessing, Hamann, Herder, Schiller, Goethe* (Cambridge, Cambridge University Press).

Norton, R. E. (1991) *Herder's Aesthetics and the European Enlightenment* (Ithaca, Cornell University Press).

Papousek, M. (1996) Musicality in Infancy Research: Biological and cultural origins of early musicality, in: I. Deliege & J. A. Sloboda (eds) *Musical Beginnings: Origins and development of musical competence* (Oxford, Oxford University Press), pp. 88–112.

Phillips, A. (1994) *On Kissing, Tickling and Being Bored* (London, Faber).

Riethmuller, A. (2002) 1933 and the Fiasco of Cultural Identities in Music, *Word and Music Studies*, 4:1, pp. 181–193.

Rasollofondraosolo, Z. & Meinhof, U. H. (2003) Popular Malagasy Music and the Construction of Cultural Identities, *AILA Review*, 16:1, pp. 127–148.

Santner, E. (2001) *On The Psychotheology of Everyday Life: Reflections on Freud and Rosenzweig* (Chicago, University of Chicago Press).

Schlaug, G., Jancke, L., Huang, Y. & Steinmetz, H. (1994) Vivo Morphometry of Interhemispheric Asymmetry and Connectivity in Musicians, in: I. Deleige (ed.), *Proceedings of the 3rd International Conference for Music Perception and Cognition*, Liege, Belgium, pp. 417–418.

Sergiu, C. & Rautz, G. (2003) Culture and Identity, *European Integration*, 25:3, pp. 189–205.

Smith, S. L., Gerhardt, K. J., Griffiths, S. K., Huang, X. & Abrams, R. M. (2003) Intelligibility of Sentences Recorded from the Uterus of a Pregnant Ewe and from the Fetal Inner Ear, *Audiology and Neuro Otology*, 8, pp. 347–353.

Spelke, E. S. (1976) Infants' Intermodal Perception of Events, *Cognitive Psychology*, 8, pp. 553–560.

Stock, J. P. J. (2003) Music Education: Perspectives from Current Ethnomusicology, *British Journal of Music Education*, 20:2, pp. 135–145.

Thorsen, S-M. (2002) Addressing Cultural Identity in Music Education, *Talking Drum*, 84, pp. 1–7.

Trehub, S. E., Schellenberg, E. G. & Hill, D. (1997) The Origins of Music Perception and Cognition: A developmental perspective, in: I. Deliege & J. A. Sloboda (eds) *Perception and Cognition of Music* (Hove, The Psychology Press), pp. 103–28.

Walder, D. (ed.) (1990) *Literature in the Modern World* (Oxford, Oxford University Press).

Warner, M. (1998) *No Go the Bogeyman: Scaring, Lulling and making mock* (London, Chatto and Windus).

Werker, J. F. & Desjardins, R. N. (1995) Listening to Speech in the First Year of Life: Experiential influences on phoneme perception, *Current Directions in Psychological Science*, 4:3, pp. 76–81.

West, M. L. (1992) *Ancient Greek Music* (Oxford, The Clarendon Press).

Williams, R. (1961) *Culture and Society 1780–1950* (Harmondsworth, Penguin).

Zammito, J. H. (2001) *Kant, Herder, and the Birth of Anthropology* (Chicago, University of Chicago Press).

5
Improvisation and Cultural Work in Music and Music Education

DAVID K. LINES
University of Auckland, New Zealand

Improvisation and the Musical Event

This essay explores the educational significance of the medium of music improvisation. As a musical activity practised and performed daily across the world, improvisation occupies the time and focus of many musicians, particularly those who interface with jazz, rock, popular styles and many non-Western styles. In this essay, I focus on one exceptional aspect of music improvisation—its capacity to intensify and heighten the dynamic qualities of the musical moment. Due to its temporal nature, improvisational practice in music draws musicians and listeners alike into the values and nuances of a musical instance. From an educational point of view, learning to improvise enables a musician to explore new expressions of what is 'musical'. Being at the conscious 'edge' of musical creation while in performance provides musicians and listeners with opportunities to gain insights into the nature and value of the musical experience.

Bailey (1992, p. ix, cited in Nettl, 1998, p. 5) argues that an 'understanding of music at large hinges on understanding something of improvisation'. Bailey's assertion underscores an engaging characteristic of music; that it is made more understandable by means of the improvised musical experience. Improvisation favours the revealing or 'presencing' of music—in the moment. It encapsulates an aspect of the music experience that comes to us temporally, rather than as a memory, written score, C.D., or digital wave file. It is what Arom calls 'the performance of music at the very moment of its inception' (cited in Nettl, 1998, p. 11), and what Erlmann describes as the creation of a musical utterance 'at the moment of its realisation in performance' (ibid.). Improvisation, privileges the moment when music is projected into space; when it is affirmed and realised for what it 'is.' Within this context, the performative characteristic of music is experienced as a fleeting event within a broader historical context from which it comes forth. Music events are sites of engagement where new musical moments are presented to listeners with 'historical' memories and expectations. The qualities and characteristics of music events, however, have not always been recognised or affirmed. In fact, the broader phenomena of music's *presencing* have become somewhat undervalued in music studies and thinking. This state of affairs is reflected to a degree in the tendency of Western music practices to detach improvisation from other conceptions of music production and dissemination.

The very idea of improvisation is a Western construct that has arisen from a presumed detachment between pre-composition and performance (Gurlitt & Eggebrecht, 1967, p. 390, cited in Nettl, 1998, p. 11). This detachment, which has become evident in music and music education practices, has tended to distract unsuspecting musicians and music learners from what improvisation offers as a mode of musical action. Small (1987: 309) writes: 'In most of the world's musical traditions the word "improvisation" has little significance, since what we have been calling improvisation is just the normal way of musicking; they call it quite simply, playing, and the idiom in which they work is, quite simply, "the way we play."' But this is not how we commonly understand things in the classical music tradition, as it is known today. The Western fascination with pre-composed music in all its detail and organizational splendour and accompanied mythologies, has become detached from its main vehicle of dissemination—performing. In many Western music education programmes, the pre-composed work has become exulted or 'superior' to the act of musicking itself. This inverted emphasis of things musical has perpetuated a value system that has de-emphasised the particular circumstances of the musical moment. Thus, in the value systems appropriated by Western musicology and music education the characteristics of the musical moment encapsulated by improvisation—unpredictability and freedom (Nettl, 1998, p. 8)—have been negated, or perhaps even in some cases, forgotten.

Improvisation has great potential to open up our thinking about the nature of the performative event of music. How can a musical event be best described and understood in improvised settings? How might a musician approach a music event and what can be learnt about it? Such questions are germane for both musicians and music educators. A musician's conception of a musical event could assist their planning and delivery of a performance. A music teacher's understanding and vision of music's 'territory of affect' (c.f. Deleuze & Guattari, 1987) could help configure the capacities and possibilities of their students' learning.

Nietzsche writes: 'when art dresses itself in the most worn-out material it is most easily recognised as art' (Nietzsche, 1996, #179). Similarly, music improvisation comes out of a well-worn matrix of stylistic nuances and musical ways of playing and listening. Music culture is epitomised by the injection of musical ideas into a fluid region of historical and communal styles. Thus, in an event, improvisations emerge in counterpoint with the regular and irregular musical circumstances from which they arise. This amounts to a 'dialogue between a musician and his [sic] music' (Jairazbhoy, cited in Nettl, 1998, p. 16). The dialogue of a Karnatak raga in India, for instance, comes out of a broad system of music rules that are 'absorbed and used like a blueprint for moulding the edifice of each improvisatory form' (Viswanathan & Cormack, 1998, p. 231).

The 'rules' of music, however, consist not only of the scientifically defined variables of music (Blacking, 1995, p. 229) that have constituted the means of modern musical analysis: rhythm, melody, harmony, timbre, dynamics etc. Improvisatory musics draw on and enter into a dialogue with the cultural meanings and contexts. Thus, the questioning of the performative music event raises the prospect of a more expansive region of musical affect than the configurations of tones. In a similar vein Small writes:

> If musical performances establish relationships, no relationships can be established without the existence of commonly understood meanings, and there can be no meanings without rules. Where, then, do the rules come from which enable free improvisers to establish those vital relationships within the group and the intimacy that they seek? Clearly, not from outside restraints such as melodic, rhythmic or harmonic idioms, but rather from those universal patterns of human behaviour and response in which it is necessary for the players to believe implicitly, if not necessarily consciously, before engaging in such a risky activity. What happens in practice is that as the musicians play together they evolve a set of common understandings; *they invent, as it were, their own culture*—not from scratch, of which I believe the human mind is incapable, but from the creative blending of the *manner of thinking and playing* of each musician (since each will bring to the performance habits of playing, favourite procedures and habitual responses) into what can only be called *a new idiom*. (Small, 1987, p. 308, italics mine)

Small highlights the value of group relationships in improvisation settings and the mini-cultures that collective creative activities build by means of interactive thinking and playing. Improvisations cultivate a sense of dialogue between participating musicians, a dialogue that involves a blending of individual contributions that brings about something that has a wider cultural significance. Small's description is useful for it helps us to conceive of musical events as something more expansive than variations of music elements or collections of sounds in themselves. He sees the relational dimension between musicians as being a critical component in the actualisation of the music. My tenet here, however, is that we can seek to understand the resonances of musical moments even more extensively. Musical events involve the presencing of *complex* modes of cultural work. There are many dimensions of dialogical music interaction—those that are interpersonal, technological, imaginary, economic, expressive, symbolic, historical, educative etc.—that can participate in the emerging character of a given musical moment. Further, I argue, that if we take time to consider the resonating characteristics of the emerging 'melodies of cultural work,' or 'new idioms' as Small describes them, our experiences of music can become more dynamic, attuned, and life enhancing.

In the tradition now known as classical music, the organisational and artistic features of pre-composed music pieces constitute their existence as music 'works'. In this tradition, regardless of where they are performed or who performs them, pre-composed pieces rely on accurate repetitions of acoustic forms and predeterminations of music scores. Improvisations, however, emphasise the surprising and particular qualities of events. What is notable and interesting about improvisations are their uncertain or 'unforeseeable' musical orientations (Magrini, 1998, p. 168). Music making, from the perspective of improvisation, involves taking hold of this artistic uncertainty and placing it at the forefront of musical expression. What sounds will I play next? How will these sounds be played? What new worlds of meaning and resonance will come forth as 'melodies' unfold? As such, in the paradigm of improvisation, the musician places his or her focus on the processes of 'becoming'. In this sense of musicking, what we call 'mistakes' are not germane to the overall experience. Instead, the processes that stimulate the revealing and unravelling of musical relations are considered most relevant. The musical qualities of performative actions are indebted to the *ways* and *means* of music's presencing, the active relations that come into play, and the meaningful configurations and connections that emerge in sonic places that come forth.

I hold that musicality and music learning resonate with the freedoms and unforeseeable elements of musical events. Freedom implies one can project a musical action in one way, out of a wider choice of ways, or perhaps even elect not to project anything different at all. Either way, the choice of musical action penetrates the play of events. Our musical actions of choice are instances of work that affect cultural territories in numerous ways. These actions, however, are not merely the preserve of individual intention. Music is not simply a *telos* of musicers and audience outcomes. The projection of music, as encapsulated in the improvised moment, brings forth a configuration of ways, systems, differences and autonomous expressions into a wider milieu of receptive and productive forces. These temporal interactions form what Babich (2001, p. 40) refers to as the '*melos of ereignis*,' the melody of the event—the expansive and differential qualities of musical happenings. Music educators can learn to *understand*, *prepare for* and *let* these configurations come forth by meaningfully engaging in the wider territories of musical action, in their own music worlds, and the music worlds of their students.

Music and Music Education as Cultural Work

How, then, can we describe the melody of the event that comes forth, notably in the practice of music improvisation? How can we encounter the sonic place of the moment, or 'first musical space' (Lines, 2001)? I argue that this moment or 'space' includes more than music's 'texts', that is, acoustic sounds, but encompasses a broader region of possible dimensions. What is feasible or potentially emergent in a musical situation is wide in scope. Heidegger calls this 'the quiet power of the possible' (Heidegger, 1993, p. 221), the dimension or horizon of what things can 'be', by means of their relations with other beings and their propensity to become expressive. Seen in this light, the possibilities of musical expression are expanded in accordance with the relations that emerge in the sonic territories of events. This broader view of music affirms music's way of being in the world in all its possible dimensions and meanings. By means of the immense range of things possible, the 'melodies' of each event are particular and different. These 'melodies,' or living pathways of sounds, form and gather together what I will call, here, the *cultural work of music*. Further, when we pay particular attention to the preparation, dissemination and moulding of these melodic pathways in ethical situations of intent, I suggest, we engage in the *cultural work of music education.* This latter work comes out of the 'natural work' of music, the work that stimulates our musical imaginaries.

The *cultural work of music* occurs in instances when music presences itself expansively as complex and interweaving sonic vectors. Music is by no means a mere singular, or linear activity; it emerges with living and changing territories of expression, intent, feeling, function, mood, identity and cognition. The regions of engagement are heterogeneous: different, fluid, multidimensional and diverse. In music events, new sonic vectors impinge on existing sonic territories of context and meaning. As such, new spaces are opened revealing new instances of cultural work. The region of disclosure can be understood as a matrix of energy; networks of forces—sonic vectors and territories—that interact and shift in accordance with their respective qualities of difference. Viewed from this perspective, the *cultural work of music* is not only the actions of human musicking, but also takes into account the relational dimensions that make musicking possible. Music can be thought of as a medium that takes hold of a whole matrix of possibilities and dimensions.

In what capacity is the *cultural work of music* educative? Music's capacity to come forth as a sonic force brings forth qualities that enable us to appreciate and experience the emergence of cultural work in our life events. Nietzsche (1999, p. 14) writes of this in the *Birth of Tragedy in the Spirit of Music* where he contrasts two Greek deities: the 'imageless art of music', Dionysus, and the 'image-maker', Apollo. Nietzsche identifies in music's sonic force, an 'imageless[1]' natural and creative drive that stimulates our artistic selves in ways that concur with our sense of humanity and life. This natural drive, Nietzsche posits, is encapsulated in the power and energy of music and gathers its source from the very creative ground of human existence. Nietzsche sees music as an emergent creative force that energises and stimulates cultural work—the formation and reformation of sounds, images, expressions, identities, symbols and concepts. The '*melos of ereignis*' thus alerts us of our character as 'artists of life' as we participate in moments of music as cultural work. Nietzsche writes: 'Man [sic] is no longer an artist, he has become a work of art: all nature's artistic power reveals itself here, amidst shivers of intoxication, to the highest, most blissful satisfaction of the primordial unity' (ibid., p. 18). Music's natural qualities, including those we experience at times in improvisation and in other musical instances, connect us with this sense of 'becoming artistic'. Music's particular sonic and Dionysian (creative power/potential) characteristics thus educate us, inasmuch as we experience the 'workly character' of art that is integral to our being.

A *music educator as cultural worker* works with music to responsively action educative possibilities. Such a cultural worker recognises the broad reach of music's capacity as a life changing and life creating force. This includes music's propensity to simultaneously create and diffuse images and identities of meaning. He or she appreciates the personal and communal intimacy of music and the profound and educative way it can influence and mobilise our modes of expression and thinking. He or she is an educator who takes music's educative possibilities seriously and works with music to project possibilities of learning, expression and, if necessary, resistance in musical events.

Debates on Music's Text and Context[2]

The synchronic and momentary character of improvised music may indeed provide musicians and music educators with an interesting avenue in which to explore the philosophical direction of their work. But is this a direction that music theorists are pointing towards in their understanding of the musical experience? Interestingly, theoretical comments and observations from contemporary thinkers in various music disciplines do indicate a similar path of thought. One such area of debate is the seemingly polemic tension or rift that exists between two ways of considering music—as musical 'texts' (notes, sounds) and as musical 'contexts' (meanings, environments). The rift is also associated with music-genre differences; between musics that have some kind of 'improvisation basis' like pop, jazz, rock and many ethnic musics; and music that primarily focuses on pre-composition and the correct renditions and interpretations of compositions in performances—notably the Western classical tradition of music and music learning that many of us have grown up with.

The growing academic area of popular music studies, which has blossomed outside the preserve of traditional music departments,[3] has been particularly conscious of what might be termed as the text-context debate in music. For popular music educators, questions of music's context and cultural particularity has become a necessary focus, even to the point of criticism within its own academic base (see Green, 2001; Shepherd & Wicke, 1997). Aware of these issues, Tagg (2002) has sought to articulate the types of musical 'knowledge' favoured by each 'side' of the text-context divide. For him, Western music traditions favour constructional knowledge (e.g. creating, producing, performing, notation coding) over receptive knowledge (e.g. recalling, recognising, distinguishing between sounds and their cultural connotations) of which the latter, according to him, is virtually excluded in the sphere of public education. Tagg's concern is that the 'contextual awareness' aspect of musical activity is largely absent from music teaching programmes. Despite this, he asserts the 'almost tautological fact that musical text and context can only exist symbiotically' (ibid., p. 1).

Shepherd (1991: 2) thinks that inconsistencies in the way that music and music education are thought about and actioned are symptomatic of a dialectic that separates objective, mental, intellectual and rational values and epistemological categories from those that are subjective, physical, emotional and irrational. This dialectical detachment has controlled, obscured and downplayed many of the 'consequences of human relatedness' (ibid.) in music. Shepherd is aware of the debilitating consequences of this situation and the resulting loss of richness in both musical and educational experiences. He suggests that what music can provide from its own internal processes are social and cultural messages that are 'intensely personal' (ibid.) and meaningful in a myriad of ways.

Other theorists are looking at new ways of conceptualising the musical experience, taking into account the diverse and interactive nature of the art form. Italian pop music theorist Fabbri (1999, p. 11), for instance, uses the metaphor of 'space' to explain music. Musical 'space' is region where we locate our understanding and experience of music; where changing cultural codes (e.g. musical laws, rituals, religious meanings, common assumptions, economic forces) interweave and blend in artistic action. Music as 'space' promotes the idea that music moves freely across boundaries and thus works as a mediator, negotiator, resistor and transformer of cultural codes and practices. In Fabbri, we observe a way of theorising the musical experience that takes into account a fluid juncture between what we traditionally view as 'music'—the sounds—and the immediate cultural context or sound environment. Fabbri extends this point by merging the concept of musical 'style'—which he denotes as the definite spaces occupied by the sounds themselves (texts)—with 'genre', which encompasses the broader spaces of mobile and flexible cultural patterns and codes (contexts) (ibid.). In this way of thinking, style becomes a more specific manifestation of genre.

Feld (Keil & Feld, 1994, p. 76) emphasises music's worldwide processual orientation, observing that in a majority of cultures music is performance orientated, dance derived and at least partially improvised. For Feld, we must not only posit 'psychological constants' as sources of musical expression, but also 'social experience, background, skill, desire and necessity' (ibid., p. 84) as constructs that shape our realities of music. 'The listener', says Feld, 'is implicated as a socially and historically situated being, not just as the bearer of organs that receive and respond to stimuli' (ibid., p. 84). The syntactic world of music is not only culturally determined from the 'inside' in relation to the movements of tones, forms, articulations and rhythms through time, but also from the 'outside', through the interpretive forces that engage listeners, performers and composers.

Slobin (1993, p. x) restates the call to revaluate the cultural constitution of the musical experience, but his theorising also moves into questions of transience and changing identities. While he recognises both the personal and collective landscapes of musical formations, he notes that these formations are not what they seem, especially when viewed up close. Personal and communal musical structures can appear rigid from a distance, but up close they are illusive and puzzling, they have shifting outlines and mirage-like qualities that are constantly in flux. As such, they offer 'striking metaphors and tangible data for understanding societies in moments of transition' (Slobin, 1996, p. 1). Music, to Slobin, helps to 'orchestrate personal, local, regional, ethnic, religious, linguistic and national identity' (ibid., p. 1). Like changing music sound patterns—and the example of music improvisation is most pertinent here—these identity formations are shifting, mobile and interchanging.

Each of the above music theorists and researchers seek to understand the synchronicity of the musical experience in different ways—as a particular event that cannot be easily separated from the component parts that constitute that particular event. Further, they point more clearly to the need to affirm and acknowledge music as a temporal and changeable art-experience, as an art form that is continually in flux, and as a medium that draws its very existence from a shifting dialogue of expression between the components of musical spaces. These associations, configurations and particularities are living processes; they reflect changing expressions of life, desire and identity.

Conclusion

The temporal nature of music improvisation draws our attention to the nature of music events. In improvised settings we tend to notice the life affirming particularities and details that make each moment different and special. Although improvisation invites engagement into the performative characteristics of the musical experience these characteristics are not confined to improvisation alone. In fact, *all* musical experiences—listening, singing, playing instruments, dancing, acts of composing etc.—engage in performative moments, in different ways. Each musical action consists of moments where musical configurations are formed; where musical meanings are adjusted and dialogically reconfigured, alongside musical intentions and interactions.

Musicians and music educators can move beyond the dualisms of text and context in music. They can begin to consider the dialogical nature of the musical moment and explore the *cultural work* of our diverse musical interactions. They need to be able to learn to 'read', observe and perceive cultural work in music and develop a sense of artistry in the process of reading, understanding and responding to such work. In order to participate in the cultural work of music, they need to have a refined sense of the possibilities such work may turn out to become. This requires explorations into the places and spaces where musical sounds become aligned with living examples of cultural meaning. There is an element of unpredictability in this process; as we partake and respond to cultural work, we don't know in advance what the nature and quality of each expressive moment will be. The unpredictability and uncertainty of each musical moment culminates in a revealing of cultural work—not abstracted musical sounds—but rather, dialogical musical relationships, new musical idioms and cultural expressions of music. As we learn to read and respond to the cultural work of music we begin to partake in the living and resonating qualities of musical experiences as they impact on our lives. We become expressive.

As musicians our focus will be, for sure, on what we play and sing—that is, the technical and expressive production of musical sounds. But this focus will always be in tandem with the play of musical events and the living dialogues of cultural work that interface with technique and expression. As music educators, we can work with these broader configurations of cultural work by guiding students into meaningful learning events. The musical meanings our students enter into become a part of their general learning as they contemplate their identities, musical histories and the possibilities and ways they may become more expressive themselves.

Finally, I am not arguing here for improvisation to become the only form of valid musical activity. Rather, I am suggesting that all types of music involvement—music making, music listening, music use and music learning—are improvisational in a sense. Further, if this sense is affirmed, discussed, contemplated and actively sought after, music has the potential to be more fully realised as the life enhancing art form it is.

Notes

1. Schopenhauer, who influenced Nietzsche's *Birth of Tragedy*, was also fascinated by the 'imageless' characteristic of music. What interests me about Nietzsche's initial thesis of

the Dionysian and Apollinian forces, however, is the moment of engagement or identity formation and reformation, the triggering power of music to affect change.
2. See Lines, 2003 for an earlier version of this text and context debate in relation to the N.Z. Arts Curriculum.
3. Many popular music studies have grown out of media and English literature academic contexts.

References

Babich, B. (2001) The Musical Style of Philosophy: From Socrates' practice to Heidegger's parataxis, in: *Gesture and Word: Thinking between philosophy and poetry* (Evanston, Northwestern University Press), pp. 1–47.

Bailey, D. (1992) *Improvisation: Its nature and practice in music* (New York, Da Capo Press).

Blacking, J. (1995) Music, Culture and Experience, in: *Music, Culture and Experience: Selected papers of John Blacking* (Chicago, University of Chicago Press), pp. 223–242.

Deleuze, G. & Guattari, F. (1987) *A Thousand Plateaus: Capitalism and schizophrenia*, trans. B. Massumi, (London, University of Minneapolis Press).

Fabbri, F. (1999) Browsing Musical Space: Categories and the musical mind, Cited on the www on 18/08/02 at http://www.theblackbook.net/acad/tagg/xpdfs/ffabbri990717.pdf

Green, L. (2001) *How Popular Musicians Learn: A way ahead for music education* (Burlington, VT, Ashgate).

Heidegger, M. (1993) *Basic Writings*, trans. D. Krell, (San Francisco, Harper Collins).

Keil, C. & Feld, S. (1994) *Music Grooves* (Chicago, University of Chicago Press).

Lines, D. (2001) The First Musical Space: Articulating the music of the moment, in: E. Grierson & J. Mansfield (eds), *Access: Critical Perspectives in Cultural Policy Studies and Education*, 20:1, pp. 82–89.

Lines, D. (2003) Text and Context in Music: Where music dwells, in: E. Grierson & J. Mansfield (eds), *The Arts in Education: Critical Perspectives from Aotearoa New Zealand* (Palmerston Nth, Dunmore Press), pp. 161–179.

Magrini, T. (1998) Improvisation and Group Interaction in Italian Lyrical Singing, in: B. Nettl (ed.), *In the Course of Performance: Studies in the world of musical improvisation* (Chicago, The University of Chicago Press), pp. 169–198.

Nettl, B. (1998) Introduction: An art neglected in scholarship, in: B. Nettl (ed.), *In the Course of Performance: Studies in the world of musical improvisation* (Chicago, The University of Chicago Press), pp. 1–26.

Nietzsche, F. (1999) *The Birth of Tragedy and Other Writings*, R. Geuss & R. Speirs (eds), (Cambridge, Cambridge University Press).

Nietzsche, F. (1996) *Human All Too Human: A book for free spirits*, trans. R. Hollingdale, (Cambridge, Cambridge University Press).

Shepherd, J. & Wick, P. (1997) *Music and Cultural Theory* (Cambridge, U.K., Polity Press).

Shepherd, J. (1991) *Music as Social Text* (Cambridge, Polity Press).

Slobin, M. (ed.) (1996) *Returning Culture: Musical changes in Central and Eastern Europe* (London, Duke University Press).

Slobin, M. (1993) *Subcultural Sounds: Micro musics of the West* (London, Wesleyan University Press).

Small, C. (1987) *Music of the Common Tongue* (London, Wesleyan University Press).

Tagg, P. (2002) Text and Context as Corequisites in the Popular Analysis of Music, Paper prepared for conference on *Musical Text and Context*, Cremona, April 2002, Cited on the www on 18/08/02 at http://www.theblackbook.net/acad/tagg/articles/cremona.html

Viswanathan, T. & Cormack, J. (1998) Melodic Improvisation in Karnatak Music: the manifestations of Raga, in: B. Nettl (ed.), *In the Course of Performance: Studies in the world of musical improvisation* (Chicago, The University of Chicago Press), pp. 219–236.

6 Musical Meaning and Social Reproduction: A case for retrieving autonomy

LUCY GREEN
Institute of Education, London University

Music educationalists are probably agreed upon one thing if nothing else: that theory and practice in the field urgently need to embrace diversity. This might encompass the diversity of musical styles which the globalization of the music industry with one hand is making widely available, and with the other hand is threatening to swamp; the localization of traditional musics being bolstered by that same industry as well as by governments and pressure groups in response to such threats; the appropriation and re-working of global musical styles in local settings, with and without the 'help' of commercial interest; the diverse responses to and uses of musics in different places, by different ethnic groups, religions, social classes, genders, 'sub-cultures', 'scenes' and other social groups; the rapidly changing array of music technology which is impacting on approaches to music-making; or the diversity of musical reception practices and approaches to music teaching and learning. How can music education philosophers and theorists, let alone practitioners, come to grips with such factors?

At the present time, the Adornian project of discerning within music, traces of the structure and ideology of the society from which that music springs, has been largely discarded. Sociological interest in music is focusing instead on questions of how musical meanings are constructed through discourse, use, education, the media and other social practices and institutions, at the levels both of face-to-face interaction and of wider social structures (Martin, 1995; Finnegan, 1989; Negus, 1999; DeNora, 2000; Clayton, 2003). What people say about music, the uses to which they put it in their ordinary lives, and their music-making practices are all receiving interest from researchers and scholars, alongside questions about the structures and processes of the music industry and broadcasting corporations and perhaps to a lesser extent, of education. Musicology has come under attack from such quarters during the last fifteen years or so, most notably for its alleged formalism and its implicit attribution of autonomous status to Western classical music. That is, it has been accused of concentrating on the sounds of music, the musical 'text', to the detriment of music's social contexts and uses, and for harbouring an assumption that the value and significance of the musical text rise above particular social and historical conditions. But we must be careful not to swing too far in the opposite direction. To consider the discourse and use surrounding music without taking into account the ways in which the musical text is organized, can altogether miss out the quality of the very object of consideration, so that in the end it could be food or clothes that are under discussion, rather than music with its own peculiar properties.

In this article I propose a theory of musical meaning and experience which takes into consideration the dialectical relationship between musical text and context, and which is flexible enough to apply to a range of musical styles. Through this theory I examine the roles played by the school music classroom which, despite the multiplicity of musical styles now incorporated into schooling, continues to contribute to the reproduction of existing social relations in the wider society. I consider how music itself can be understood to construct and communicate apparent 'truths' about ourselves and society and what role the classroom plays in perpetuating those 'truths'. Finally I argue for a partial but necessary reinstatement of the much-maligned notion of musical autonomy as a critical moment in any attempt to change things.

Musical Meaning and Experience

What causes us to recognise a particular concatenation of sounds as being music? If we hear the sounds of a lorry backing into a side-street, or a steel-pan being tuned, we don't consider them to be music. In order to do so, the listener has to be immersed in a complex range of social conventions, which are discernible in relation both to the organization of the sounds themselves, and to the social contexts surrounding their production and reception.

Sound is the raw material from which music is made. For music to come into existence and for musical experience to occur, this raw material must be organized in such a way as to have relationships which are perceived in the mind of a listener. For example, the listener might notice features such as patterning, opening and close, whole and part, beginning and end, repetition, similarity, difference, and so on. These features are perceptible in several ways. One is that the flow of musical materials through time is organized in such a way as to cause listeners to anticipate future sonic events, as L. B. Meyer (1956) so persuasively demonstrated with reference to Western classical music, and which can equally be referred to many other classical, popular and traditional musics. We wait for the final chord or the next note after the pause, we expect the music to break out into a melody at the next strong beat, we hear the string flourish or the drummer's extended up-beat as an announcement of the reprise, and so on. Not only does music raise expectations for what might be going to happen next, it also causes us to make retrospective connections between present and past events, so that the present makes the past meaningful; and the musical past colours the present just as much as the present raises expectations for the future. In many musics, perhaps even most, expectation and retrospection seem to play a relatively small part in the experience. On one hand, experience is focussed on the quality of the sounds: texture, timbre, a crack in the voice, a pitch inflection so slight as to be barely noticeable; on the other hand, experience takes in a wide field of processual flow, such as the feeling of being carried along on a relentless beat. But of course that quality, or that sense of travelling along, nonetheless only comes into existence in relation to what went before and what comes afterwards at any particular moment.

The mental acts involved in processing music backwards and forwards in time, and attending to the quality of the moment or processual flow, involve the making of meaningful connections between parts of the music being heard. But these connections are not restricted to the particular piece of music in question, for they arise from the listener's previous experience of a number of pieces of music that together make up a style, sub-style or genre. Thus the connections can cut across from one piece of music to another. I am not referring here to a postmodern concept of intertextuality; indeed what is meant by intertextuality has been going on between pieces of music, by necessity, since the first music emerged into history. For no music can exist, that is, no music can be perceived as music, without reference to a higher-order organizing factor, or what can be termed a style; and virtually all music has always 'borrowed', imitated or directly implanted components from other pieces. Perception of the connections within and across pieces of music is learnt, acquired through repeated listening and therefore, through some level of familiarity with the style of the music in question. If the listener does not have familiarity, relatively few meanings will be conceived. Therefore a piece of music which is highly meaningful or very rewarding to one individual, might be relatively meaningless or lacking in interest to another. Any one piece of music can give rise to a multiplicity of possible meanings.

I refer to the meaningful connections that are forged within and across musical pieces, as 'inherent musical meanings' (Green, 1988; 1997). The word 'inherent' has at least two meanings in the English language. It can mean that a property of an object is essential, ahistorical or natural, which is quite the opposite of how I am using the term. It can also mean that a property of an object is contained within the object, but without any suggestion of this containment being essential, ahistorical or natural. This is how I am using the term. 'Inherent musical meanings' are 'inherent', in the sense of being contained within the musical object, in relation to the historically-constituted, logical properties of the meaning-making processes. These processes involve meaning-making constituents, or to put it crudely, 'signs' which are made of musical materials (a chord, a note, a phrase); and meanings-being-meant corresponding with 'referents' (the anticipated chord or note, the recognized melody) that are also made up of musical materials. Both 'signs' and 'referents' are incorporated, embodied, or they inhere and are thus inherent within the raw materials that constitute the music in question. However, they are of course entirely socially constituted, and recognition of them, as I have already suggested, is dependent on listeners' acquired familiarity with the stylistic norms of the music in question. To return to the example of the lorry backing into a side-street or a steel-pan being tuned: such sounds could only become music and therefore only carry musical meaning by virtue of a complex set of social conventions. The organization of the materials into meaningful relationships, or what I call inherent musical meanings, is one such convention.

Someone could object to my claim that musical experience relies on the listener making connections between the past, present and future of the musical materials, as follows: that if we turn on the radio and hear only the shortest snatch of sound, less than a second, we can still tell it is music that we are hearing, rather than, say, a spoken voice, a lorry turning or some other sound. We can tell this even though we are quite unable to make any connections between the snatch of sound that we heard and any ones that preceded it or followed after it. How then can we recognise the sound as music, if it is the case that such recognition requires a perception of inherent meanings arising from making connections between parts of the music as they pass in time, as suggested above? One response is to say that we do not actually have a musical experience in that situation. Rather we recognise that the snatch of sound comes from one or more musical instruments or sung voices, and we assume that because it was heard on the radio, putting two and two together, it must be part of a piece of music.

This is so, but there is in fact something else going on which is of much deeper significance. For our assumption that the snatch of sound comes from a piece of music derives from a quite different aspect of musical meaning, an aspect that relates not to the interrelationships of musical materials, that is not to musical inherent meanings; but to music's social context and its mediation as a cultural object through historical social institutions. In other words, it derives from musical meanings which point outwards from the musical text towards concepts, relationships or things that exist independently of it. I refer to such meanings as 'delineations', (Green, 1988; 1997) in other words, as meanings which are loosely suggested or metaphorically sketched by the music in relation to its social context. Factors such as the clothes and hairstyles of the musicians, their listeners or fans; the venues in which the music is relayed; the social or political values associated with the music, which may or may not be embodied in lyrics; the musical practices of the listeners, and indeed other social practices connected with them, and so on, all come into play.

Any particular piece of music may mean something we can relate to, something we dislike, something we desire and so on. Individuals will have a multiplicity of responses to musical delineations, some of which are shared and generally agreed upon by the majority of people in any particular society or social group; others of which will be entirely idiosyncratic. For example a National Anthem delineates the nation, monarchy, president or whatever is relevant to practically everyone in and beyond a particular nation; but to some individuals it can delineate pride whereas to others it delineates shame; to some love, to others hatred. Not only are there obvious examples such as National Anthems, wedding songs, football songs which acquire generally-recognized conventional meanings, but there are far more subtle levels of delineation, such as the sound of a particular flute, the way an electric guitar is distorted, a rhythm, a vocal inflection, the precise bend of a pitch; all of which can carry delineated meanings which are conventionally recognized to a greater or lesser extent. A piece of music may also delineate a particular event or feeling that arose on one occasion for one particular individual when she was listening to it, that has nothing whatsoever to do with the meanings conventionally attributed to it by the rest of her society.

Some sociologists of music have argued that it is not possible to fully appreciate a particular piece of music unless one is an insider to, or at least unless one has some insider-knowledge of the culture in which the music was originally produced. Detractors from this position have pointed to the capacity of music to carry across times and places, allowing people from one culture to respond with enjoyment to music from other very different cultures (see the debate between Vulliamy & Shepherd, 1984, 1985 and Swanwick, 1984). Notwithstanding fundamental disagreements, both sides would tend to agree that one can have a fuller, richer understanding if one is an insider; and that if not, the acquisition of some knowledge about the social context in which the music was originally produced is likely to enhance the listening experience. But it is not only the context of production, for unavoidably, the context of *reception* also contributes to the music's delineations. No music can ever be heard (that is, heard-as-music) outside of a social context. Taking music out of its original context of production and putting it into even a completely new and different context of reception does not cause it to lose delineated meanings; it merely replaces some delineations (related to the context of production) with others (related to the context of reception). We can still have a musical experience even if we know absolutely nothing about the original social contexts, so long as we can recognise the piece as being a piece of music in the first place.

For that recognition to take place we must rely on the perception of inherent meanings. But I have suggested that unless the listener has some familiarity with the style, then no experience of inherent meanings will occur. So to return to the example of the snatch of music on the radio: it is precisely the radio, the social conventions surrounding radio broadcasting, or other circumstances such as the concert platform, the gathering of dancers in the centre of the village and so on, in combination with the musical inherent meanings, that tell us it is music we are hearing. In short, recognition of the social, collective definitions of what counts as music is a necessary component of what makes something music. No music can exist at all without its transmitting some delineation or other. Musical delineation is not merely an add-on to inherent musical meaning. On the contrary, it goes on at a fundamental level from the very first moment of recognition of sounds as being music at all. Delineation is therefore as fundamental to musical meaning as inherent meaning and indeed, without experience of musical delineation, no musical experience could come about at all. For without some understanding of the fact that music is a social construction, we would ultimately be unable to recognise any particular collection of sounds as music. So, when we listen to music, we cannot separate our experience of its inherent meanings entirely from an awareness of the social context that accompanies its production and/or reception.

Past commentators have occasionally misunderstood or objected to this understanding of musical meaning, because, they say, the difference between the two aspects of meaning is not clear-cut. I wish to respond to that in two ways, firstly by disagreeing with it, then by agreeing with it. The distinction is clear-cut in a logical sense, in terms of the processes by which the meaning is made. As I suggested earlier, with inherent meaning the 'signs' and the 'referents' all consist of musical materials. A sound refers to another sound either in the same piece of music or beyond it in another piece, or within the style in general terms. With delineated meaning, the 'sign' is made up of musical materials, that is, sounds, but the 'referent' is made up of non-musical constituents related to the social context of the music's production and reception. In short, with inherent meaning the process of signification occurs from sound to sound, whereas with delineation it occurs from sound to non-sound. That encapsulates the logical distinction between the two types of meaning.

Secondly, however, I agree that in other ways the two meanings are not distinguishable, and indeed it is precisely the difficulty of distinguishing between them that interests me most. The point of making the distinction is to contribute to a *theoretical* understanding of musical experience; but we do not tend to distinguish between the two types of meaning, or to separate them out *experientially* when engaging in music. This presents no problem for the theory to my mind, quite the opposite in fact, for it is quite normal as well as helpful to make theoretical distinctions between things that we find hard to distinguish experientially. Take the example of love. We can theoretically distinguish between different types of love: sexual love, parental love, filial love, love between siblings, love between friends, and so on. We can also make distinctions between other cognate areas, for example liking, desire, lust. But experientially it is not always easy to separate these feelings out from each other, and indeed that difficulty leads to a great deal of confusion and complexity in our lives. But that does not mean we give up the idea of making the distinctions theoretically, for there are so many cases where they are clear and helpful. The fact that other areas exist where they are confused, only serves to remind us of the complexity of human culture, and that theory is a mere tool to help us achieve a better understanding of that complexity, rather than undermining theory *per se*, or refuting a particular theory. So it is with the dialectical theory of musical meaning which I am putting forward here.

Although as I have argued, our prior experiences and our social circumstances will greatly affect our responses to music, they cannot be said to be wholly determining factors. For even though music relies on social convention for its existence, this does not mean that it has no objective properties which would carry across different social contexts, or which lend themselves more-or-less forcefully to particular types of response or meaningful experience. To that extent music can be said to have objective properties existing independently of convention. Music is not merely a symptom of our musical practices and meanings, but it acts back on us, through its capacity to influence our beliefs, values, feelings or behaviour; or as Moore (2002), DeNora (2000) and E. Clarke (2003) put it, adapting the concept from Gibson (1986, pp. 127–43), it *affords* different responses. As a simple example: if an adult in any country that I can think of, asks young children to dance to some fast, loud music with an explicit beat, the children are likely to jump around vigorously; if she asks them to dance to some soft, slow music, they will glide about gracefully. To what extent have the children learnt these responses from conventional usage of music in the particular social context to which they are accustomed; and to what extent are these responses natural and universal? It would be hasty to altogether throw out the idea that the responses retain some natural or universal elements. An example of the different types of funeral music or music used in death-rites that can be found in different cultures is often used to point to the social constructedness of musical meanings: that in some societies such music is slow whereas in others it is fast. But this does not mean that the same characteristics of music (fast or slow) afford different responses in different social contexts; rather it means that the responses to death and bereavement are different, or are expressed differently.

The Dialectics of Musical Meaning and Experience

The theory which I am putting forward posits a dialectical relationship between the two types of musical meaning identified. Musical experience, in this model, cannot occur at all unless both aspects of meaning are in operation to some extent or other. However, this is not to imply that both types of meaning always co-exist to the same degree, or that we are always *conscious* of both, or even either, of them. Indeed, our responses to each aspect of musical meaning can be in contradiction, each aspect can have a different effect upon musical experience as a whole, and more interestingly, each can influence and overpower the other.

In order to think through these claims, it is helpful to understand our responses to each aspect of musical meaning in terms of polar extremes, although in practice of course individuals will experience a variety of subtle shades at different points along each pole. Chart A (below) is intended to provide some graphic aid to thinking through these matters. With regards to inherent meaning, we can have a highly affirmative, or positive response. This will occur when we are very familiar with the style or the particular piece, we understand its nuances, and we are carried along securely or pleasurably in its ebb and flow. The greater our familiarity with the style of the music, the more affirmative the experience is likely to be. For when we are familiar with the normative stylistic terms of reference in a piece of music, we are able to distinguish disruption from normality and resolution from disruption. If the music surprises us with, say, an unexpected event, we understand it. Although our expectations may have been negated, we assimilate the negation in terms of a wider field of presence related to other parts of the music and to the style, and thus we enjoy it: without negation, disruption, difference and so on, at whatever level, no inherent musical meaning could arise. Only through these and through our understanding of them do we relate meaningfully to music. Hence ultimately, our negation is understood in the light of its own affirmation: we are negated only because we understand, to whatever extent, the style of the music; and we are thus affirmed in our overall musical experience as it takes place in time.

At the other extreme, there is a negative response. This is likely to occur when we are unfamiliar with the musical style, for we are then less likely to understand the music, and may have difficulty making sense of it or responding to its internal similarities and continuities, differences and changes. An event which would surprise and delight a listener who has greater familiarity, will go completely unnoticed, so the music seems uneventful and dull. In such circumstances, the capacity of a piece of music to engage our interest is relatively limited. Not being aware of

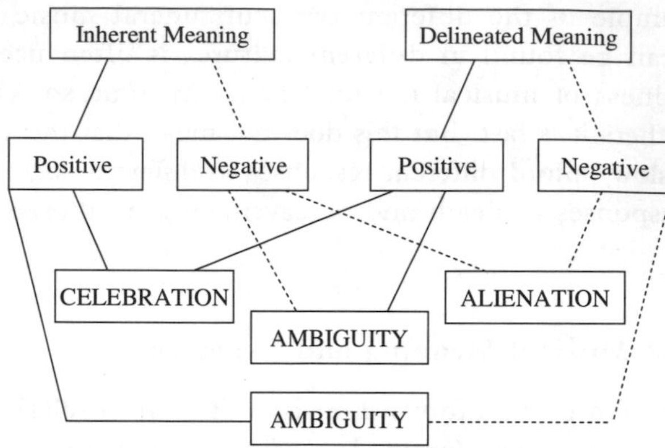

Chart A (Adapted from Green, 1988, p. 138 and 1997, p. 251)

what is and is not normative, we cannot readily distinguish disruption or its resolution, are unable to hear constituent parts as things in themselves, and cannot relate them to other constituents within the piece or across pieces. We therefore receive few, or merely confused, inherent meanings; we cannot engage with the music, are rarely negated and rarely affirmed. Such an experience can be boring, but it can also be more forceful and quite painfully aggravating or irritating. When musical style is this unfamiliar, we may well find the music random or incoherent. Our experience is fragmented, tossed to and fro on apparently unrelenting, arbitrary waves of meaningless movement.

Such an experience can be illustrated by an anecdote of a music student in a class on the twentieth-century atonal composer Schönberg. On listening to the vocal and instrumental piece 'Mondestruncken' from his *Pierrot Lunaire*, she declared she found the music incoherent, chaotic and random, and that listening to it was like a form of slow torture. Unfamiliarity with Schönberg's compositional procedures and the style of the music in general, had prevented her noticing a high level of organization of the musical materials, for example a distinctive seven-note motif which is uninterruptedly repeated four times in the flute at the beginning, repeated again and taken up in varied forms by other instruments throughout the rest of the piece. As a result of her unfamiliarity with such stylistic factors, amongst others, she received few meanings from the music, which is one reason why she had such a negative response to it.

We are uplifted, affirmed, bored or aggravated by music's inherent meanings in as many different ways as the diversity of musical style and of our individual understanding and prior experiences imply. Similarly, we can have a range of responses from positive to negative in relation to delineated meaning.

At one extreme we have a positive response when we feel the music in some way expresses our feelings, when we identify with the music because it delineates our social class or supports our political values, when it affirms our preferred clothing, hair-style, our age, ethnicity, gender and many other factors. At the other extreme we can have a negative response when we feel the music delineates social or political values of which we disapprove or from which we want to disassociate ourselves, social groups from which we are excluded, and so on. To illustrate such responses here are two snippets from Bennett's ethnographic work with Asian youth and their relationship with Bhangra music in Newcastle, UK in the late 1990s. Some used it to celebrate 'tradition', and valued it as a family music crossing generations; others rejected it as a way of articulating their separateness from these same traditions and family values. For example:

> It's good to go to a bhangra event because … it brings back memories … it's like tradition. It's the same with the dancing like. There is a traditional dance … nowadays some people just move how they want to. But I think it [the traditional bhangra dance] does matter in some ways, 'cause it gives you a buzz to be doing something a bit traditional. (Bennett, 2000, p. 111)

Alternatively:

> I was brought up listening to bhangra, because that's what my parents listened to … there was nothing else to listen to really. Then, as soon as I got to about thirteen or fourteen … I had different friends, white friends, and a different kind of atmosphere. I started listening to their tapes and I'd find out what I really liked which is dance music … Now I can't stand bhangra. (Bennett, 2000, p. 117)

What is meant by 'I can't stand bhangra'? Is it that the person is aggravated by the inherent meanings of the music, or negated by the delineated social values the music carries? It would not be unreasonable to assume that our responses to inherent and delineated meanings usually correspond. If we dislike the one we are likely to dislike the other. For example, if we are already negative to music's delineations, we are unlikely to be affirmed by its inherent meanings; and indeed, unlikely to get ourselves in a position to become sufficiently familiar with its inherent meanings for affirmation to take place. If school children are perfectly sure that Western classical music is intended only for 'boffins' and very boring adults (delineations), they are likely to dismiss its inherent meanings as being equally boring. They will therefore avoid listening to it and for that reason will continue to be unfamiliar with its inherent meanings; and for that reason in turn are highly unlikely to suddenly get a kick out of listening to the Scherzo of Beethoven's Ninth Symphony. Conversely, if our responses to inherent meanings are already negative, it is likely we will dismiss the delineations too. Some classical musicians today still believe that popular music is wholly simplistic and very easy to play. The pop-musicological challenge to that perception includes the point that such listeners seek the 'wrong' qualities in the music, expecting to hear motivic development for example; and in so doing, miss out on hearing the 'right' qualities, such as timbral change, rhythmic inflection or texture (Middleton, 1990; Brackett, 1995). The Schönberg student is another example, because not only did she find the inherent meanings tortuous, she dismissed the whole enterprise of modernist abstract art and atonal music as pretentious.

What I term 'celebration' is experienced when a positive experience of inherent meanings is accompanied by positive inclinations towards delineations. Contrastingly, 'alienation' is experienced when a negative experience of inherent meanings is accompanied by negativity towards delineations.

But sometimes the two aspects of musical meaning are in contradiction, and this will engender an experience of 'ambiguity'. There are two ideal types of ambiguity. In one of these, the experience of inherent meaning is negative, whilst that of delineated meaning is positive. For example, we can think of a person who dislikes Mozart's music and hears it as boring, frilly and superficial. As a result he hardly ever listens to it, which means in turn that his familiarity with the style is quite low. All in all such factors are liable to make him negative towards the inherent meanings. But at the same time, he can nonetheless approve of and identify with the delineations: the practice of taking important overseas business colleagues to the opera, perhaps (he would never consider taking them to a rock gig!); the social-class values with which the music is associated in his mind, and so on. He is thus positive towards the music's delineations.

Alternatively, experience of inherent meaning can be positive whilst that of delineated meaning is negative. In such a case we can think of the classical music-lover who is totally familiar with the inherent meanings of Wagner's music, say; who has perhaps listened to, played or sung his music for many years, and has thus developed a profound knowledge of the style, allowing her to be thoroughly affirmed by the inherent meanings. But, simultaneously, she has strong antipathies to Wagner because of his renowned anti-semitism and the harnessing of his music by Nazi Germany; or perhaps she simply dislikes going to the opera because she thinks the rest of the audience are 'stuffy'; or she is critical of most operatic plots because she finds them sexist, racist, and so on.

Not only may the quality of the response to each type of meaning contradict the other, but something else can occur which is perhaps one of the most provocative aspects of music, and raises some interesting issues for music education. This is that the response to one aspect of meaning can overpower, influence and even change the other.

On one hand, delineation can override inherent meaning. For example, a late nineteenth-century Scandinavian music critic was in the habit of writing very positive reviews about a particular composer. After many reviews, he found out that the composer was a woman. He carried on writing good reviews, but his language changed. Instead of using words like 'strident', 'virile' or 'powerful', he began to use words like 'delicate' and 'sensitive'. What had happened was that the gender of the composer had entered the delineations of the music for this listener, as a problematic aspect that challenged contemporary assumptions about gender, musical practice and compositional creativity. This new delineation then affected the way that the critic heard the inherent meanings (Green, 1997).

On the other hand, the notion that inherent meaning can act back to change our perception of delineation appears at first to be a logical impossibility. For inherent meaning is devoid of content; it exists as a virtual aspect of musical experience, which can itself only occur if there is also a delineated content. However I will argue at the end of this article that experience of inherent meaning can indeed change, and challenge, our musical responses to and presuppositions concerning delineation; and that it is in this moment of musical autonomy, that the most critical power of music resides.

Musical Experience and Social Reproduction

Music education in schools for most of the twentieth century took it for granted that the musical experience and needs of all children were fundamentally the same. All students were required to engage in music whose inherent meanings ranged from being affirmatory for some of them, to being wholly alienating for others; and whose delineations corresponded or conflicted with the students' social class and family backgrounds, self-images, public or private identities, values and desires. Music education is intended to enhance and appraise students' musical abilities, but at the same time there may be something else altogether going on. This proposition can be considered on two levels, one reflecting the experience of the individual student, in all the diversity that implies; and the other concerning the production and reproduction of large-scale social groups and corresponding patterns of advantage and opportunity, to which the education system makes such a powerful contribution. I will briefly consider these two levels and in so doing, illustrate the role of the music classroom in the production and reproduction of two social groups in particular, class and gender.

There is little disagreement nowadays that in its concentration on Western classical music for at least the first three-quarters of the twentieth century, music education participated in the construction and perpetuation of certain ideologies about musical value that privileged this musical style. These ideologies involved placing a high value on qualities said to be possessed by classical music, notably those of its autonomy from particular social interests and contexts; its corresponding ability to express a 'universal' human condition; its eternality, which was also related to its universality; and its formal complexity, (which was paradoxically related to the social convention of notation, on which it relies for its transmission [Green, 2003]). The school classroom afforded greater opportunities for educational success in music to those children from social class backgrounds that equipped them with commensurate practices and values regarding classical music. This occurred partly with regards to access to resources such as musical instruments and private tuition. Indeed, the assumption that such access was a pre-requisite of musical success was even written into exam syllabi, explicitly in the 1950s, then implicitly, right up to the middle of the 1980s (Green, 1988).

This was by no means only a question of access, for pupils' relationships to musical meaning are a more trenchant factor. Affirmation by the inherent meanings of the music being studied is as advantageous as affinity with the music's delineations, allowing for possible 'celebration' by the music in the classroom. These positive responses to both inherent and delineated meanings, of course derive largely from students' having family and social class backgrounds in which classical music is listened to and valued, so that they are already well equipped in Bourdieu's terms, with what the school demands but does not provide (Bourdieu, 1973, p. 80). Many of those pupils who did not have such backgrounds appeared to lack both interest and ability in music, concealing the fact that a small but significant minority of them were deeply involved in other musical styles related to quite different learning practices outside the school, such as playing in pop, rock or jazz bands (Green, 2001). But it was not only the musical practices in which pupils were or were not engaged that caused this fissure in the institutional recognition and reward of musical ability. For musical experience itself, in which pupils found themselves being celebrated or alienated, or through which they had ambiguous musical experiences, is more fundamental. I will return to the significance of this at the end of the article.

Another factor in the music classroom's production and reproduction of social groups concerns the invisibility of the reproduction processes. These were perhaps buried even more deeply, and ironically so, by virtue of an appearance of increased equality of opportunity which started to occur in the late 1980s, when a wider range of music was included in the school curriculum in many countries (Green, 2002). For since popular, jazz and 'world' musics were, at last, accepted in the classroom, this appeared to afford greater opportunities to pupils from a much wider range of social groups than hitherto. But there were two problems here. One was that teachers still tended to operate within an aesthetic of classical musical autonomy, only they referred this aesthetic to a wider range of musics. So popular musics, jazz and 'world' musics were assumed to have some amount of autonomy, universality, eternality and the capacity to express the human condition, especially in their ability to cross cultural boundaries. Such a position therefore appeared to place equal value on a wider range of musics, whilst actually continuing to uphold an aesthetic position that was fundamentally derived from classical paradigms, and was not necessarily applicable to most of these 'other' musics in the world outside the school (Green, 1999). The other problem was, and continues to be, that teachers tend to be largely trained in classical music themselves, and to adopt twentieth century-derived classical pedagogical approaches, which ride roughshod over the informal learning practices by which most of these other musics have always been transmitted. Thus, although there is new content in the music classroom, the teaching strategies mitigate against its authenticity. The musics in that sense exist inside the classroom as shadows of their 'real' forms (Green, 2001).

The majority of pupils who choose to sing and play classical music, or the music provided and organized by their teachers in schools, especially in extra-curricular activities, are girls. They are also widely regarded by teachers as being more successful at music, more tolerant, hard-working and reliable than boys. Meanwhile boys are generally said to avoid music because of its 'cissy' connotations, restricting their involvement to those areas of musical activity that signal the least approval, and the least supervision, by teachers (Green, 1997; Hanley, 1998). However, as distinct from the hard-working obedience of girls, it is not *despite* but *because of* boys' negative attitudes, that teachers attribute boys with the qualities of creativity and genius which girls are seen to lack (Green, 1997).

Again this involvement of music in reproducing age-old gender assumptions does not stop merely at the level of pupils' musical practice and teachers' perceptions of it. It goes further, in that the music involved takes on corresponding delineated meanings. As the discourse of both pupils and teachers shows, to a large extent classroom-approved music comes to delineate femininity, and more radically, effeminacy. By the same token, popular music, or any music that is not included in the curriculum or extra-curricular activities, and not taught by the teacher, delineates masculinity, and beyond that, machismo. It is not merely a matter of 'feminine' practice that girls play the violin, or of 'masculine' practice that boys play the electric guitar; but musical experience itself, and with it, the very construction of gender as a symbol of self, are at stake. The music in which girls and boys are involved acts back through these gendered delineations, to bring a symbolic affirmation, or a problematization of their gender identity. So as with social class reproduction, musical experience itself, in the context of the school, actually produces and reproduces not only gendered musical practices but gender identities and with them, gender itself.

By similar processes other social groups are produced and reproduced in the music classroom. For example, many schools incorporate 'world music' to reflect and celebrate the ethnicity of their pupils. But, as Bennett's work illustrates (above), this can backfire. Alden (1998) found that primary school children in London concealed their 'true' Hindi popular music identity and pretended to prefer the pop charts, to avoid being stigmatized by the 'white', mainstream culture, which prevailed in their classroom, despite the school's anti-racist policies and multi-cultural curricula. Other social groups, from large-scale religions to small-scale local scenes, can be similarly affirmed or denied by the music classroom, forming themselves not only through its purview, but precisely, in contradistinction to the music and musical experiences that the classroom offers.

In classrooms, some pupils will find themselves musically celebrated by positive relationships to both inherent and delineated meanings; others will be alienated, and for others, musical experience will be ambiguous. The reasons are not to do with innate musical ability, but are the result of family and social class background, membership of different social groups, and prior listening experiences. But I have been suggesting that it is not merely that the music classroom makes available, rewards or negates musical experiences; something else is going on which is more interesting and more powerful. Since music itself carries meanings for us, therefore reproduction occurs through musical experience itself. As I argued earlier, the distinction between the two aspects of musical meaning that I have suggested in this article is a logical one, but when we engage with music the two aspects come to us experientially as one unified whole. We do not usually, and often cannot, distinguish the one from the other, just as we find it hard sometimes to distinguish different kinds of love from each other. Because of this, the delineated meanings of music appear to come to us as if they were a part of the inherent meanings, the 'music itself'. So our responses to inherent meanings appear to be visceral; the inherent meanings appear to contain the delineated meanings as if those meanings did reside inside the music. Thus they seem to be immediate, that is, un-mediated by history and convention, not constructed, but natural, unquestionable and 'true'.

Retrieving Autonomy

If music is such a conservative force, and music education along with it, do either of them also have the capacity to change things? This is where I wish to reach for that discarded concept of musical autonomy. Where the concept becomes problematic is when it goes so far as to completely deny the importance and relevance of music's social contexts or delineations, focussing instead on the musical text or inherent meanings in ways that either explicitly or implicitly suggest that these are the only 'real' or 'important' aspects of music. Such an approach does indeed beg for adjustment so that social and cultural influences on both the production and reception of that text are included in any examination of its full significance. However there are three provisos to this.

One is that there can surely be nothing 'wrong' with musicologists focussing entirely on musical texts and ignoring social contexts, so long as it is done in the recognition that they are only concerning themselves with some, out of many possible, aspects of the music (Green, 2000). Secondly, historical musicology has in any case always concerned itself with the social contexts in which the music studied was originally produced, and with the music's reception at the time of origin and beyond. It may be that such work did not concern itself with certain *aspects* of those contexts, such as the roles of women in music; but that is a different matter. Thirdly, it is only because music does indeed retain some level of autonomy from social contexts that it can exist at all. Music cannot be *whatever* people say it is. Any attempt to suggest that it can be, and thus to altogether deny its autonomy, ironically ends up as a position of idealism (which is the very accusation levelled at the autonomists, but for different reasons!). For it presupposes that music has no objective properties, that its materials are immaterial, so to speak, as if music could be made out of any material whatsoever, organized in any way, and still be counted as music. It is partly because we cannot see or touch music, that it is often regarded in such a light; but music is of course an object like any other object in the world, fleeting perhaps, but nonetheless material. And as I suggested earlier, in relation to Gibson's terminology, certain music affords certain responses rather than others.

Not only is it unwise in a logical sense to totally dismiss the concept of autonomy, but it might also lead to overlooking one of the most critical capacities made available by music. (This notion is more fully developed in Green, 1997, pp. 249–56. D. Clarke, 2003 suggests a similar perspective.) For example, imagine a social and historical context in which it is generally assumed that a class of teenaged school pupils will not be capable of singing with conviction in an opera, since they are exclusively and jealously interested in pop music; or a context in which it is assumed that women cannot play orchestral instruments confidently, since they are too feeble; or one in which it is assumed that women cannot compose music that is 'strident', 'virile' or 'powerful'; or that white people cannot sing the blues authentically ... Then imagine a situation where you see and hear these very things going on, and where the inherent meanings of the music hit you, not as being somehow lacking, feeble or inauthentic, but the opposite: as musical affirmation.

Such moments, arising from a virtual experience of inherent meanings logically set free from delineations, can explode the apparent 'truth' of the old, taken-for-granted delineations. We touch a quality of musical experience which, precisely because of its logical freedom from delineation, at the same time exposes the inevitability of delineation. The previous assumptions about teenaged school children, women, race or whatever surface. The delineations about them are made audible. Then a host of new delineations, new conceptions, both of music and of teenagers, women, race and so on become possible. It is through such experiences of inherent meanings as logically separable from delineation, and thereby as potentially open to any content, that new musical and social horizons can appear.

So in that sense I would say that music *can* cross boundaries, and has done so many times in its long history. This is one reason why music education continues to be worthwhile: for although education has reproductive effects such as those I have considered earlier, it also offers us the potential to challenge our understanding and awareness at a deep, symbolic level, through bringing together new and previously disparate meanings and experiences. Of most particular significance here is that such moments may be most forceful when we engage with music not only as listeners but as music-makers. In making music, students have a direct effect upon inherent meanings, indeed bring them into being, and are thus able to imbue the music with a delineated content of their own. The potential freedom, or autonomy of such content from previously taken-for-granted assumptions and definitions is thus potentially exposed. It is precisely by acknowledging music's logical moment of autonomy from social contexts, that we reveal how readily music becomes filled with social content and significance. At the same time therefore, this perspective carries a caution: against making any assumptions about how music is understood by others.

References

Alden, A. (1998) *What Does It All Mean? The National Curriculum for music in a multi-cultural society* (unpublished MA dissertation, London University Institute of Education).

Bennett, A. (2000) *Popular Music and Youth Culture: Music, identity and place* (London and New York, MacMillan's Press).

Bourdieu, P. (1973) Cultural reproduction and social reproduction, in: R. Brown (ed.), *Knowledge, Education and Cultural Change* (London, Tavistock).

Brackett, D. (1995) *Interpreting Popular Music* (Cambridge University Press).

Clarke, D. (2003) Musical autonomy revisited, in: M. Clayton *et al.* (eds), *The Cultural Study of Music: A critical introduction* (New York and London, Routledge).

Clarke, E. F. (2003) Music and Psychology, in: M. Clayton *et al.* (eds), *The Cultural Study of Music: A critical introduction* (New York and London, Routledge).

Clayton, M., Herbert, T. & Middleton, R. (eds) (2003) *The Cultural Study of Music: A critical introduction* (New York and London, Routledge)

DeNora, T. (2000) *Music in Everyday Life* (Cambridge, Cambridge University Press).

Finnegan, R. (1989) *The Hidden Musicians: Music-making in an English town* (Cambridge, Cambridge University Press).

Gibson, J. (1986) *The Ecological Approach to Visual Perception*, (first printed in 1979) (London and Hillsdale, NJ, Lawrence Erlbaum).

Green, L. (1988) *Music on Deaf Ears: Musical meaning, ideology and education* (Manchester and New York, Manchester University Press).

Green, L. (1997) *Music, Gender, Education* (Cambridge University Press).

Green, L. (1999) Ideology, in: B. Horner & T. Swiss (eds), *Key Terms for Popular Music and Culture*, (New York and Oxford, Basil Blackwell).

Green, L. (2000) On the Evaluation and Assessment of Music as a Media Art, in: R. & J. Sefton-Green (eds) *Evaluation Issues in Media Arts Production*, (London, Routledge).

Green, L. (2001) *How Popular Musicians Learn: A way ahead for music education* (London and New York, Ashgate Press).

Green, L. (2002) From the Western Classics to the World: Secondary music teachers' changing perceptions of musical styles, 1982 and 1998, *British Journal of Music Education*, 19:1.

Green, L. (2003) Why 'ideology' is still relevant to music education theory, *Action, Criticism and Theory for Music Education*, 2:2 (December), pp. 3–21, http://mas.siue.edu/ACT/index.html.

Hanley, B. (1998) Gender in Secondary Music Education in British Columbia, *British Journal of Music Education*, 15:1.

Martin, P. (1995) *Sounds and Society: Themes in the sociology of music* (Manchester and New York, Manchester University Press).

Meyer, L. B. (1956) *Emotion and Meaning in Music* (Chicago and London, University of Chicago Press).

Middleton, R. (1990) *Studying Popular Music* (Milton Keynes, Open University Press).

Moore, A. (2002) *Rock: The Primary Text: Developing a musicology of rock* (London and New York, Ashgate Press), originally published in 1993 as *Rock: The Primary Text* (Buckingham, Open University Press).

Negus, K. (1999) *Music Genres and Corporate Cultures* (London and New York, Routledge).

Swanwick, K. (1984a) Problems of a Sociological Approach to Pop Music in Schools, *British Journal of Sociology of Education*, 5:1.

Swanwick, K. (1984b) A Further Note on Sociology of Music Education, *British Journal of Sociology of Education*, 5:3.

Vulliamy, G. & Shepherd, J. (1984a) The Application of a Critical Sociology to Music Education, *British Journal of Music Education*, 5:1.

Vulliamy, G. & Shepherd, J. (1984b) Sociology and Music Education: A response to Swanwick, *British Journal of Sociology of Education*, 5:1.

Vulliamy, G. & Shepherd, J. (1985) Sociology and Music Education: A further response to Swanwick, *British Journal of Sociology of Education*, 6:2.

7 Musical Understanding, Musical Works, and Emotional Expression: Implications for education

David J. Elliott
New York University

Consider three descriptions of 'pure' instrumental music. First, *New York Times* critic Allan Kozinn (2002) describes the outer movements of Mahler's Ninth Symphony as 'anguished cries from the heart' (p. 1). Kozinn elaborates:

> In the opening movement, the stretches of introspective pathos and lyrical flights of nostalgia ... were as powerful in their way as the frantic explosions of despair that make up the movement's heart. (p. 1)

In a discussion of Aaron Copland's Piano Concerto, Bernard Holland (2003) notes how Copland manages to use 'harmonic conflict as an expression of optimism, not despair' (p. 1). Similarly, Paul Griffiths (1999) praises Jean Barraque's Piano Sonata for the ways it 'oscillates between rampaging passages and others that ... go on being repeated in what is almost a maddening depiction of futility ... or when the music becomes so violent as to be at once angry and chilling' (p. 1).

Though common, these emotion-filled descriptions of instrumental music are philosophically problematic. How can passages of instrumental music be expressive of anguish, optimism, futility, violence, or anger? Sounds are not living organisms. Sounds do not feel; sounds do not 'have emotions'. Of equal philosophical interest is the next question: Do listeners feel the emotions they claim to hear in musical patterns?

These questions gain additional importance when we ask them in the context of music education. For example: Can we and should we teach listeners to hear musical expressions of emotion in music? Can we and should we teach musical performers, composers, arrangers, and conductors to hear, interpret, and create musical expressions of emotion?

Wilfried Gruhn, an eminent German educationist and music researcher, believes we can and should. He explains his position in relation to students learning to sing an India *rag*:

> learning how to sing a *rag* always depends on studying with a guru for a long time. The student listens intensely to the guru, learns to imitate him, learns all details and nuances of a song by rote and, finally, becomes independent of the guru. ... The guru's intent is to develop the student's ability to hear, grasp and express the emotions evoked and mediated by the

> *rag* in his or her own artistically unique and characteristic manner ... One's ability to mediate the musical emotions expressed by the musical details of the *rag* is the core of one's understanding of the *rag*. This 'understanding' is reflected by one's performance of the *rag*. In other words, the strongest 'knowledge' of a *rag* is reflected in and by the quality of a person's interpretive performance. (Gruhn, in press)

Many parents, students, music teachers, and music education professors believe that 'musical understanding' is equivalent to one or more of the following: knowing how to read musical notation; knowing facts and concepts about music history and music theory; and/or knowing how to 'sound out' notated music on instruments or one's voice. Contrary to what most non-musicians might assume, music teachers seldom think about whether or how sonic-musical patterns can be expressive of specific emotions. Accordingly, teachers seldom teach students how to hear, interpret, and create musical works in relation to (what I call) 'expressional' musical meanings (Elliott, 1995, pp. 143–151) and the role of such meanings in our enjoyment of music.

The purpose of my discussion is to outline a concept of musical works and musical understanding that addresses the importance of developing students' abilities to grasp and create musical expressions of emotion. In the first section of this paper I summarize a multilayered concept of what to listen *for* in musical works.[1] I follow this with a more detailed examination of musical expression theories. Lastly, I offer a concept of musical understanding and recommendations for developing students' abilities with regard to musical expressions of emotion.

Musical Works

In *Music Matters* (Elliott, 1995) I develop a 'praxial' philosophy of music and music education. A key tenet of this philosophy is that music listening is not the auditory equivalent of a 'copying' process; rather, music listening is a cognitive-affective construction process. Suffice it to say here that concentrated episodes of music listening involve several forms of thinking and knowing (which I outline later in this essay). Of course, people differ widely in their ability to hear (construct), interpret, and/or make sense of musical patterns. Nevertheless, most people in most cultures develop the basic, non-verbal thinking processes they need to identify and follow 'their' preferred kinds of musical style(s) by means of regular, informal music listening. However, to move beyond a novice level of music listening requires more than casual exposure to recordings or concerts. It requires additional types of formal and informal learning. This is so, I contend, because musical sound patterns can be heard-*as* 'carrying' or presenting several simultaneous dimensions of meaning for listeners' understanding and enjoyment. In other words, a 'musical work' is neither all 'out there' nor all 'in the mind'. Human experiences of artistic-sonic patterns lie at the intersection of human consciousness and humanly made musical sounds.

If so, and if we acknowledge that listeners are, in the end, completely free to listen to any music in any way they wish, what can we say about guiding listeners' attention and developing their understandings of what musical works may offer for their enjoyment? I wish to suggest that if music teachers and music students keep in mind that *there is no one way to listen for all music everywhere*, and if the following seven-dimensional 'map' of musical works is used as a flexible guide, then students are more likely to experience a fuller measure of the meanings that musicing and listening involve.

a) *The Performance-Interpretation Dimension*

Works of music are sonic-social events of a special kind. Musical works are performances: auditory-social events that are intentionally generated by the informed actions (overt and covert; professional and amateur) of human agents to be intentionally conceived as such by other human agents (music makers and/or listeners). Thus, music listening is a matter of listening for a performance-interpretation of some kind: either a performance-interpretation of a written composition, or a remembered work, or an improvisation. Most listeners do not simply want to hear performers produce the sounds that constitute a work; rather, listeners usually want to hear how this-or-that performer and/or ensemble interprets a given work.

b) *The Design Dimension*

Every musical work involves a composed or improvised musical design or structure. Learning to 'follow' a piece of music in terms of its unfolding sonic architecture is (for many listeners) a key aspect of enjoying, understanding, and appreciating a musical work. We can subdivide the architecture of musical works as follows: the syntactic parameters of musical design include melody, harmony and rhythm; the non-syntactic parameters of musical design include timbre, texture, tempo, articulation, and dynamics. Listeners mentally construct the relationships among and between musical patterns as interpreted and performed by music-makers.

In most styles of music worldwide, syntactic and non-syntactic musical patterns are not just any old sounds; rather, musical patterns are sounds organized by means of practice-specific standards and principles. In other words, most music-makers do not invent the materials of music each time they compose, improvise, perform, arrange, or conduct. In most cases, music-makers begin with a delimited set of materials (pitches, timbres, durations and intensities) that are already 'musical' because they have been pre-selected and pre-organized in relation to specific systems of pitch organization, rhythmic organization, and so on. In short, the sonic building blocks of musical works are already 'musical' before musicians begin to organize these materials into works of music by means of composing, arranging, improvising, performing and/or conducting.

Unfortunately, Western music academies and school music programs today tend to privilege the design dimension of musical works to the exclusion of all others. This is so because Western music schools are products of Enlightenment beliefs that put scientific understanding above all other forms of knowing. Thus, music teachers are trained to teach students to listen to, 'analyze' (and thereby 'understand') music by breaking pieces down into sections and 'elements' (melody, harmony and so forth). Of course, this longstanding, pseudo-scientific approach to musical works also serves to privilege Western European 'fine art' music in the school music curriculum.

c) *Stylistic Traditions and Standards*
Joseph Margolis (1993) points out that 'musical properties are culturally emergent *incarnate* properties' (p. 152). The sounds of vocal and instrumental music are 'historically referential' (p. 152): they always refer in the sense that they are 'about some part of a pertinent [musical-cultural] history' (p. 152). What is composed, arranged, performed, conducted, or improvised in the context of a particular musical practice is *musical* sound, not mere sound. Margolis sums the point: 'Music possesses historied properties—not merely properties (that is, ordered sound)—that are the precipitates of creative efforts that have their own history and intentional energy' (p. 150).

Indeed, every auditory aspect of a musical work is inexorably tied to some artistic-musical-historical tradition. Thus, the successive and simultaneous sound patterns of a musical work not only relate intra-musically (to each other), they also relate inter-musically by manifesting stylistic features in common with other works in the same musical tradition of practice.

d) *Musical Expressions of Emotion*
The musical designs and performances of many (but not all) musical works are rightly heard as being expressive of specific emotions (e.g., musical expressions of sadness or happiness) and/or musical expressions of such broad affective patterns as tension and release, conflict and resolution, and so on. Indeed, making and listening for musical expressions of emotion are eminently musical things to do, depending on the musical practice and work involved. This is the dimension of meaning I will focus on in more detail below.

e) *Musical Representations and Characterizations*
The musical designs and performances of some (but not all) musical works include musical representations of people, places, and things. In fact, composers and arrangers have many means of creating musical works that combine musical and so-called extra-musical materials.

f) *The Cultural-Ideological Dimension*
Musical works constitute and are constituted by cultural-specific knowings, beliefs, and values. This is so, I suggest, because (a) all forms of musicing are inherently artistic-social-cultural endeavors, (b) musical works are social-cultural constructions, and (c) music makers and listeners live in particular places and time periods. In short, music listening and musical works always involve cultural-ideological meanings. At the very least, and because syntactic and non-syntactic musical patterns evince their practice-style affiliations, musical works delineate their broader historical and cultural links (e.g., their historical times and places of composition).

g) *The Narrative Dimension*
As Christopher Small (1998) points out in *Musicking*, it is common and reasonable for listeners to hear the unfolding of a musical work as an emotional/pictorial/literary narrative in which (basically) a composer (a) establishes musical stability, (b) upsets this stability by means of various musical devices of variation and

development, and (c) returns his or her musical structure to stability. Such 'narrative' composing and listening has unending possibilities if we grant that all dimensions of a musical work (listed from a–f, above) can be combined to achieve such ends.

Summarizing to this point, I suggest that the multidimensional concept of musical works I outline above is sufficiently comprehensive and flexible to accommodate the works of many (if not most) musical styles. At the same time, I am the first to admit that there may be musical works past, present, and future that involve additional dimensions not accounted for above. Moreover, I wish to underline that this multidimensional view is not carved in stone. This concept and its seven categories are heuristic devices.

Still, I contend that if music teachers and music students keep in mind that there is no one way to listen for all music everywhere, and if the above map of musical works is used as a flexible guide, then students may experience a fuller measure of the meanings and enjoyment that listening and music making involve.

Let me now turn to a more detailed discussion of the fourth dimension of music I sketched above.

Musical Expression of Emotions

A majority of contemporary music philosophers—including Peter Kivy, Stephen Davies, Francis Sparshott, Jennifer Robinson, and Jerrold Levinson—hold, as I do, that music can be expressive of specific emotions. As I mentioned early in this essay, Wilfried Gruhn and I also believe that musical understanding includes knowing-that and knowing-how musical patterns can be expressive of emotions.

That said, the idea that musical understanding includes the ability to hear and interpret musical expressions of emotion is a serious philosophical problem for two main reasons. First, philosophers disagree about *how* musical patterns can be expressive of emotions. Second, philosophers also disagree about whether listeners feel the same emotions they allegedly hear in musical patterns. Additionally, however, if we arrive at reasonable answers to these two questions, what would this mean for the everyday practice of music teaching and learning?

Let me begin by examining selected views on the first two questions.[2] Peter Kivy (2001) argues that just as we routinely experience some faces, postures, or movements as presenting or resembling emotion characteristics (e.g., a sad-looking face), so too do listeners hear musical patterns as expressive of joyfulness, melancholy, or sadness. Kivy is not saying that music refers outside itself; he is saying that an expression of (say) sadness is a property of the musical sounds themselves. In other words, attentive listeners identify 'heard qualities of the music' in the same way listeners hear musical passages as 'dissonant, chromatic, major, minor' and so on (Kivy, 2001, p. 73). Moreover, Kivy insists that sad-sounding music does not make a listener feel sadness anymore than a St. Bernard's sad-looking face makes its master feel sad.

Colin Radford (cited in Kivy, 2001, pp. 75–76) agrees that musical patterns possess specific emotional qualities, but he differs with Kivy in arguing that listeners *tend* to experience these same qualities when they hear them. Radford's argument begins with his claim that because (say) 'sunless days depress people' it makes sense to state that sunless days 'possess' qualities such as 'depressing' (Kivy, 2001, p. 75). Stated in musical terms, Radford argues that musical patterns can and do possess specific emotions as 'perceived qualities' (e.g., joyfulness or melancholy) and that these heard qualities have a tendency to cause listeners to feel these same emotions.

Like Kivy, Stephen Davies (2003) holds that 'music expresses emotions by presenting or exemplifying the appearances of emotions' (p. 129); 'music is naturally expressive of emotion because the dynamic character of music is experienced as significantly similar to human behavior expressive of emotions' (p. 132). Davies observes that in everyday life we 'read' appearances of emotions to understand how other people feel (e.g., family members and friends). However, says Davies, the difference between interpreting a particular appearance of emotion (such as sadness) in a friend and hearing sadness in music is that in music our interest is in the *musical* 'appearance' of an emotion for itself (p. 130), not in the 'owner' of that emotion. Thus, like Kivy, Davies denies that a sad-sounding passage of music causes listeners to feel sadness.

Davies (2001) goes on to suggest that the kinds of emotions expressed in music may go beyond those 'that can be worn by appearances' to include more complex emotions, such as hope (p. 144). Davies believes this is possible due to the dynamic nature of music as a phenomenon that unfolds in time. That is, just as emotions often follow each other in time (e.g., happiness followed by surprise, foreboding, and sadness), a composer can create a progression of identifiable emotional expressions such that his or her musical expression of hope is more likely to be heard as such by attentive listeners. As Davies says:

> [B]y judiciously ordering the emotion characteristics presented in an extended musical work, the composer can express in his music those emotional states that are not susceptible to presentation in mere appearances. (p. 144)

In addition to the arguments put forth by Kivy and Davies, I argue elsewhere (Elliott, 1995) that musical expressions of emotion occur within specific musical-cultural contexts. Thus, our ability to hear a musical expression of (say) melancholy in a slowly descending chromatic line may be contingent upon hearing these sounds as tones-in-a-system. The expressiveness of a musical pattern may therefore be thought of as a musical 'figure' (expressive pattern) against a musical 'ground' (e.g., the Western tonal system, or the North Indian system of ragas). To hear the expressive musical figure, a listener must first be familiar with the musical ground in which the figure is embedded and in relation to which it reveals itself.

At the very least, in order to grasp instances of musical expressiveness a listener must have an informal understanding of the practice-specific principles underlying a particular musical system. In addition, to cognize a musical pattern as expressive of an emotion based on resemblance, a listener must be tacitly or verbally familiar with the vocal customs and/or gesture customs that musical patterns resemble.

These reflections bring us to another aspect of musical expression. What people know as 'their music' is usually an outcome of long traditions of music making and listening. This suggests that when listeners call music 'sad' they do so, in part, because they have come to know musical sadness when they hear it. In other words, certain musical patterns and contextual cues become associated with musically conventional expressions of sadness (happiness and so on). Sparshott (1987) calls this 'expressiveness by convention' (p. 58). That is, certain musical patterns sound sad to listeners in a given culture because the musicers and listeners in that culture have developed certain conventions of making and listening to sounds over time that, to them, sound like: (a) the sounds a sad person might sing or play to express their sadness, or (b) the sounds that people will want to hear on the occasion of a sad funeral, a happy celebration and so on. In other words, people tend to transfer the emotion words deemed suitable in particular circumstances (e.g., a wedding or a funeral) to musical patterns used in these circumstances.

In addition, musicers and listeners often associate specific musical patterns with identifiable emotions. Consider, for example, how some Western composers have combined the timbres and textures of trombones with melodic patterns that are expressive of somber dignity, deep foreboding, jovial good humor, and romantic love. In my view, such musical expressions of emotion are as 'real' as the musical conventions that inform the composition, orchestration and performance of trombone passages in such works as Mozart's *Zauberflote*, Bartok's *Concerto for Orchestra*, Dvorak's *Symphony No. 5* ('From the New World'), Ravel's *Bolero* and Tommy Dorsey's theme, *I'm Getting Sentimental Over You.*

Let me tie these ideas together. The thinking of several philosophers suggests that musical patterns can indeed be expressive of human emotions because (a) musical patterns can and do bear resemblances to expressive human gestures and (b) vocal music can and does partake of the inherent emotional qualities of the human voice. Also, humans have a tendency to invest the looks and sounds of things with emotional qualities. Additionally, we learn to make and apprehend musical expressions of emotion by means of musical conventions and associations.

Altogether, I suggest that an important value of music making and listening inheres in the human use of musical patterns for emotionally expressive purposes. Musical patterns provide the artistic means to extend the range of our expressive powers beyond those we find naturally and ordinarily.

Human Consciousness

To me, the central weaknesses of most theories of musical expression trace back to the tendency of thinkers (e.g., Kivy and Davies) to fasten on one explanation of musical expression and to ignore what contemporary brain-mind scholars know about the nature of human consciousness. In short, I believe that human listeners can and do respond emotionally to musical patterns on many levels because the human brain-mind is enormously complex, plastic, and multilayered. Thus, humans can 'take in', process, understand, and feel many simultaneous levels of 'information' (in the broadest sense of this word).

For one thing, data perceived via our senses does not mirror reality in a one-to-one relation. Human consciousness 'adds' information from personal learning and experience to recognize, identify, or understand something to be something (Gruhn, in press). Psychologist Jeffrey Gray (1998) makes the same point in a different way when he argues that consciousness depends on the ways our brains make comparisons between the unconscious sensory data we take in and our individual past and present memories and intentions. Similarly, Anthony Damasio (1999) maintains that consciousness arises from an interaction between brain processes in the context of a neural model of the self. Accordingly, Zeman (2002) calls these theories 'interactive':

> [C]onsciousness depends upon a dialogue between diverse regions of the brain which are usually associated with more or less independent psychological functions, like perception, emotion, memory and action. (p. 291).

How does this happen? Gruhn (in press) answers that 'this can only happen in a communicative context where participants exchange information.' Gruhn continues:

> In a social and cultural setting, a child (for example) perceives pictures, sounds, words, objects, and so forth. 'Just' through the 'normal' processes of being actively engaged in perception, a child learns to cognitively-psychologically associate meaning with demonstrated and perceived objects. Neurologically, these processes depend on a physiological process by which one develops mental representations. The 'concrete' neurological substrate of the development of representations is bound to the growth of synaptic connections (synaptogenesis) between neurons in the brain. (Gruhn, in press)

If Gruhn, Gray, Damasio, and other scholars of human consciousness are correct in saying that cognitive representations can only develop within the gross wiring of the brain, and that 'these representations can be described in terms of synaptic density and neuronal connectivity' (Gruhn), then the relationships between the nature of musical understanding and musical expressions of emotions become a little easier to understand.

How so? In his recent book, *Synaptic Self*, Joseph LeDoux (2002) explains that the human brain is organized into processors called neural systems that function independently of one another to some extent (p. 302). For example, we have multiple systems for attention, memory, emotion, cognition, motivation, intention and so forth. Accordingly, humans can perform several tasks simultaneously, in parallel:

> Life requires many brain functions, functions require systems, and systems are made of synaptically connected neurons. We all have the same brain systems, and the number of neurons in each brain system is more or less the same in each of us as well. However, the particular way those neurons are connected is distinct, and that uniqueness ... is what makes us who we are. (LeDoux, 2002, p. 302)

LeDoux goes on to explain that one remarkable feature of our synapses is that they are *plastic*: they are open to modification by 'selection and/or instruction and construction' (p. 307); thus, our personal histories with particular 'objects' (e.g., musical patterns) modify the synapses in the several brain systems involved in processing that stimulus. So,

> when an emotionally arousing stimulus is present, other stimuli that are also present acquire emotion-arousing qualities ... and actions that bring you in contact with emotionally desirable stimuli or protect you from harmful or unpleasant ones are learned. (LeDoux, 2002, p. 303)

Additionally, our multiple neural systems learn and store info about the same experience. Thus, 'a kind of shared culture develops and persists in each individual brain-mind because parallel and malleable neural systems encode each experience from specialized perspectives' (LeDoux, 2002, p. 309).

Musical Understanding: Ten Forms of Knowing

With the above thoughts in mind, I wish to suggest that musical understanding involves at least (a) five *kinds* of knowing in the category of 'music making ability' and (b) the same five kinds of knowing in the category of 'music listening ability'. The kinds of knowing I mean are procedural knowing, verbal knowing, experiential knowing, intuitive knowing, and meta-cognition (or supervisory knowing). Since these kinds of knowing are largely self-explanatory, and since I explain them in detail elsewhere (Elliott, 1995, pp. 49–106), I will only add a few remarks here.

First, I conceive music listening as a covert ('mental') form of procedural knowing in which a listener's brain-mind 'adds' structure and meaning (based on a listener's informal and formal experiences) to the sonic information that arrives at her ear by means of music makers. The other four kinds of knowing inform and enrich the covert action of listening. This is especially the case in learning-to and knowing-how to hear musical patterns as expressive of emotions: all five kinds of knowing must be informed and engaged to hear musical expressions of sadness, happiness, and so forth.

Second, and given what we now know about human consciousness, I believe it's reasonable to claim that, over time, the various forms of knowing in my '5+5 model' weave together seamlessly in the actions of fine musicians who learn know how to hear and create the many dimensions of meaning that a musical work can present for our listening enjoyment.

Third, in view of the work of LeDoux and his colleagues (1994) I believe it is very likely that listeners hear (or 'construct'?) musical expressions of emotion as part of their listening processes and that listeners *can* feel these same emotions at various times, depending on a wide range of variables (cognitive, affective, cultural, and so forth). As Francis Sparshott (1994) says:

> [T]here seems no reason a priori to suppose that only one relationship should hold between musically formal structures and the active and affective lives they relate to, or that they should relate distinctively to any specific range of such phenomena, or that such relationships as obtained should be reducible to any system. (p. 24)

Implications for Music Teaching and Learning

It follows from the above that music teachers ought to make a central place for engaging students in listening *for*, reflecting on, interpreting, performing, and creating musical works that are expressive of emotions.

More specifically, I recommend that teachers deliberately select works that offer clear examples of 'emotions-in-musical-patterns'. Second, it is imperative that we 'target' students' attention to instances of musical expression and, then, present students with interpretive problems to solve in performance projects, composition projects, arranging projects, and so on. Indeed, learning to make and hear musical expressions of emotions is not something that happens automatically for all students. We must teach-*for* this kind of awareness, ability, and sensitivity.

Teachers can accelerate such learning by providing regular demonstrations of expressive music-making through their own performing and/or by comparing and contrasting recorded examples of expressive and non-expressive music making.

Also, emotive descriptions of musical works have an important role to play in music teaching and learning. That is, I recommend that teachers use 'emotion words' and emotional analogies in order to focus students' attention on the expressive features of musical patterns. Just as formal medical terminology is unable to render everything a patient may want to know about his health, a strictly formal approach to musical analysis is insufficient to capture all the dimensions of a musical work, especially the expressional dimension.

Please note that this is *not* a recommendation to assign emotive descriptions to all music everywhere. There are reasonable ways of knowing when musical patterns are expressive of emotions. This knowing is chiefly a matter of considering the ideas of the music philosophers I discussed above and knowing the traditions and standards of the musical style to which a given work belongs.

In sum, making and listening *for* musical expressions of emotion are eminently musical things to do. As music educators, we need to reflect upon and teach this dimension of musical meaning more carefully, deliberately, and creatively than we have in the past.

Notes

1. For a detailed explanation of this concept, see Elliott (1995), chapters 4, 6, and 8.
2. For a detailed survey of musical expression theories, see Davies (2001).

References

Damasio, A. (1999) *The Feeling of What Happens: Body and emotion in the making of consciousness* (New York, Harcourt Brace).

Davies, S. (2001) Philosophical Perspectives on Music's Expressiveness, in: P. N. Juslin & J. Sloboda (eds), *Music and Emotion: Theory and research* (Oxford, Oxford University Press).

Davies, S. (2003) *Themes in the Philosophy of Music* (Oxford, Oxford University Press).

Elliott, D. J. (1995) *Music Matters: A new philosophy of music education* (New York, Oxford University Press).

Gray, J. (1998) Abnormal Contents of Consciousness, in: H. H. Jasper (ed.), *Consciousness at the Frontiers of Neuroscience* (Philadelphia, Lippincott-Raven).

Griffiths, P. (1999, July 11) A Piano Sonata Created from Fire and Ice (*The New York Times*, Section 2, p. 30).

Gruhn, W. (in press) Understanding Musical Understanding, in: D. Elliott (ed.), *Praxial Music Education: Reflections and Dialogues* (New York, Oxford University Press).

Holland, B. (2003, September 18) How Classical Composers Defined an American Sound (*The New York Times*, Section E, p. 8).

Kivy, P. (2001) *New Essays on Musical Understanding* (Oxford, Clarendon Press).

Kozinn, A. (2002, March 4) Nostalgia and Cries of Anguish (*The New York Times*, Section B, p. 7).

LeDoux, J. (2002) *Synaptic Self* (New York, Viking).

Margolis, J. (1993) Music as Ordered Sound, in: M. Krausz (ed.), *The Interpretation of Music* (Oxford, Clarendon Press).

Small, C. (1998) *Musicking: The meanings of performing and listening* (Hanover, NH, University Press of New England).

Sparshott, F. (1987) Aesthetics of Music: Limits and grounds, in: P. Alperson (ed.), *What is Music? An introduction to the philosophy of music* (New York: Haven Publications).

Sparshott, F. (1994) Music and Feeling, in: P. Alperson (ed.), *Musical Worlds: New directions in the philosophy of music* (University Park, Pennsylvania, Penn State University Press).

Zeman, A. (2002) *Consciousness: A user's guide* (New Haven, Yale University Press).

8
The Wow Factor? A Comparative Study of the Development of Student Music Teachers' Talents in Scotland and Australia

ALASTAIR MCPHEE, PETER STOLLERY & ROS MCMILLAN
University of Glasgow; University of Aberdeen; University of Melbourne

Introduction

There has been a considerable degree of debate in recent years about the nature of musical intelligence and what constitutes musical gift. In connection with this, a number of differing perspectives have emerged. The first of these may be described as the psychological perspective (e.g. Sloboda, 1985; Storr, 1992; Snyder, 2000)—although within this, there may be discerned a number of subdivisions. For example, one could view the issue from the point of neuropsychology (e.g. Gardner, 1993; Rauscher, 1995; Schlaug *et al.*, 1995, etc): or from the viewpoint of perception (Schiffman, 2000). Clearly, the emotional perspective would be another area within which music could be approached (Robertson, 2000). In terms of musical education, one might, for instance, look at the curriculum (e.g. Paynter, 1982), or at how musical ability develops over the programme of the educative experience (e.g. Moog, 1976; McDonald & Simons, 1989). Recent research has drawn contemporary psychological and educational perspectives together, and has shown that there are considerable links between the two areas. A metacognitive claim for music is finding increasing acceptance as a result of neurological and neuropsychological research, and it has been considered in a recent paper (Stollery & McPhee, 2002) involving two of the authors.

The concept of musical gift may also be seen to be rooted in a number of other debates. There is a general interest in the education of gifted pupils, and this interest is world-wide (Kirk *et al.*, 2000). However, for our present purposes, we define musical gift as:

> A situation where receptive, creative, responsive and technical skills are at a highly developed level. (Stollery & McPhee, 2002: 90)

Musical giftedness has been identified in a number of different ways. For example, a checklist-based approach has been advocated for some years and continues to be supported by some investigators (Hartounian, 2000). This approach is also one which has found favour amongst those investigating general high levels of ability amongst children (e.g. Passow, 1979). Nevertheless, there are others who advocate a more developmental approach, in that rather than seeing children as *born* gifted—children can *become* gifted (Skinner, 1991). For the purposes of this paper, this is a very important distinction. And the logical concomitant of this position is that if giftedness in music is not simply the preserve of an elite few, then it is possible for it to be developed in many more, through teaching. In the context of this debate, Michael Howe believes that excellence may depend not only on inherited factors, but also on opportunities for learning and the way in which these are presented to individuals (Howe, 1990). It is the opinion of Davidson, Howe & Sloboda (1997) that while biological factors do have an undoubted role to play, we should not see the gifts and talents area in purely deterministic terms. Rather, we should also see it in terms of the environmental factors which influence development.

An important commentator in the area of musical excellence and the psychology of music is John Sloboda (1990). If musical excellence can in fact be developed by teaching, then Sloboda takes the view that there are a number of 'myths', which we need to explore. These 'myths' include the following:

- To be excellent in music, one has to be excellent to begin with;
- If one works hard, this will eventually lead to the attainment of excellence.

Further, if one is to attain excellence, then musical training from experienced musicians who have themselves displayed the appropriate qualities is essential. However, we are not looking at a situation where the idea that excellence can be developed through teaching, has replaced or supplanted the earlier model that excellence is innate: there are still contemporary analysts such as Eastop (2001) who hold firmly to the older view.

We may therefore arrive at a position where it can be seen that there are really two positions amongst commentators in this area. The *first* of these is that musical gift is possessed by a few of the population, who may be seen as constituting an elite. These people require to have their inherent talents developed in a special way in order to maximise the potential which they represent. The *second* view is that musical gift is innate in all of us, and that the task of the educator is to ensure that this particular intelligence is drawn out and developed to the fullest extent.

Educating the Musically Gifted

It is possible to see reflected in the provision made for the education of musically gifted children the working out in practice of these two positions. To exemplify this, we shall use the situation in Scotland as a case study. There have been a number of studies undertaken in this field, both within the state sector and private institutions (McPhee, 2000). If we look first at the position that musical excellence is the preserve of a few, we can see, for example, the possibility of conservatoire-based provision through the Junior School of the Royal Scottish Academy of Music and Drama (RSAMD, 1998, 2001). Here, there are opportunities for young people who wish to develop their potential in music within the context of an internationally reputable institution. It is of interest that applicants for this particular provision are required to undertake entrance auditions and tests which serve to identify those within whom excellence, or the potential to be excellent, is thought to reside. Further, they are given tuition by practising, professional musicians in the various elements which they have chosen to study. In this, the positions identified by Eastop, and by Sloboda in his 'myths', are seen to be operative.

School Education of Musically Gifted Young People

A number of studies of the provision made within Scotland for the enhancement of musical excellence have been undertaken (e.g. McPhee, 2000; Stollery, 1997, etc.). From these, we see that the two polarities are in fact represented: there are institutions which are designed to cater for an elite (e.g. RSAMD, 1998, 2001) and to develop their musical ability to a very high level indeed—and there are others which strive to bring out musical excellence in all their pupils, where it may be seen to be ripe for development. It is interesting that the Cameron Report (Scottish Education Department, 1975) in which the interests of gifted young musicians and dancers in Scotland were considered, was of the opinion that the first model of elite provision was the more appropriate. However, since then a number of mainstream comprehensive schools have developed provision which indicates that the second model of the development of talent in large numbers of students is being successfully undertaken through the provision of ensemble opportunities and other means (McPhee, 2000). Likewise, in Australia, there exist opportunities at school level for the development of 'elite' musicians, and for the development of musical talent in mainstream schooling through similar ensemble provision and general instrumental and musical instruction.

The Conditions In Which Excellence May Develop

If, as we state, it is possible that musical excellence or musical intelligence can be in fact developed through teaching, then it may be possible for us to identify those experiences in life which are more conducive to its development than others. Similarly, it will be possible for us to identify those which act as barriers to it. We have, in our earlier work, chosen to call these *crystallising* and *paralysing* experiences, respectively. Thus, crystallising experiences will be those which have, in the musically educative and developmental history of the individual, served to enable growth in musical ability. Likewise, the paralysing experiences will be those which have served to stultify or to prevent it.

Our first research was carried out in 2001 at the conference of the Scottish Network for Able Pupils (Stollery & McPhee, 2002, op.cit.). Here, we presented a paper on musical gift to an audience of professional educators, all of whom were practising musicians, and we used the opportunity to gather qualitative data on the crystallising and paralysing experiences which they had themselves experienced. We asked respondents if they could describe experiences which had happened to them and which had had a significant positive or negative effect on their musical development. The format used was that of a free text box. There was no questionnaire used, and at this particular session, there was no debriefing of the responses—although there was a very full and interesting discussion of the issues.

The responses to the crystallising experiences showed a distinct pattern, and the following appeared to be most significant to respondents:

- Parents affording opportunities, through instrumental provision and opportunities for exposure to music in various forms;
- Pupils given high self-esteem through reinforcement and praise;
- Motivation from a 'gifted' teacher;
- Motivation provided by other members of the family—siblings, etc—participating in musical activities;
- Motivation from a successful performance in front of an audience;
- Working with other musicians at the same and at different stages;
- Realising that one has the ability to respond to music.

We identified from these responses that there was a general reference to the provision of opportunity, rather than attempts to shut potential down. Those who thought that they had achieved, had done so when they had been given the opportunity. We then turned to the paralysing factors, and here a number of key areas were suggested:

- Being embarrassed in front of a group by poor or inadequate performance;
- Ridicule from peers (e.g., for carrying an instrument to school or not conforming to the social norms of that particular group);
- Poor teaching/boredom from tutors who operated a deficit model, with resultant destruction of confidence;
- Lack of opportunity to become involved in musical activity;
- Negative comments about playing;
- Negative effects about formal examinations in music and the processes leading to them;
- Costs of tuition in financial terms;
- Low importance attached to music by school or family;
- Time required for the practice thought necessary to be proficient;
- Pressure to perform to a high standard before confidence had matured;
- Inappropriate or boring repertoire;
- Ill informed personal comments by staff.

There was a range of features from the analysis of this admittedly small and unrepresentative sample which we thought important. Firstly, the number of comments relating to the paralysing or negative aspects were roughly in the proportion of two to one against those which were crystallising or positive in tone. Secondly, it was clear that there was great importance attached to the provision of opportunity for musical development. Thirdly—and for the purposes of this paper, perhaps most importantly—it was clear that the quality of teaching and tuition was of great relevance in deciding whether an individual's development was affected either in a positive or in a negative way.

If, as we have seen, teachers and teaching can play a critical role in musical development and thence into the attainment of musical excellence, it is therefore important to look at the development of music teachers themselves. Modelling is of great importance in looking at the ways in which people develop (Papalia *et al.*, 2001): music teachers themselves are not immune from this process. Thus, it is also interesting to look at developing teachers of music and to see to what extent their own development had been affected by the factors which our earlier study had identified. The authors of this paper are centrally engaged in the education of music teachers in Scotland and in Australia—in terms of both music studies and education studies—and the opportunity was present to look at our own students to see the extent to which crystallising and paralysing processes had influenced their own progress and development. (In fact, the institutions in which two of the authors of this paper are employed—the Universities of Aberdeen and Glasgow—are two of only three in Scotland involved in the undergraduate education of potential teachers of music.) It was thought that such research, besides shedding some light on these processes as they affect our own students—and therefore a substantial number of the music teachers about to go into careers in Scotland, and in Australia—would allow further illumination of the crystallisation and paralysing processes in general.

Methodology

The methodology chosen was as follows, and was based upon the findings of the first study (the SNAP conference). Students in Scotland were gathered together in their year groups and the purposes of the study were outlined to them. They were then asked to undertake a similar process to that which had taken place at the conference—that is, they were given free text boxes and asked to list those factors which had been significant in terms of their development in either a positive (crystallising) or a negative (paralysing) way. All responses, in line with the original study, were anonymous. This was to allow students to make comments free from fear that in some way they could be identified and feedback given to tutors or other interested parties. They were provided with additional guidance as and when necessary by the researchers. The research data was then collated and the results were entered on spreadsheet grids listing each response and the frequency with which it occurred. The grids allowed analysis by comment and by institution. From these spreadsheet grids, two questionnaires were developed, listing the factors which had crystallised or paralysed the experience of the Scottish students. These questionnaires were then given under guidance to student teachers of music at the University of Melbourne in Australia, in order to determine the extent to which experiences were similar in the two countries and cultures. Students were invited to tick as many factors as they thought applied to them: thus, it was possible for students to identify a spectrum of factors from all to none as applicable. In all, responses were received from 86 students in Scotland and from 46 students in Australia.

Results

In contrast to the pilot study, the number of crystallising responses from student teachers was much greater than the number of paralysing responses. In total 218 crystallising responses were received from the 86 Scottish students and 390 from the 46 Australian students. Similarly, 156 paralysing responses were received from Scotland and, coincidentally, 156 from Melbourne. Responses were also rank ordered in terms of the frequency of each response: this was the case for data both from Scotland and from Australia. Results are tabulated as follows:

Discussion

Perhaps the most immediate result likely to engender debate is the substantial number of responses delivered by the students in Australia compared to the number delivered by students in Scotland. This is *pro rata* true of both crystallising and paralysing factors. There may be two possible explanations for this phenomenon. The first of these is that the methodology, which set out to align the responses from the Australian students with those of the Scottish ones, might have pre-disposed the Australian students along the paths which had been laid out by their Scottish counterparts. In other words, the fact that particular crystallising factors had been *suggested* might have encouraged the Australian students to identify factors other than those which they might have thought of if presented with a free text box. But that in itself does not explain the bulk of the responses received from Australia. There were instances of 2 students, for example, who found it possible to identify all the crystallising factors as relevant to their own situations. Several others identified a majority of the factors as relevant, and there were only a few who checked

Table 1: Crystallising responses

Factor	*Scotland ranking (Response frequency)*	*Australia ranking (Response frequency)*
Inspiring/Encouraging music teacher	1 (38)	6 (31)
Family influence and encouragement	2 (30)	5 (34)
Good school Music Department	3 (24)	8 (30)
Performing opportunities/ensemble contexts	4 (21)	1 (41)
Musical environment at home	5 (20)	10 (19)
Availability of/affinity with instrument	6 (16)	4 (33)
Performing opportunities incl solo opportunities	7 (15)	6 (31)
Hearing/watching others perform	7 (15)	3 (38)
Positive feedback on performance/exam success	9 (10)	9 (29)
Personal reasons—e.g. financial	10 (9)	11 (17)
Positive peer influence	11 (7)	14 (15)
Opportunities for travel abroad	12 (6)	15 (14)
Opportunities for composing/inventing	13 (4)	11 (17)
Feel good factor	14 (4)	2 (39)
Starting early	15 (1)	11 (17)

Table 2: *Paralysing responses*

Factor	Scotland ranking (Response frequency)	Australia ranking (Response frequency)
An over-critical music teacher or one who demanded too much from you	1 (27)	8 (10)
A poor music teacher	2 (24)	3 (17)
Not having money available to buy instruments and/or get tuition	3 (14)	8 (10)
Pressure to do well and to achieve high standards/practise hard	4 (13)	1 (19)
Personal reasons—e.g. illness, lack of motivation	5 (12)	10 (8)
Lack of encouragement and interest from your family	6 (11)	12 (4)
Negative influence from other young people at school	7 (10)	12 (4)
Lack of support in the school	8 (8)	5 (11)
Lack of opportunities to play with other young people	8 (8)	4 (14)
The school discouraged me from doing music in favour of other subjects	8 (8)	12 (4)
Pressure from music exams	11 (6)	5 (11)
You were held back by classmates who were not as good at music as you	12 (5)	11 (7)
Being made to perform in front of others	13 (4)	12 (4)
Low self esteem	14 (3)	5 (11)
Having to take part in competitions or not doing well in them	15 (2)	15
Being nervous about performing	16 (1)	2 (18)

off a very small number of factors. It is therefore possible to posit the view that the Australian students may well have undergone formative experiences which were *in general* more weighted towards crystallisation than those of the students from Scotland. The data does not lend itself completely to either explanation: it is possible to surmise that either or both of the reasons outlined above may be operative.

When the crystallising factors are examined, by response frequency and rank order, it becomes clear that there are significant differences between the students in Scotland and their counterparts in Australia. Whereas Scottish students ranked the importance of an inspiring teacher as first, those in Australia chose the provision or availability of ensemble contexts for their performance skills (ranked fourth by the Scottish students). Similarly, the Australian students placed a lower emphasis on the importance of family interest and encouragement (5th) than the Scottish students, who ranked this in second place. This encouragement was more important to both groups than the existence of an overtly musical environment at home. Although there were some instances where both sets of students aligned their preferences—for example in the provision of performing opportunities for solo work or for opportunities for travel or the availability of an instrument—there were also instances of major discrepancy. Perhaps no instance illustrates this better than the 'feel good factor'. Whereas the Australian students ranked this as second, the Scottish students relegated it to fourteenth place. Likewise, Scottish students seem to be much more influenced by their peers than were their Australian colleagues.

Finance seems to be of equal importance in the lives of both groups, but it is perhaps heartening to observe that neither group places this factor at the head of its priorities. Listening to—or watching—performance by others is more important to the Australian students, who ranked this factor as third in importance, than it is to their Scottish counterparts. Other factors such as opportunities for travel and starting early seemed to rank comparatively low in the estimation of both groups.

School or education-related aspects were ranked higher by the Scottish students than by the Australians. The primacy of the importance of an inspiring or encouraging teacher amongst the Scottish cohort has already been remarked upon. Likewise, Scottish students placed importance on the school music department as a crystallising element in their development. It is fairly clear from the data that the Scottish students tend to emphasise home and school factors, whereas Australian students rank music-specific ones higher. This is interesting, as it may reflect the greater importance to the students in Scotland of the social circumstances under which they approach their musical education and training. On the other hand, it may equally reflect on a greater independence on the part of the Australian students which enables them to see beyond these social factors and into their own feelings and perceptions.

When the paralysing factors are considered, it is obvious that there are other divergences. Consideration of the paralysing factors can be useful, as it can act as a check on whether the perceptions of crystallising aspects is borne out: in other words, whether the negative influences in a student's formation are the obverse of the positive ones. In that respect it is clear that the influence of the teacher on students in Scotland is just as important in terms of paralysing their musical formation as it is in crystallising it. Scottish students place more emphasis again on standards of teaching and on quality of inspiration and encouragement than Australian students do. The perception that internal factors personal to the student are perhaps more important in general terms to the Australian sample than the social/interactional ones are to the Scots, is borne out by the fact that the Australian students find pressure to achieve the greatest factor in paralysis: likewise, they attach a high rank of importance to anxiety in performance and find the negative pressure to perform in examinations difficult. Perhaps most interesting of all in this context is the intimation by the Australian students that low self esteem is a paralysing factor. This does not seem to affect the perceptions of the students in Scotland to the same extent: indeed, very few of them identified this factor as significant in their experience. Australian students, on the other hand, seem to be less affected by an over-critical music teacher than their Scottish colleagues. Scots again commented on situational aspects such as family support as being important to their musical development. While Australians also developed this response, they did not do so to the same extent. Scots were more likely, too, to be affected by negative comments and pressures at school than the Australians were.

Lack of opportunities for ensemble playing was more serious for Australian students than for the Scottish group. This may reflect the situation in the schools: schools in Scotland have moved over recent years to establish ensemble groups in a number of contexts, both classical and popular. Some reinforcement for the view that Scottish students are better supported in schools is given by the fact that there were more Australian responses citing lack of school support as a paralysing factor than Scottish ones.

One interesting finding is that the factor ranked third in terms of the Scottish responses was the lack of available finance for resourcing a musical career. While availability of finance did not figure largely in the crystallising responses—in other words, the fact that money was available for instrument purchase and for tuition did not in itself predict substantial musical development—it does seem to figure as a paralysing agent. Moreover, the issue of availability of resources is more important to the Scots than to the Australians. Fortunately, neither group of students feels held back by the slower progress of classmates—thus perhaps pointing to an awareness of musical talent and how to cope with it amongst the teaching forces of both nations.

Commentary

While our sample in the present study is a larger one than that which was used in our previous work on this topic, it is nevertheless one which has to be treated with some care when conclusions are being drawn. Although the students involved in the research are studying music in higher education and although many of those involved in the Scottish cohort are students at the national conservatoire and those in Australia had received a conservatoire education in a variety of institutions including the Faculty of Music, all of the students are being educated to become teachers of music rather than professional performers. Thus, although it is assumed they are very competent and excellent in terms of their performance skills they may in some quarters not be seen as the pinnacle of musical giftedness in Scotland. Such students might well have had a highly specialised musical education, perhaps in a dedicated institution, rather than the broader curriculum more generally offered in that country. This, in turn, will to a certain degree affect the responses which the students have given us. Secondly, the sample, being education students, might well be expected to be more aware of pedagogical issues than another sample composed of music students receiving no education input. It would be an interesting exercise to see how such students would respond. Thirdly, the students are bound to be affected by institutional factors in terms of the programmes which they are currently pursuing and the personalities which they encounter on these programmes—and there is, particularly in the responses indicating the importance of composition to some students, evidence that this is happening. However, the sample may also be seen as fairly homogeneous in that these are young—and occasionally more mature—people who are pursuing a common aim in their musical studies and for whom there will be a certain similarity in the learning outcomes of the programmes. In this sense, then, we feel that it is valid to attempt some generalisation from the evidence which we have obtained in this research.

The results would seem to indicate three main findings: firstly, that student music teachers in Scotland identify social and contextual factors as important in their musical development; secondly, that their colleagues in Australia place greater importance on internal personal factors; thirdly, that both groups identify areas over which the schools that they attended have influence, as critical in their development. The task of this section of the paper is to examine these findings and to look at reasons for them.

In terms of the indication that social factors are important in the development of the Scottish students, one can speculate on a number of possible reasons. Students of music in Scotland tend to come from mixed backgrounds, but there is a preponderance of students from middle class backgrounds in training for music teaching, and this fact is recognised by the national conservatoire in its development of access programmes to ensure a more even social mix (RSAMD, 2001). Therefore, it might appear to be reasonable to assume that solid family backing and in some cases a solid family musical environment would be of assistance in crystallising music development. Against this, it could well be argued that the same factors would apply in the case of the students from Australia, where arrangements for the financing of studies are perhaps harsher.

Secondly, the indication by the Australian students that they valued music-personal specific factors more highly in terms of their development is interesting. This may point to a greater independence—but against this is the fact that the Australians were more likely to suffer from poor self-esteem and nerves in performance. What is clear, however, is that in terms of both the groups of students there are cultural factors—for example, related to expectations and social contexts—at work in terms of their musical development; and this may in itself be the most important result from this research.

Thirdly, the importance of school-specific factors to both groups of students is important and interesting. It is clear that both groups are affected by inspiring music teachers in terms of the crystallisation of their development and equally affected by poor ones in terms of the paralysing of their development. To a large extent, this is a predictable finding. However, a caveat has to be added in that it must be recognised that teaching—particularly instrumental teaching—may well occur outside the school environment. The finding that the role of the teacher and the school is of critical importance in the development of musical excellence is one which is supported by other research (Sloboda, 1985 op.cit.; Swanwick, 1988, etc.) Our study has reinforced this, and, given the fact that our sample is composed of aspiring teachers of music, perhaps gives it an extra edge. The commentary by many of our students on the importance of teaching style gives focus to the importance of pedagogy in framing conditions and an ethos within which the crystallisation of musical ability can occur. This, likewise, has been commented upon by others (e.g. Swanwick, 1988, 1994.) It is therefore important that firstly, our students keep in mind the extent to which their own development was either hastened or hindered by appropriate or inappropriate pedagogy, and that they rehearse the correct skills in their own teaching. It is also clearly important that institutions of teacher education should impress upon students the creation of a suitable teaching style and a fertile classroom ethos (Farmer, 1979).

It is very interesting to observe that the importance of ensemble opportunities is very high for the Australian cohort, but perhaps more taken for granted by their Scottish colleagues, who placed emphasis on the importance of a good music department—again a social, contextual feature rather than a personal specific one. Nevertheless, it is clear that such opportunities are of critical importance in the formation of musical talent in a generic sense, and there are implications for school pedagogy and management here.

Conclusion

This paper commenced with the idea—part of contemporary debate—that even if musical ability is not necessarily innate, then it is possible for it to be developed in an individual through teaching, to a high degree. This idea was further expanded to investigate the factors which may either work positively (crystallise) or negatively (paralyse) towards that musical development. The investigation was carried out within two distinct systems of musical education, the Scottish and the Australian, to introduce a comparative element and to identify which factors might be culture specific and which more generic and universal.

The findings indicate that there is indeed a range of factors which are universal in musical development. These include the importance of good teaching and opportunities for development with other young musicians. These aspects of social learning are perceived as of much greater importance to those who participated in our study than solo opportunities. Secondly, there are factors which are culture-specific and which relate to the social and contextual environments in which musical learning takes place. Such factors include family encouragement; the encouragement of peers and the opportunities for musical development provided by schools.

This paper has merely scratched at the surface of a much larger debate, about the nature of activities which are undertaken in order to foster and develop musical talent. Consideration of where, and how, that development should start and take place—needs to be taken forward. Further research is also needed in terms of the aetiology of musical development and it would be an interesting exercise to establish which of the crystallising and paralysing factors are most important at different stages in this process. This should constitute a further stage in the contemporary research agenda.

References

Bentley, A. (1966) *Musical Ability In Children and its Measurement* (London, Harrap).

Davidson, J., Howe, M. J. A. & Sloboda, J. A. (1997) Environmental Factors In The Development Of Musical Performance Skill Over The Life Span, in: D. Hargreaves & A. North, (eds), *The Social Psychology Of Music* (Oxford, Oxford University Press) pp. 188–206.

Eastop, P. (2001) Teaching Self-Teaching, in: C. Paechter, M. Preedy, J. Scott, & J. Soler, (eds), *Knowledge, Power and Learning* (London, Paul Chapman Publishing).

Farmer, Paul (1979) *Music in the Comprehensive School* (London and New York, Oxford University Press).

Gardner, H. (1993) *Frames Of Mind: The theory of multiple intelligence* (London, Fontana).

Hargreaves, D. J. & North, A. C. (1997) *The Social Psychology Of Music* (Oxford, Oxford University Press).

Hartounian, J. (2000) Perspectives of Musical Talent: A study of identification criteria and procedures, *High Ability Studies*, 11:2, pp. 137–160.

Howe, M. J. A. (1990) *Sense and Nonsense about Hothouse Children: A practical guide for parents and teachers* (Leicester, BPS Books—The British Psychological Society).

Johnston, D. (2002) Scottish Local Government Reform and Instrumental Music Instruction, *Scottish Educational Review*, 33:2, pp. 133–141.

Kirk, S., Gallagher, J. & Anastasiow, N. (2000) *Educating Exceptional Children* (New York, Houghton Mifflin).

McDonald, D. & Simons, G. (1989) *Musical Growth and Development* (New York, Schirmer Books).

McPhee, A. D. (2000) *The Identification of Children Gifted in Music and Ways in Which Their Needs Are Met: An example from Scotland*, paper presented at the Scottish Association for Music Education 4th Scottish Conference on Music Education; Dundee, 8th September 2000.

Moog, H. (1976) The Development of Musical Experience in Children of Pre-school Age, *Psychology of Music*, 4:2, pp. 38–45.

Mills, J. (1985) Gifted Instrumentalists: How can we recognise them? *British Journal of Music Education*, 2:1, pp. 39–49.

Papalia, D., Olds, S. & Feldman, R. (2001) *Human Development* (New York, McGraw Hill).

Passow, A. H. (1979) *The Gifted and the Talented, Their Education and Development: By the yearbook committee and associated contributors* (Chicago, NSSE, distributed by the University of Chicago Press).

Paynter, J. (1982) *Music in the Secondary School Curriculum: Trends and developments in class music teaching* (Cambridge and New York, Cambridge University Press, For the Schools Council).

Rauscher, F., Shaw, G. & Ky, K. (1995) Listening to Mozart Enhances Spatial-Temporal Reasoning: Towards a neurophysical basis, *Neuroscience Letters*, 185:1, pp. 44–47.

Robertson, P. (2000) Why Does Music Affect People as it Does? *RSA Journal*, 3:4, pp. 66–74.

The Royal Scottish Academy Of Music And Drama (RSAMD) (1998) *Junior School Prospectus*, Editions 1998–2001 (Glasgow, RSAMD).

The Royal Scottish Academy Of Music And Drama (RSAMD) (2001) *Outreach Development of Junior Academy* (Glasgow, RSAMD).

Scottish Education Department (SED) (1975) *Gifted Young Musicians and Dancers: Report of a working group set up to consider their general and specialised education* (The Cameron Report) (Edinburgh, Her Majesty's Stationery Office).

Schiffman, H. R. (2000) *Sensation and Perception* (New York, John Wiley).

Schlaug, G., Lutz, J., Huang, Y. & Steinmetz, H. (1995) *In vivo:* Evidence of structural brain asymmetry in musicians. *Science*, 1995, 267, pp. 699–701.

Schwartz, L. L. (1975) *The Exceptional Child: A primer* (Belmont, California, Wadsworth).

Skinner, D. (1991) 'Mozarts in our Midst?' *Times Educational Supplement* (06/xii/91).

Sloboda, J. (1990) Musical Excellence—How does it develop? in: M. J. A. Howe (ed.), *Encouraging the Development of Exceptional Skills and Talents* (London, BPS Books for the British Psychological Society).

Sloboda, J. (1985) *The Musical Mind: The cognitive psychology of music* (Oxford, The Oxford University Press).

Snyder, B. (2000) *Music and Memory* (Cambridge, MIT Press).

Stollery, P. & McPhee, A. (2002) Some Perspectives on Musical Gift and Musical Intelligence, *British Journal of Musical Education*, 19:1, pp. 89–102.

Stollery, P. (1997) *Scaling the Heights: Report on research findings for Scottish Network for Able Pupils project* (Glasgow, St Andrew's College and SNAP).

Storr, A. (1992) *Music and the Mind* (London, Harper Collins).

Swanwick, K. (1988) *Music, Mind and Education* (London, Routledge).

Swanwick, K. (1994) *Musical Knowledge, Intuition, Analysis and Music Education* (London, Routledge).

9
Music Education, Performativity and Aestheticization

Constantijn Koopman
Radboud University of Nijmegen and The Royal Conservatory of The Hague

In this paper I discuss two prominent phenomena in postmodern society which influence the position of music education: performativity and aestheticization. In the first part of the paper I shall argue that performativity threatens to marginalise music and music education. The conditions created by performativity are opposed to those in which the arts thrive (1.1). From the artistic point of view, performativity should be combated rather than endorsed. Attempts to justify music education by appealing to the performative results of music education will be shown to be misguided (1.2). The second, longer part of the paper will deal with the many-sided phenomenon of aestheticization, which at first sight seems to be contrary to performativity. After having given a survey of major aestheticization processes (2.1), I will take up the question whether aestheticization positively influences music education (2.2). This leads to further qualifications of aestheticization demonstrating that aestheticization and the arts do not accord in important respects (2.3). This is corroborated by the fact that there is a significant connection between performativity and aestheticization (2.4). Finally, in the conclusion the implications of the discussion for music education will be examined.

1 Performativity

1.1 Performativity and the Arts

Among the forces dominating our culture today, performativity is perhaps the one felt most strongly in music education. 'Performativity' derives from the verb 'to perform', which has two source-meanings. First, 'to perform' means to carry through in due form, with purpose undertaken and itself completed as a central aspect; second it means to accomplish entirely, achieve or complete (Stone, 1997, p. 300). These meanings resound in the postmodern concept of performativity employed by Jean-Francois Lyotard. The elements of completion and perfection, as well as the element of measurement, come together in the interpretation of performativity as efficient agency (Lyotard, 1984, ch. 11). 'Performativity' thus refers to the drive for goals to be achieved in ever more efficient ways. Social systems organise themselves in such a way as to optimise efficiency and productivity, defined as the state in which a minimum of input leads to a maximum of output.

Although efficient agency might appear to be very positive indeed, performativity turns out to be a totalitarian force; it tends to take possession of all kinds of practices. According to Lyotard, scientific practices are driven by the desire for enrichment rather than by the desire for knowledge. What is at stake is not so much truth as the improvement of technology, that is, the improvement of performative achievements in relation to the realisation of products. Likewise, justice becomes associated with performativity: the chances that a command is considered to be just increase with the chances that it is being carried out, and these chances increase with the performativity of the prescriptor (Lyotard, 1984, ch. 11).

Performativity also affects the position of the arts, though in a different way.[1] The mechanisms of efficiency and productivity are opposed to the conditions under which the arts thrive. Artistic activity cannot be forced into a scheme in which clear goals are defined, after which appropriate means are established and put to use in most efficient ways. In the arts there must be room for the free exercise of imagination. The artist does not usually start with a clearly confined conception of what he is going to produce. She needs time to explore, to try out, to adjust, and sometimes to start again from the beginning. Maximising productivity and minimising efforts is, as pop art shows, not completely unknown in the arts, but it is the exception rather than the rule. Similarly, reception in the arts has little to do with efficiency. One does not engage in art (as art) with a specific aim or interest but one opens oneself to what the work of art has to offer. We allow ourselves time to explore and contemplate the work of art. There is no minimizing the input; in fact the distinction between input and output makes no sense at all. Artistic experience is a whole, we do no put attention and perception in and get emotions and pleasure out.

The antithesis between the artistic domain and efficiency thinking is clearly exposed in the analysis of the arts by Hans Georg Gadamer (1977). He explains the artwork as play, symbol, and feast. As play the artwork appears as autonomous movement. By its movement artistic play does not pursue any external aims but movement as movement, which signifies a phenomenon of surplus, of self-presentation of livingness (p. 30). As feast art replaces the 'normal' pragmatic experience of time—the experience of time as 'time for something'. This is the time of which one disposes, which one fills with some kind of activity. Instead of this, the arts feature a different type of time: fulfilled time. When the feast starts, the present is being fulfilled by the celebration. It is not that someone has had to fill in empty time but rather, conversely, time has become festal when the time of the feast has arrived. The calculating way in which one disposes of one's time is brought to a standstill in the act of feasting (Gadamer, 1970, pp. 55–56).

In the arts, then, time does not function as a means to achieve some purpose or goal. Rather, time is allowed to be fulfilled by autonomous and intrinsically valuable artistic experiences. We now can see the precarious position of the arts. In a society in which efficient, goal-directed action provides the norm, artistic activity becomes an extravagant mode of behaviour, particularly if efficiency is measured in terms of money. From such a perspective music and the other arts are at best considered as a luxury or even as parasitic practices, using up the profits gained in other areas. Performativity tends to marginalise the arts, presenting them as activities at odds with the serious commerce of life.

1.2 Performativity and Music Education

The status of music education in institutionalised settings like schools suffers from the rhetoric of performativity. Again and again the question is raised what the benefits of music education are, what use it actually has. Advocators of music education often yield to the pressure of justifying music in terms of what is seen as performative results. Various kinds of positive effects of music education have been claimed: improvement of mathematical insight, reading skills, concentration, social skills, the development of creativity and a positive self-image, the channelling of emotion health, etc.

Such arguments are unconvincing. Hardly any of the claims about the positive outcomes of music have been established by research (cf. Koopman, 1996; Koopman, forthcoming). Moreover, if positive results can be demonstrated, the problem of efficiency remains. It seems impossible to defend that music education is, for instance, the most efficient way of improving particular cognitive or social skills.

One argument given in favour of arts education is that, rather than promoting concrete skills, the arts constitute an important factor in humanising the educand. According to John White (1998), the arts deserve a place within the curriculum because they foster self-knowledge, reinforce our ethical values, and bind us together as members of communities. When we experience a play or a novel 'from the inside' we are confronted with all kinds ideas, emotions, conflicts, resolutions we would not easily experience in ordinary life. Art works give us a broader and deeper sense of what human existence is about. By dwelling in art works we both expand the knowledge of ourselves and the world, and we gain a new awareness of our ethical values and our place within the community. Although they cannot easily be demonstrated by empirical research either, these claims to self-knowledge, reinforcement of ethical values and social cohesion are indeed sophisticated. They relate the value of artistic engagement to the unique nature of the arts themselves and thus render the question of efficiency as irrelevant. No alternative activity can confront us with our human condition in this way.

One problem is that, since it features no plot enacting lifelike situations, most music does not seem to be able to promote self-knowledge and ethical awareness in a concrete sense. White (1998, p. 195) acknowledges this but he thinks that as a mirror of our psychic constitution as a whole music might be more valuable than other forms of art. The more fundamental limitation of the types of justification mentioned is that they conceive the value of music as instrumental. In these arguments musical activities are seen merely as means to some further end: knowledge, ethical awareness, social coherence. The intrinsic value of musical engagement is neglected.

Can we make a case for the value of music in a non-instrumental way? System theory suggests that we cannot, because it takes performativity to be something which is beyond human control (cf. Lyotard, 1984, ch. 4). Whatever people think about them, systems will develop autonomously in the direction of optimising the global relationship between inputs and outputs. This would mean that justifications of music education in alternative terms, for instance, in terms of its contribution to a fulfilled life, are unrealistic; social systems will evolve in the direction of maximal efficiency and practices that do not comply with the logic of performativity will be obliterated.

One need not surrender to this pessimism, however. In fact, system theory does not provide any arguments to say that mechanisms of performativity are indifferent to our efforts to promote a just society and a happy life. Rather it rules out the role of rational agency governed by free will from the outset. In other words, system theory gives us a one-sided representation of reality. It ignores the fact that the intentions of human beings can make a difference. No matter how powerful the forces of capitalism have been, people have succeeded in countering its inhumane consequences. Social action and social policy have secured a reasonable level of prosperity for masses of people who would be worse off under capitalism in its crudest form. And recently, movements opposing forms of capitalist globalisation have gained considerable influence.

In a similar way, proponents of music education should be aware of the power of efficiency thinking and reflect on the appropriate way to deal with it. My suggestion is that by completely accommodating the rhetoric of usefulness and efficiency, the profession digs its own grave. We can only be successful if we manage to divert discourse from instrumentalism and efficiency-thinking to questions of humanistic education and fulfilment. It should be pointed out that, while music fits into a different kind of discourse than performativity—the discourse of play, feast, imagination, contemplation, of sharing experience—it can make a vital contribution to the life of many people. Music's contribution to humankind resides in the rich experience it provides to people who allow their time to become fulfilled instead of always employing it as a means to attain goals ahead. Music celebrates the full experience here and now, whereas instrumental behaviour always sacrifices the quality of the present to an imaginary state in the future.

2 Aestheticization

2.1 Aestheticization Processes

A second characteristic of contemporary society, which is particularly interesting in relation to the arts, is aestheticization. 'Aestheticization' refers the processes in which the aesthetic more and more permeates all kinds of domains. Whereas performativity is not conducive to artistic practices, aestheticization by contrast appears to be in accordance with them. It emphasizes and promotes precisely that which the arts exploit: the aesthetic. We shall see however, that things do not turn out to be as simple as that. Aestheticization denotes a wide range of developments associated with the concept of the aesthetic, which cannot all be positively related to the arts. First, we shall provide a sketch of various aestheticization processes largely based on the work of Wolfgang Welsch, whose analysis gives a clear overview of many strands of the phenomenon.

Welsch starts his exposition with the aesthetic furnishment of reality. This is most clearly visible in the urban environment where almost everything has been subjected to a face-lift. Shopping centres have been fashioned to be elegant, chic and animating. This trend has not been limited to the urban centres but has spread to the outskirts and to the rural areas. 'Hardly a paving-stone, no door-handle and no public place has been spared this aestheticization-boom' (Welsch, 1997, p. 2). Even ecology has largely turned into a branch of beautification. Welsch suspects that, if Western societies were able to do so, they would transform our entire environment (urban, industrial and natural) into a hyper-aesthetic scenario.

While Welsch emphasizes the visual aspects of our the aestheticized world, there is no doubt that the auditory is just as involved. In the last couple of decades we have become used to music's omnipresence in our urban culture. Not so long ago, to be able to hear a symphony or a string quartet was a special opportunity. Live performances were practically the only source of musical encounters. One's experiences were limited by the availability of musicians in one's vicinity. The arrival of the radio and the gramophone, and later the television and the CD-player changed this radically. Music lost its quality of fleetingness; musical experiences can now be organized at will and can be repeated as many times as one wishes. The complete availability of music has been accomplished by the arrival of internet sites from which it can be downloaded. Music from any historical period and any place of the world is now continuously at our disposal. And we do avidly use this availability. Listening to their favourite music is for many people a major and daily source of enjoyment. Music, of course, is not only a private enjoyment but it has won its place in the public atmosphere. We encounter it in cafés, malls, plazas, workshops, airports, and in dozens of other places. The musical furnishment of reality has the function of making people feel at their ease but also of neutralizing or counterbalancing the increasing noise modern life carries with it. Walkmans and CD players in cars combat the traffic noise, while easy listening music has the upper hand on many shop-floors.

With aestheticization, Welsch says, the world reveals itself as a realm of experience. Everything we do becomes an experience: shopping, sojourning in a café or at a railway station, etc. Every day we go from our experience-office to experience-shopping, relax with experience-gastronomy and we end up at home with experience-living (Welsch, 1997, p. 2).

But aestheticization not only involves the furnishment of reality but it also affects its very constitution (Welsch, 1997, p. 5). More and more it is the media, especially the television, which determine our sense of reality. When zapping between the channels, we see many different versions of the world. The reality of television is optional, exchangeable, disposable, escapable. The images of the media no longer offer a documentary guarantee of reality, but are rather arranged and artificial. Increasingly reality and virtual reality become indistinguishable. Through the media, reality is becoming a tender, which down to its substance is virtual, manipulable and aesthetically 'modellable'.

Whereas the aesthetic increasingly influences the way we see the world, the hegemony of knowledge has also been challenged. Western philosophy and science have always been dominated by the quest for true knowledge, conceived as an accurate representation of objective reality. This idea became problematic when Wittgenstein (1953) abandoned his earlier view of language as the logical picture of reality (Wittgenstein, 1922) and replaced it by the concept of language as a variety of language games. Developing the ideas of Wittgenstein, Richard Rorty (1979; 1989) challenges the view of knowledge as 'the mirror of nature'. The world has no intrinsic nature that can be captured by language; it does not spontaneously split itself up into facts (1989, ch. 2). There is no true world out there. The concept of truth applies to our descriptions of the world, not to the world itself.

With Jacques Derrida (1976), the sign is no longer a transparent medium for communicating about independently existing entities. The signifier takes priority over the signified. Signifiers no longer function as vehicles for representing the signified but instead one signifier provokes the other, producing an endless chain of signifiers in which the signified never gains full presence. The signified exists only as a trace which never reaches its termination point. Any suggestion of a reality existing independently of language is excluded by this view of semiosis.

If scientific and philosophic knowledge can no longer be conceived as the contemplation of eternal truths, the pursuit of knowledge becomes a much more mundane activity. But even as a factor that secures the progress of human society, knowledge has been overestimated according to postmodern philosophers. For Lyotard the enlightenment philosophy of the removal of ignorance and slavery through the ideals of knowledge and equality is one of the 'grand narratives' that have lost their credibility. While adhering to the ideals of democracy, Richard Rorty also rejects the idea of growing rationality and historical progress. He is convinced that the role of philosophy and knowledge in culture has been strongly overrated. In his view, the importance of the arts in 'the conversation of mankind' is hardly less important than philosophy and science. All these aspects of human culture play an equivalent role in keeping our horizon open (cf. van Reijen, 1987, p. 182).

Not only has the superior status of science and philosophy over the arts been called into question, it has increasingly been found that our conceptions of reality, knowledge and truth are aesthetic at heart. Welsch (1997, pp. 19–24) refers to this development as epistemological aestheticization and he gives various examples to substantiate the case. According to Friedrich Nietzsche, our conceptions of reality do not merely contain aesthetic elements, but they are entirely aesthetic in nature. Reality is a construction that we produce like artists with the means of fiction—ways of vision, projections, images, and phantasms. Paul Feyerabend declared that, fundamentally, science proceeds in the same way as the arts: it is style-bound. Rorty pleads for an aestheticized culture, a culture which knows that its foundations are cultural artefacts and are thus produced in an aesthetic way. Not only has the significance of aesthetic considerations been pointed out by philosophers but it has also been acknowledged by scientists themselves. At decisive points in their work, Bohr, Einstein and Heisenberg argued in aesthetic ways and Poincaré stated that aesthetic rather than logical potency constituted a good mathematician's central talent. James Watson's discovery of the DNA structure was founded on the aesthetic premise that the solution would have to be of great elegance. Welsch concludes that whereas in the past aesthetics was considered to deal with secondary, supplemental realities, the aesthetic nowadays belongs to the very foundations of knowledge and reality (cf. Welsch, 1997, p. 24).

Ethics are no less permeated by aesthetic considerations. Individuals increasingly relate to each other aesthetically (Welsch, 1997, pp. 6–7). In a world where traditional moral rules fade away, table manners and etiquette seem to give us at least something to hold on to. Aesthetic competence compensates for the loss of moral standards. At a deeper level, Welsch perceives that for our modern conscience all forms of life, orientations and ethical norms have taken a peculiar aesthetic quality; no longer do they feature as obligatory standards but instead as historical, social or individual designs. Moral systems are to be considered as formations of artistic stature and the criteria one adopts for deciding between different moral systems are, in the final analysis, aesthetic in nature. Ethics, Welsch (1997, p. 19) suggests, is on the way of becoming a sub-discipline of aesthetics.

Elsewhere, Welsch writes that in this media-dominated postmodern world in which every difference between appearance and being fades away, we can only react and think in an aesthetic way. Aesthetic thinking nowadays is the genuinely *realistic* mode of being because only it can cope with the aesthetic constitution of reality (Welsch, 1990, pp. 164–165).

2.2 Does Aestheticization Support Music Education?

We need not endorse Welsch's most radical conclusions—that knowledge as well as ethics are founded upon aesthetic concepts and that the aesthetic is the only realistic mode of being left to us—in order to agree with his claim that there has been a clear tendency toward aestheticization during the past decades. Now, what does this tendency towards aestheticization mean for arts education in general and music education in particular?

At first glance, one might think that tendencies of aestheticization provide a positive impulse to music education. Because they live in an aestheticized world, children will have a better starting position when they begin music classes. They have already developed the aesthetic mode as a dominant orientation and they have gained a lot of aesthetic experiences. More importantly, the position of music education appears to be enhanced: if the aesthetic comes to the fore, so will education in the arts. Contrary to its marginal position up to now, music now features as a subject that directly connects to a central fact of postmodern existence: the aesthetic way of life. As the status of the aesthetic rises, so do the arts, in which the aesthetic experience is cultivated more intensively and purely than anywhere else.

Moreover, Welsch argues that the arts have a special role in acquainting us with the postmodern condition of plurality. Since the aesthetic mode prevails in postmodern culture, art becomes a model for postmodern society: the plurality we experience in the arts, characterised by radical heterogeneity, corresponds to the constitution of postmodern society. Nowhere else can we study and experience pluralism better than in the arts. They teach us what is important in society with its different forms of life: recognition of the different, prohibition of infringement, uncovering of implicit oppression, resistance to structural unification and facilitating transitions without assimilation (Welsch, 1990, pp. 164–165).

But things are more complicated than this positive picture suggests. To begin with Welsch's argument, note that he conceives arts education in an instrumental way. The arts are the most appropriate medium for teaching lessons about what is important in the plural society. The focus is not on the arts themselves but on how to act in postmodern life. The arts are not so much a unique realm of experience as a useful model for society at large. As with all instrumental justifications of music education Welsch's argument implies a choice for certain genres at the cost of others. If taken seriously, the argument would amount to focusing only on the works that expose the 'virtues' of plurality. Moreover, Welsch's argument would merely provide a temporary justification for arts education. Once people have become used to and adapted the values of pluralism this reason for including arts education into the curriculum would expire.

This leads to a further issue: *in a world where everything is approached in an aesthetic way, the special position of the arts appears to dwindle and the need for arts education seems to vanish.* Far from being beneficial to the arts, aestheticization might increasingly undermine its special status. If aesthetic experiences can be had anywhere and every time, why is there a need to give special attention to the arts? Aren't the arts reduced to just one of many ways of behaving aesthetically? If this were the case, there would seem to be no reason why the arts should be conferred a privileged status in our educational system in comparison with other aesthetic phenomena.

2.3 Qualifying Aestheticization

What, then, is the status of the arts in an aestheticized world? Do the arts really become indistinguishable from other types of aesthetic behaviour?

A first point to be made is that the concept of the 'aesthetic' as employed within the arts does not coincide with the way it is used by theorists of aestheticization like Welsch. While 'aesthetic' denotes a very broad domain within the arts, it has even wider denotations in discourse about aestheticization. Welsch (1997, pp. 8–15) points out that in the first place 'aesthetic' refers to the *sensuous*. The aesthetic has two sides, a subjective one and an objective one. One the one hand we have *sensation*, which is related to pleasure and is emotional in nature; on the other hand there is *perception*, which is directed to objects and is cognitive in nature. Aesthetic *pleasure* transcends the level of the 'vulgar-sensuous', the direct pleasures related to our direct vital needs. It is a reflexive pleasure, one which judges its objects not as necessary or useful, but as beautiful, harmonic, sublime or superior. On the cognitive side, the side of perception, aesthetic refers to the relations between the elements of the object. Here the concepts of *form* and *proportion* come to the fore. *Beauty*, the aesthetic predicate par excellence, relates to the perfecting form of the sensuous (Welsch, 1997, p. 13).

In this way Welsch demonstrates how from the basic notion of the aesthetic as the sensuous the key concepts of aesthetic discourse—sensation, perception, feeling, pleasure, form, proportion—arise. But his scope does not restrict itself to these concepts so familiar in the philosophy of art. He goes on to relate the aesthetic to various other concepts, which results in a very broad conception of the aesthetic. The aesthetic now also includes the pretty, the styled, the cosmetic (besides the beautiful); staging and lifestyle (in personal behaviour and advertisement); virtuality (the mediation of the world by the media), the illusory, the fictional; the qualities of being produced (the *poiëtic*) and changeable; the non-obligatory (Welsch, 1997, pp. 8–9, 13–17).

It is important to realize, then, that much of what Welsch and others writing about aestheticization deem 'aesthetic' has little to do with the arts. 'Aestheticization' does not mean that those features in which the arts excel spread to the rest of human culture. The concept of the aesthetic takes on different connotations and stands for other kinds of experiences within the various domains that are affected by aestheticization. The virtual world presented by the TV and the computer highlight different features than those normally associated with art. (Of course some artists have recently embraced virtual reality but by setting out to make works of *art* within the new media, they aim at something qualitatively different from standard experiences within this domain.) Aestheticization in relation to lifestyle denotes fun, entertainment and 'enjoyment without consequences' (Welsch, 1997, p. 3) rather than the more demanding engagement serious art requires. And in the context of material technologies aestheticization signifies that materials have become so malleable that they can be formed in accordance with all kinds of wishes. Here, aestheticization refers to the creation of new materials for practical uses, not to the shaping of materials into artistic forms.

Aestheticization of culture, then, cannot simply be connected to the types of aesthetic experience that are cultivated within the arts. It often means that something new or different, related to alternative connotations of the term aesthetic, has been accomplished rather than that features of the arts have directly been adopted. And when indeed characteristics of the fine arts are highlighted in other areas we often see a loss of quality. Welsch (1997, p. 3) observes that with the aesthetic furnishment of reality only the most superficial elements of the arts are adopted and then realised in a rather inferior manner. 'Beautiful ensembles drift into prettiness at best, and the sublime descends into ridicule'. This everyday aestheticization by no means realises the aim of avant-garde programmes (like those of Cage and Beuys) to extend and break down the limits of art. The reverse is the case: traditional artistic characteristics are being carried over into reality, daily life is being stuffed with 'artistic character'. Kitsch is furthered instead of progressive art.

The paradoxical fact is, moreover, that aestheticization leads to *anaesthesia*, as Welsch (1997, pp. 25–27) points out. A basic aesthetic 'law' states that we do not only need stimulation and invigoration but also interruption, repose, and zones of quietness. This means that massive beautification is doomed to failure. Complete aestheticization results in the opposite: numbing and indifference. It is therefore aesthetic reasons which speak in favour of breaking the aesthetic turmoil. Welsch pleads for the development of a 'blind-spot' culture. Aesthetic reflection encourages us to be aware of the twofold relationship between consideration and exclusion. To see something is simultaneously to oversee something else. We should develop our sensibility so as to become aware of differences and exclusions. In a separate essay on the 'culture of hearing' Welsch calls attention to the need for reorganising our *auditory* environment (Welsch, 1997, pp. 160–163). Accepting the noise of modern life, as has been recommended by Russolo and Cage, is no option for him. To counter auditory anaesthesia noise should be avoided where possible, unavoidable noises should comply with the no-nuisance principle and silent zones should be created. This policy includes all kinds obligatory music, which Welsch finds a nuisance rather than an achievement of contemporary society. Revitalising our auditory environment is all the more important because he suspects that the complete domination of the visual will gradually give way to a much more auditive culture (Welsch, 1997, pp. 150–163).

Welsch's ideas about the threat of anaesthesia and desirability of a blind-spot culture have interesting implications for music education. They suggest that aestheticization tendencies do not simply imply the improvement of people's aesthetic sensibility. People may become numbed and as far as they do not, they will still have to develop their sensibility for the blind spot.

2.4 Aestheticization and Performativity

A further characteristic of aestheticization related to the superficial character of the 'beautification' of reality, is that it frequently serves economic purposes. The aesthetic is being employed to stimulate the sale of commodities. By giving products an aesthetic look the unmarketable becomes marketable and the already marketable two or three times more so. Products that have become stylized aesthetically are taken up into the logic of fashion and thus the need for replacement will arise long before the already in-built obsolescence renders them unserviceable. Also, products which have become increasingly unsaleable on moral or health grounds (as with cigarettes) become saleable again once they have been given an aesthetic aura. Increasingly the relationship between the article and the packaging is being reversed: the packaging with its aesthetic aura is now the consumer's primary acquisition, while the article is merely incidental. The aesthetic becomes the guiding value; rather than acquiring the article, you buy yourself into the lifestyle with which the advertisement has associated it (Welsch, 1997, pp. 3–4).

Here we see performativity and aestheticization coming together. At first, the tendency toward aestheticization may seem to be opposed to performativity. Where performativity stands for thinking and acting in an efficient and instrumental way, aestheticization appears to refer to taking things easy, to engaging in things for the pleasure we take in them. But we have seen above that 'aesthetic' covers a very wide range of phenomena, which do not all share the characteristic of self-sufficient activity. Moreover, we now find that performativity in its economic form heavily controls our 'aestheticized culture'. Jean Baudrillard and Frederic Jameson take the radical view that all cultural products have been absorbed by capitalism (cf. Van den Braembussche, 2000, pp. 344–356). Not only has the cultural sign become a product with a market, its logic also merges with the logic of the commodity. Just as with the commodity the utility value has been superseded by the exchange value, the signified of the cultural sign gives way to the signifier. Commodities are produced as (aesthetic) signs, while the cultural signs are produced as commodity, as exchange value. It is not only that commercial products are rendered more saleable through aestheticization but also that art works are more and more seen as commodities, as objects dominated by their exchange value. This happens to classical art works like paintings by Van Gogh and (recordings of) Beethoven's symphonies but the cultural industry has also produced new art forms like the video clip, the TV series, the B-film and other kinds of mass art with much larger economic potential. In this way the autonomy of the arts gives way to the force of economic performativity. Artistic considerations, creativity and innovation by no means disappear but they are restricted by commercial desiderata. Economic interests pose limits to what can be done in the arts: art works should have direct appeal and provide ready entertainment; they should not be incomprehensible to large groups, nor should they leave the public with confusion or vexing questions.

Conclusion: Implications for Music Education

Postmodern insights into performativity and aestheticization result in a rather gloomy picture of the position of the arts. The forces of performativity are inimical to activities that do not fit the means-ends scheme of goaldirected action. Consequently, performativity thinking tends to present the arts as a luxury. Aestheticization, though it appears to promote the aesthetic dimension of our lives, often has opposite consequences. Superficiality often reigns, overfeeding leads to anaesthesia, and the aesthetic is often controlled by economic performativity.

This shows that aestheticization processes by no means render aesthetic education superfluous. I see two major functions of music education, which gain new significance and urgency in the light of aestheticization as well as performativity: life enhancement and furthering a critical attitude.

Life Enhancement

Aestheticization feeds us with all kinds of would-be experiences, experiences which are superficial, short-lived and end with disappointment (cf. Welsch, 1997, p. 2). Consequently, the need for real, authentic experiences only becomes more important. Music education's function of enhancing experience, then, is even more topical than it was before. Music education can provide an antidote to the superficiality and the anaesthesia of modern life. Restoring and developing sensibility as well as extending the range of authentic experiences should be major aims of music education today. Pupils should be led to overcome the musical cliché and to become sensitive to new possibilities of meaningful sound. Like other domains of reality, music has been profoundly infected by the trivializing influence of commercialism but there remain plenty of opportunities for 'real' musical experiences. These experiences can be found in solo performance, in making music together, in composing but also in listening (even in listening to some commercially produced CD's). By initiating people in first-class musical activities music education offers them a major form of life fulfilment for the present and for the future.

Critical Attitude

Music education as the cultivation of musical sensibility and authentic experience should not limit itself to guiding pupils towards the kinds of musical practices which can provide these. It should also teach them how to guide themselves. People in postmodern society are flooded by all kinds of music with all kinds of functions, both manifest and hidden. Music is often used as a manipulative force. As we have seen, it serves the purpose of boosting commodity sales—no radio or TV commercial functions without music. In social, political and religious contexts music is used to promote a mood of 'belonging'. National, religious, and classical hymns (e.g., Beethoven's Ode to Joy), club songs and pop songs are effectively used for this goal.

Music can thus serve to shape and confirm one's identity, social, ethnic, political, and religious. Music places us in the world in very specific way. As Christopher Small says, when fully engaging in communal musical activities, we are in fact making a statement: 'This is who we are' (Small, 1998, p. 134). Music is one of the most effective ways of influencing our sense of identity because it not only operates on the cognitive but also on the emotional and somatic level. Music's workings are strong but largely irrational. Because of these attributes and because music is so powerful in shaping our dispositions, direct musical engagement should be complemented by critical reflection.

What functions does music have in our society? Which ones are welcome, which are neutral, and which are harmful? How is music used to manipulate me and what can I do to prevent this? How can I prevent myself falling prey to the anaesthetizing effects of my auditory environment? What part does music play in my life and how does it position me in relation to other people?

Such questions are important issues to deal with in music education. Pupils should learn to perceive, think and judge critically about music, both in relation to the intrinsic value of music and in relation to the uses and abuses of music in society. For people who get the chance to develop their musical sensitivity, who have good opportunities to participate in authentic musical activities, and who also take a critical stance toward their auditory environment, the prospects of leading a fulfilling musical life may not be as bleak as postmodern philosophy suggests.

Notes

1. This part of the paper emphasises the opposition between the arts and performativity. The impact of economic performativity on the arts is discussed in 2.4.

References

Derrida, J. (1976) *Of Grammatology*, trans. G. Spivak (Baltimore, Johns Hopkins University Press).

Gadamer, H. G. (1977) *Die Aktualität des Schönen. Kunst als Spiel, Symbol und Fest* [The Topicality of Beauty. Art as Play, Symbol and Feast] (Stuttgart, Philipp Reclam).

Koopman, C. (1996) Why Teach Music at School?, *Oxford Review of Education*, 22:4, pp. 483–494.

Koopman, C. (forthcoming) *Art as Fulfilment: On the justification of arts education.*

Lyotard, J.-F. (1984) *The Postmodern Condition: A report on knowledge* (Manchester, Manchester University Press).

Reijen, W. van (1987) Postscript to J.-F. Lyotard's *Het Postmoderne Weten* [The Postmodern Condition] (Kampen NL, Agora).

Rorty, R. (1979) *Philosophy and the Mirror of Nature* (Princeton, Princeton University Press).

Rorty, R. (1989) *Contingency, Irony and Solidarity* (Cambridge, Cambridge University Press).

Stone, L. (1997) Educational Reform through an Ethic of Performativity: Introducing the special issue. *Studies in Philosophy and Education*, 18, pp. 299–307.

Welsch, W. (1990) *Ästhetisches Denken* [Aesthetic Thinking] (Stuttgart, Reclam).

Welsch, W. (1997) *Undoing Aesthetics* (London, Sage).

White, J. (1998) The Arts, Well-being and Education, in: P. H. Hirst & P. White (eds), *Philosophy of Education: Major themes in the analytic tradition*, Vol. IV, Problems of Educational Content and Practice (London, Routledge).

Van den Braembussche, A. A. (2000) *Denken over Kunst* [Thinking about Art] (Bussum NL, Coutinho).

Wittgenstein, L. (1922) *Tractatus Logico-Philosophicus*, trans. C. K. Ogden (London, Routledge and Kegan Paul).

Wittgenstein, L. (1953) *Philosophical Investigations*, trans. G. E. M. Anscombe (Oxford, Blackwell).

10
The Global Musical Subject, Curriculum and Heidegger's Questioning Concerning Technology

Janet Mansfield
University of Auckland and Auckland University of Technology

In a global cyber economy embedded with inequalities in power relations, cyberspace and its technologically mediated environments give birth to new paradigms of subjectivity and identity. The global musical subject is defined and framed within global empires and techno-culture in ways not unrelated to political interests. 'Being musical'—the protection of musicality—becomes a critical issue where technology orders and constructs a politics of musical knowledge. The New Zealand music curriculum, no less than other subject areas, resonates with reflections of global 'progress' at a local level under the strategies of the global knowledge economy and music education falls into line under the globalizing constructions of knowledge. Therefore, what becomes imperative for music educators as cultural workers is an awareness of political and strategic conceptions of musical knowledge and a familiarity with the discourses through which the work of music education is enframed. Where technology enters hegemonic and universalist discourses of musical knowledge as in music curricula, the relationship between global communication and technology requires recognition. Unquestioned past curriculum certainties come under scrutiny.

The accountability so revered by rapidly globalizing audit culture under neo-liberal policies of 'growth and development' locks music educators into attempting to describe how music knowledge fits a 'knowledge economy'. How can such knowledge procedurally and theoretically, be conceived of in terms of economic commodity? Will it 'innovate' or contribute to national wealth? Department programmes are, contradictorily, squeezed to advertise themselves as contributing to competitive advantage at a time when they are marginalized within curriculum policy. As an intervention claiming a space for contestation in musical cultural and curriculum issues, I use Heidegger's philosophy as he articulates it in his famous essay 'The Question Concerning Technology'. Heidegger writes of poiësis and art's saving power in the confrontation of the essential unfolding of technology. His questioning with regard to modern technology may assist us in retaining a necessary continuing questioning stance in the politics of musical knowledge, now within the discourse of technology and commodity culture.

The Global Musical Subject

Music education exists and is enframed internationally and locally. The political, economic and social milieu is one produced in part by global neoliberalism. In this environment governments warp as systems of often invisibilised global power re-inscribes a modernist individualism upon the global musical subject. Barbara Kruger's painting '*I Shop Therefore I Am*' springs to mind when considering the sounds and symbols of the market, its ideologies and their impact upon the reconstituted musical subject. Sites of creativity are co-opted in technologies of cultural packaging and we need to give some thought to the ways in which music and music education are implicated in this.

The notion of *globalization* is helpful in understanding the conditions under which musical knowledge is constructed. In emphasising the notion of *globalization* Grierson, (2003, pp. 3–4) points to Pearsall's (1998, p. 780) discussion where '*global* is "of or relating to the whole world; worldwide"; from *globus* a spherical object; with globe derived from Latin *globus*'. She indicates the common usage of terms such as '*globalist, globalize, globality*, and *global age*' again referring to the writings of a number of authors (Featherstone, 1990, 1992, 1995, 1996; King, 1991; Hirst & Thompson, 1996; Scott, 1997; Albrow, 1997, 1999; Giddens, 1999). Grierson states: '*A globalized world order, global networks, global capitalism, global economy, global technologies, global citizen, global culture, global village* have become familiar descriptors of economic, political, educational, cultural, and social conditions of the twenty first century' (2003, p. 4). Further, she points to globalization's reigning power and authority in local and global strategies and discourses of domination, normalization and marginalization.

Under globalizing musical culture, modernism's unifying universalist principles and ethos which had assumed that music practice was merely the product of free, autonomous individual expression, have been unsettled and replaced by relativistic perspectives and questions of 'difference'. However, simultaneous yet contradictory processes occur relating to globalization as the twenty-first century begins. While national identities or origins are becoming increasingly 'unfixed' and confounded in the wake of global flows of people, capital, cultural practices, products, and meanings and their pilgrimages across and between countries, modernism's homogenising tendencies still permeate. Today, people and institutions are connected along many and various lines of interactions across borders of nation states. As a result, national, ethnic or religious groups, professions, businesses and cultures become further and further enmeshed. In such conditions, bodies of knowledge become decentred. While modernism has been associated with experiment, a search for the new and transgression, postmodernism too, is associated with processes of decentring of bodies of musical knowledge. Such processes are exemplified by Gebesmair & Smudits when they suggest:

> The international ambitions of the 12 note style; the grand narrative of the evolution of tonality has been challenged, and an emphasis has shifted to cultural context, reception and subject position. Together, these have conspired to eat away at the status of canonical composers and categories of high and low music (Gebesmair & Smudits, 2001, p. ix).

In the latter two decades of the twentieth century musicology has experienced turmoil as various dimensions of difference, including gender and sexuality, enter music scholarship (see Solie, 1993; Gebesmair & Smudts, 2001). Critical, philosophical and theoretical models of music education and the arts generally, have begun to draw upon poststructuralism, cultural studies, postmodernism, semiotics, psychology and sociology (see Mansfield, 2000; Grierson & Mansfield, 2003; Lines, 2001, 2003; Naughton, 2001; Stock, 1994; Gebesmair & Smudits, 2001). Thus, musical cultures and music education are today situated in a context in which 'a cybermedia corporate complex' (Eisenstein, 2001) operates. We need, therefore, to pose critical questions as to the ways in which transnational practices and their resulting power configurations incidentally and apparently unproblematically mould or enframe music education. International boundaries are spanned by current socio-economic, political and cultural formations and it is the ways in which music education *takes account* of the impacts of these processes on its sites of practice that become matters of importance. If we are concerned with *musical cultures*, then how local and regional musical cultures might be affected by global transnational culture industries become matters of importance and interest for music educators. Conditions of music production and distribution are constantly altering in a highly technological globalized world as creative cultural resources are appropriated from different parts of the world by roaming musical marketeers (Gebesmair, 2001; Binas, 2001). Sounds altered, extended and sampled, by composers, engineers and scientists who through the 'virtual' studio may both specify and manipulate sound (see Scaletti, 1999, p. 7) form a kind of commodity and cultural capital which may be drawn upon commercially and nationally for market purposes within a competitive global economy.

In an age where packaged music becomes a commodity, these trends must shape possibilities for artistic and musical cultural expression and production and be affected by the increasing gaps between wealthier and poorer nations. Bearing this in mind, a critical theory of music education would engage in the questioning of these global technological processes for their impact upon music educational sites. When we promote the advantages of globalization and its new (modernist) metanarratives for music education, do we *also* question the appallingly unequal power relations in cyberspace?[1] For example, convolution processes that require hours of computer time may be questioned for their ideological connections to the interests of certain commodifying communities. The existence of sound/audio manipulators and sound crafters within the context of globalized technological advances mean that critical philosophical questions need to be brought to the music educators' table. How are these kinds of materials packaged, marketed and used within music education at present and what are the implications of their use? How might music and art education contribute to revealing the moral and ethical dimensions of a 'hyperaesthetics' of technoculture? (see Lunenfeld, 1996). It becomes increasingly clear that the music educator's cultural and curricular knowledge involves a facility with deconstructive practices in respect of the electronically produced musical product or commodity.

Under conditions of globalization, musical signifying practices composed of diverse cultural musical references express identities that are often multiple and contradictory, yet form a positive statement of hybrid musical identity, despite the likelihood that the cultural referential qualities of globally circulating samples of beats and rhythms may be weak or poor. This is a here and now identity, one which steps outside Hegelian reality and the binarisms of modernism.[2] Democratic inclusive practices of DJs who include bi-cultural and multi- cultural musical styles from around the globe 'from salsa to reggae ...' (Hernandez, 2001, p. 70) both challenge and confirm cultural assumptions behind marketing categories. Hernandez (2001, p. 70) in *Global Repertoires* refers to 'genre-jumping and travelling music'. Novel and eclectic musics both confront, test and confirm cultural assumptions, and inevitably broadening cultural flows produce musical hybridity as the unified categories of traditionally imagined musics based upon nation and state are destabilized. These hybrid musical styles confound original configurations of different genres. Music 'of the moment' has its day. (see Lines, 2001, 2003).

The musician as *bricoleur* (Kearney cited in Pearse, 1992, p. 250) engages in practices which are implicated in the continuous processing of auditory or musical symbols. Such processes demand an escalating 'simulation of reality' which is obtained simply through representing increasingly diverse and culturally identified specific musical practices. Engels Schwarzpaul refers to these processes in respect of ornament as types of 'practically dissolved lifeworld' (2001, p. 277). In such circumstances, the processes of commodification of culture inherent in globalizing market culture, lead to meaning becoming 'non-referential, unmediated and indeterminate' and the blunting of the tools of the bricoleur and often, a 'low-level aesthetic referential quality' (Engels-Schwarzpaul, 2001, p. 229). This, I think, is what might result from music that results from simulated musical experiences where works are assembled by musicians in the absence of one another. Bill Martin in *Avant Rock* (2002, p. 248) writes of a 'disembodied sensibility' to much of this music 'at a time when contingency asserts itself as never before'. He argues that there is an 'unavoidable fragility to this music of our time' (p. 248) and that 'one irony of some of the new music that is made entirely in the cybernetic domain is that, even while a significant part of it is meant as "body" music, it is far away from being tactile in its creation' (pp. 228–9).

Music educators may well heed Jenny Wolmark's comments in her book *Cybersexualities*, where, in examining the politics of identity and subjectivity, she calls for an examination of the positive and negative features of 'hybrid cyber-identities' (1999, p. 241). Wolmark (1999, p. 241) points to Donna Haraway's text 'Manifesto for Cyborgs' arguing that Haraway's,

> cyborg metaphor produces a complex model of the networks of shifting alignments and associated consciousness that are necessary for an oppositional and differential politics; as she puts it, 'differential consciousness can be thought of as a constant reapportionment of space, boundaries, of horizontal and vertical realignments of oppositional powers'.

Such oppositional politics may be imagined in postmodernity where received approaches of music are challenged by revolutionary and radical subjectivities commanding a disruptive power and expression in new musical spaces of articulation, radical form and disorientation. Musical signifying practices may include, for instance, romantic and mystical expressions, impetuous rhythms, 'throbbing cadences', pulsating tempos', 'assemblage[s] that pulsate with menace, cynicism and perversion' (Whitley, 2000, pp. 97–98). Subjectivity is both subject and object of the 'fetishistic, the harmonically static, the heavily repetitive ... the extraordinary' (Whitley, 2000, p. 100) where ambiguities of sexuality, female identity and boundaries of gender are disputed and challenged in new performative moments and desire expressed through intensely dynamic music. The insistent, the urgent and the religiously animated, the oddly juxtaposed and 'figurative displacements' signify desire—the disarticulation, the *bricolage*—'of the punk aesthetic' (see Whitley, 2000, p. 105). 'Differential consciousness exists rhizomatically and parasitically' (Sandoval, 1999, p. 259) and as such it functions as a tactical device for deconstructing fixed categories, in the process of which it reorders existing ways of thinking about the relationship between dominant and subordinate cultures and ideologies' (p. 242).

The *musical subject* is reconstituted somewhat in the contemporary global environment. Cyberspace and its technologically mediated environment spawns new paradigms of musical subjectivity and identity. Subjectivity, rather than being fixed and unified is contradictory, fluid and ambiguous and the signifying practices of these new decentred musical subjectivities are addressed and expressed in cross-overs, mixed and new musical genres. The global musical subject is often one whose cultural roots are located at the intersection of two or more cultures. The relationship between globalization and music is played out through the new patterns of migration on the production and consumption of local national musical forms.

While technological advances enable diasporic populations to retain close links with their original home countries and institutions, the reality of their situation within the larger demography of their host counties presides. Normalising processes of musical hegemony are powerfully exerted through canonistic approaches and homogenising marketing categories of exposure. These operate as powerful interventions in immigrant's attempts to retain their musical cultural ties with their countries of origin. Questions of authenticity in music are debated constantly in this site of competing discourses and the political struggle over how society will be experienced and organised is felt no less in the constructions of the music curriculum. In the following section, a critical awareness of a technologically mediated music education environment is adopted and the question to be asked is, 'When frames of technological literacy' are imposed in music education, 'does the exercise of power in pedagogic practices produce governable subjects to suit the purposes and practice of the governing body?' (Grierson, 2000, p. 476). The New Zealand example illustrates a likely pattern of curriculum development in other OECD countries under neo-liberal policies of economic globalization.

Technology in the New Zealand Music Curriculum

A number of authors have documented the wider educational 'reforms' that occurred in New Zealand with the restructuring of educational administration in the late 1980s to 1990s (see Peters, 1995, 1996; Olssen, 1990, 1996; Fitzsimmons, Peters & Roberts, 1999; Grierson, 2001; Mansfield, 2001). The pervasive effect of neo-liberalism and economic liberalism has been felt as a result of the thrust toward globalization and the internationalizing state. Curriculum has thus been embroiled within this project and the introduction of technology into the curriculum has not been unrelated to an imposition to act as a 'transmission belt' for the world economy.

Technological enframing procedures impinge upon institutional sites such as schools, where discourses of official music educational 'knowledge' are conditioned and may be un-interrogated in terms of their impact upon the *musical subject*. School practice enacted through new curriculum prescriptions have obeyed these technological ordering processes as musical production is increasingly framed on technology's terms. The policy document *Digital Horizons: Learning through ICT—a strategy for schools* (Ministry of Education, 2002, p. 3) which revised the Information and Communication Technology (ICT) Strategy for New Zealand Schools, stated its aim of 'helping schools to extend their use of ICT to support new ways of teaching and learning' (Brown, 2002, p. 1). Globalizing processes and interests have promoted the new orthodoxy and presence of technology in the curriculum generally and in the music curriculum in particular. Its representation in the music curriculum is undeniable. Technology is mentioned early in the Music Curriculum (see Ministry of Education, *The Arts in the New Zealand Curriculum*, 2000, p. 52) which states: 'Music encompasses ... sounds generated by conventional musical instruments and *electronic technologies*'. Students are to 'appreciate the aesthetic qualities, in the sounds of the natural and *technological* environments' (my emphasis).

Students are to be technologically literate, for 'literacy in music', according to the document (Ministry of Education, 2000, p. 53) 'involves the development of knowledge and skills relating to ... technologies and musical structures'. A measurable 'literacy' in music implies the mastering of technological 'conventions' which are thus normalized within the document in relation to 'creating' and 'performing' and critically evaluating musical compositions' and performances. 'Literacy' in music is therefore linked to particular communities, those involving technology and commodity culture. Particular *business* partnerships using technology therefore link 'literacy' in music and art to notions of 'creative industries' and creative communities. The politics of musical literacy are left unproblematized, as are questions of access to sophisticated technology. Following 'the imperatives of commodification and empire', communities form on the basis technology's reproducibility capabilities and, as Bill Martin in *Avant Rock* (2002, p. 212) argues, at the point where a small number of corporations control almost all the media, things begin to look a little 'conspiratorial'. The formation of the 'literate' music community, composed of 'developing' 'literate' musical subjects appears to have a clear relationship to certain technological capabilities. Further, the help of schools is required to rein the musical subject (student and teacher alike) into the technological vortex. One way this is done is through curriculum prescriptions. We need, therefore, in a music education which nourishes the *musical being* aspects of life, to question the nature of the relationship between these communities (which organize collective musical memory), (Mowitt, 1987, p. 182) and technologies. The curriculum intends, it would appear, to set the occasions for the 'developing' musical subject to form 'literate' music communities tied to technological capabilities. We must interrogate the connections between the technologically 'literate' music community produced by the school and the imperatives of commodity and empire.

Level 7 of Music (Ministry of Education, 2000, p. 62) states that: 'Students will analyse and investigate ways in which *communications media* and *technology* influence sound and meaning in music' and that they [students] will use '*critical analysis* to inform and *evaluate performances*'. But how, we may ask, is 'critical analysis' being framed or interpreted? Questions asked from within the ideological framework of policy will not allow for the critical questions to be asked and, as Peters argues (Grierson & Mansfield, 2003) 'there is no place to stand outside the system'. Again in a similar vein, Marshall suggests, technicist questions require technicist answers (2001). 'Critical analysis' is used (only) to 'inform and evaluate a wide range of performance' (Ministry of Education (2000, p. 69). That is, critical analysis is to inform *performance* and to evaluate *performance*, the musical '*work*', not to examine the discourse of music education—now within the discourse of technology and commodity culture. That is, students are to be kept unaware of the politics of musical knowledge for the absence of such profoundly critical questions is submerged within the normalizing procedures of state curriculum documents. 'Criticality' ought to involve dialogue, which can hardly proceed from the idea of a universalist consensus implied within the curriculum imperatives of developing 'musically technologically literate' students or from the idea of a 'prior-being-in-truth' (Kögler, 1996, p. 84) where the value of 'truths' emanating from 'technological literacy' in music is assumed. If the wings of dialogue are clipped by technological rationality, criticality does not occur.

The music curriculum within *The Arts in the New Zealand Curriculum* (Ministry of Education, 2000) embeds a universalist claim to 'truth' about the value of technology, (a universal consensus) or from an 'idea of a prior-being-in-the-truth' (Kögler, 1996, p. 84). Under such circumstances there is little opportunity for understanding to become a reciprocally challenging process with the other where there may be also, neither guarantee of a comprehensive truth, nor a further assured goal of a final consensus. Thus, what Kögler refers to as 'the power-determined character of understanding' and 'power-determined meaning constitution' (1996, p. 84) is apparent in arts 'knowledge' through the pervasion of technological—based or conditioned 'arts literacy'.

Where students are to understand 'Music in Context' (Level 8 Ministry of Education, 2000, p. 69), the document states:

> Students will investigate the purposes and significance of music in society and research a range of styles and genres in music in relation to past and present contexts. Students will research the ways in which *technology mediates* the composer and the performer and the audience in contemporary contexts.

Once again, there is no space for criticality. 'The ways technology mediates the composer' implies a technicist answer. A critical pedagogy would presumably ask questions relating to the protective dimension of Beings that is needed including questions on the 'lived relations of domination' (Haraway, 1991, p. 4). A critical musical pedagogy would also require the deconstruction of the digital bit which affects memory (see Mowitt, 1987).

Under 'Developing Ideas in Music', the Music curriculum states:

> Students develop an awareness of different sounds and the potential of sound for resourcing and generating ideas and for communicating feelings. They use aural skills, imagination, and develop a knowledge of structural devices, musical instruments, technologies, and the elements of music to improvise, compose, and notate music with increasing sophistication and refinement. (Ministry of Education, 2000, p. 54)

Thus, 'technologies' condition the discourse of music education through 'improvisation and composition' and performance, and their 'increasing sophistication and refinement' ('Developing Ideas in Music', Ministry of Education, 2000, p. 54). Such phrases and as 'sophistication and refinement' (Ministry of Education, 2000, p. 54) are loaded and emotive phrases now linked to technology's capabilities and its specialized communities. Again, under 'Developing Ideas in Music', 'students will use musical elements, instruments, and technologies to improvise and compose simple pieces' (Ministry of Education, 2000, back cover chart). 'Official' musical knowledge as prescribed in curriculum, now becomes linked to the use of technologies and weds the 'developing' musical subject and her 'skills' to the discourses of the 'creative industries' and their commodities or products. Heidegger's questioning with regard to modern technology may assist us in retaining a questioning stance in relation to the politics of musical knowledge, which is now, as suggested earlier, within the discourse of technology and commodity culture.

Heidegger's Questioning Concerning Technology

German philosopher, interpreter of Nietzsche and critic of Western metaphysical modes of analysis, Martin Heidegger, indicated the grave consequences of pervasive and dominating modern prescriptions of thought. These generalize, he suggests 'so as to apply to things, equipment and work' (1993a, p. 157). Such dominating preconceptions, he argues 'shackles the reflection on the Being of any given being' (Heidegger, 1993a, p. 156) and he warns us to 'take heed of' the 'boundless presumption' embodied in such thoughts (1993a, p. 157). The gravity of Heidegger's thinking on the domination of technology in modern life and the need for an ongoing questioning of what the questions might be concerning technology is developed in his seminal essay, *The Question Concerning Technology* written in 1945 and revised in 1955. He states:

> Thus questioning, we bear witness to the crisis that in our sheer preoccupation with technology we do not experience the essential unfolding of technology, that in our sheer aesthetic mindedness we no longer guard and preserve the essential unfolding of art. Yet the more questioningly we ponder the essence of technology, the more mysterious the essence of art becomes .... The closer we come to the danger, the more brightly do the ways into the saving power begin to shine and the more questioning we become. For questioning is the piety of thought. (1993, p. 341)

Heidegger's views in his seminal essay *The Question Concerning Technology* are helpful regarding art's role in the protection or safeguarding of *Being*—in this case, 'being musical'. Given the fact that schools are in *loco-parentis*, a critical music pedagogy might ask questions relating to the protective dimension of musicality. '*Poiësis*', argues Heidegger, may enable us to defy the 'essential unfolding of technology' (Heidegger, 1993, p. 309). He wants to criticize the essence of technology for being unconcerned with protecting Being. When we take this tool (technology) for granted assuming its disinterestedness or neutrality we do not understand its true nature and we are unaware of its enframing and manipulative qualities. For Heidegger:

> ... the essence of technology is by no means anything technological. ... Everywhere we remain unfree and chained to technology, whether we passionately affirm or deny it. But we are delivered over to it in the worst possible way when we regard it as something neutral; for this conception of it, to which today we particularly like to pay homage, makes us utterly blind to the essence of technology. (Heidegger, 1993, pp. 311–312)

Discourses of music education conditioned and interpreted within the Creative Industries and 'education-for-sustainability' paradigm of knowledge are tied to global technological advance. Dominating assumptions embedded within the music curriculum indicate that within music education the 'natural' human resource of musicality—'a primary product'—can and must be worked upon, or, in Heidegger's terms, 'set upon' to produce 'higher value products' (Ministry of Education, 1995, p. 6). Through a *technological musical literacy*, referred to in the New Zealand music curriculum, nature is set upon and challenged. Heidegger states: in *The Question Concerning Technology*:

> What is modern technology? It too is a revealing. Only when we allow our attention to rest on this fundamental characteristic does that which is new in modern technology show itself to us ... And yet the revealing that holds sway in modern technology does not unfold into a bringing forth in the sense of *poiësis*. The revealing that rules in modern technology is a challenging [*Herausfordern*], which puts to *nature the unreasonable demand* that it supply energy which can be extracted and stored as such. (Heidegger, 1993, p. 320)

How is music education to 'add value'? We are implored to jump through the technologically deterministic hoops, to conquer, hoard, and turn into investments—objects—the human 'resources' of musicality. If *being musical* involves the ability to perceive, appreciate, and produce melodies and rhythms, why, in the predatory moves for order is the absenting of the body from the sight and site of sound of musical production (its disembodiment) neither stated, recognised, made problematic nor revealed? The neutrality of technological literacy is assumed. We are to master, through an apparently neutral technological literacy, the musical 'human' resources of the subject and, as Marshall states with reference to *Technology in the New Zealand Curriculum* (Ministry of Education, 1995), 'to extract, store, and invest' in such resources (2000, p. 122). The question of technological 'literacy' which now colonizes the arts as sites of creativity, avoids the question of what Heidegger terms, its 'essence'—the challenging setting upon nature of the essence of technology. The 'primary product' of musicality becomes objectified and is to be processed into higher value products. Not only does the *Arts in the New Zealand Curriculum* (Ministry of Education, 2000) not acknowledge the 'interestedness' of the notion of technological literacy within arts literacy, but the actual value-laden nature of technological literacy is not mentioned. As Marshall (2000, p. 124) points out, the *Technology in the New Zealand Curriculum* document (1995) places knowledge and understanding of the capabilities of technology 'prior to environmental, social and cultural issues'. Critical musical and arts literacy is not the intention, but rather a functional literacy.

Heidegger argues that in modern technology, there is a *challenging* or *demanding* of nature, not just a bringing forth or revealing of what is in nature, as in ancient technology (see Marshall 2000, p. 126). In modern technology, a demand is placed upon nature, to do more than reveal nature, (musicality) but to order it as standing reserve. For Heidegger, this demanding of nature was captured within the notion of enframing (*ge-stell*). Music education as enframed technologically, will be, in Heidegger's thinking, challenged to not merely reveal and nurture musicality but to order it as 'standing reserve' (1993, p. 325). The musical subject thus becomes part of the standing reserve. Where technology is used for the production of CDs and tapes of recorded music for use in music 'education' in schools, musicality, in Heidegger's terms is kept in reserve, challenged, used, for production within the studio by others. The use, in schools, of such packaged resources, is likely to mean less use of musical instruments, a reduction in the physicality of music-making.

Heidegger's anxiety about the coercive and oppressive nature of modern technological culture is expressed further when he states:

> Enframing means the gathering together of the setting-upon that sets upon man, i.e., challenges him forth, to reveal the actual, in the mode of ordering, as standing reserve. Enframing means the way of revealing that holds sway in the essence of modern technology and that is itself nothing technological (Heidegger, 1993, p. 325).
>
> ... The rule of enframing demands that nature be orderable as standing reserve. (pp. 327–328)
>
> We are questioning concerning technology in order to bring to light our relationship to its essence. The essence of modern technology shows itself in what we call enframing. (p. 328)

Which of our activities now lead us to think about musicality as standing reserve? In the case of music education, what is in 'nature' is not brought forth, or revealed in the use of 'quick-fix' commodities for it involves a controlled, minimal and diminishing musicianship. Composing, performing dimensions of musical being are enframed ideologically and musicianship may be unperformed—largely intact. In Heidegger's terms, the 'concealed' will not come into 'unconcealment' (p. 318). He states in the essay, *The Question Concerning Technology*:

> ... Bringing-forth brings out of concealment into unconcealment. Bringing-forth propriates only insofar as something concealed comes into unconcealment. This coming rests and moves freely within what we call revealing [*das Entbergen*]. The Greeks have the word *alétheia* for revealing. The Romans translate this with *veritas*. We say 'truth' and usually understand this with correctness of representation. (Heidegger, 1993, p. 318).

If musicality will not come into presence, the site of *poiësis* is endangered because it is ordered. The *being musical* aspect of the musical subject's identity, is unnurtured, unprotected in the musical subject. Marshall notes that 'what was wrong with modern technology, according to Heidegger, is that it reduces humanity to the state of a clever animal, with no obligation to shelter things or protect their *being*' (Marshall, 2000, p. 128). Given that teachers within state education are charged with the protective role of being *in loco parentis* technological literacy and literacy in the arts ought not to be taken on without this sheltering and protection of *musicality and its being.* If 'everything including humanity is turned into a standing reserve', and 'man himself is changed in this ordering and controlling of standing reserves' (Marshall, 2000, p. 128), the musical subject is changed in that access to music-making. He or she then becomes the clever animal in the form of the music student mastering *technological musical literacy*, the DJ, the studio technician manipulating digital musical technology. Opportunities for students to play instruments, to sing, to make-music are lost or grossly diminished—unprotected.

Nature is set upon and challenged. Again, Heidegger claims: 'This setting-upon that challenges the energies of nature ... is always itself directed from the beginning toward furthering something else, i.e. toward driving onto the maximum yield at the minimum expense' (Heidegger, 1993, p. 321). Further, he states:

> Enframing is the gathering together which belongs to that setting-upon which challenges man and puts him in a position to reveal the actual, in the mode of ordering, as standing-reserve. As the one who is challenged forth in this way, man stands within the essential realm of enframing (p. 329).

The musicality of the musical subject is set upon, stored up, saved, framed, to be used, under-used, 'distributed ... switched about ever new' (Heidegger, 1996, p. 322). In this situation *poiësis* as revealing, occurs only within a particular ideological context. The musical 'work' is produced to stand by, to be in stock as commodity to sooth the largely untouched musicality of the masses who listen only. A modernist aesthetic ideology is thus reinscribed. The presence of absence is everywhere. Bodies are abstracted from the site of musical production. The musicality of the musical subject is in standing reserve for purposes of manipulation. The musical subject is ordered to produce an object, and alongside the object, to stand by with his/her 'natural' resource—musicality. When resources (by extension nature and culture) are exploited, its subject matters are alienated and transformed. As Heidegger argues: 'Where enframing hold sway, regulating and securing of the standing reserve mark all revealing (Heidegger, 1993, p. 332). For the musical subject, where enframing holds sway, *poiësis and* revealing occur within a particular scaffold which orders. Heidegger states:

> The fact that now, wherever we try to point to modern technology as the revealing that challenges, the words 'setting-upon,' 'ordering,' 'standing-reserve,' obtrude, accumulate in a dry, monotonous and oppressive way—this fact has its basis in what comes to utterance. (Heidegger, 1993, p. 323)
>
> ... Thus the challenging-enframing not only conceals a former way of revealing (bringing-forth) but also conceals revealing itself and with it that wherein unconcealment, i.e. truth, propriates. ... Enframing blocks the shining-forth and holding sway of truth (p. 333).

He implores us to 'stand and guard' or protect the essential unfolding of art (p. 341), and this includes music. That is, in our terms, the musicality of the musical subject in its 'essential unfolding'. He wants 'reflection upon technology and decisive confrontation with it' (p. 340) and suggests that this occurs best in the realm of art. Heidegger sees the saving power of art and the poetical:

> Could it be that the fine arts are called to poetic revealing? Could it be that revealing lays claim to the arts most primally, so that they for their part may expressively foster the growth of the saving power, may awaken and found anew our vision of, and trust in, that which grants? (Heidegger, 1993, pp. 339–340).

Following Heidegger's philosophy, critical music curriculum scholarship must therefore, engage with 'decisive confrontation' in its reflection upon technology. When the musical subject becomes technologically enframed, musicality in action is reduced and the goals of transformative possibilities for radical, critical pedagogy become illusive. However, when students discover ideologies of listening, playing, performing, and musicianship and their social, cultural, historical contingencies within an adequate theory of representation, there is space for resistance and transformation. It is within alternative and resistance strategies that Heidegger's sites of poiësis are to be found. Poiësis, I suggest, may be found within a music education wherein 'questioning builds a way' (Heidegger, 1993, p. 311).

Concluding Remarks

I have discussed the framing of the musical subject, and, applying Martin Heidegger's philosophy, I have argued that modern technology's enframing capabilities and tendencies have consequences for music education discourses as well as for music educators in the postmodern condition. Through a discussion of the democratizing and enframing processes involved in technology in the music curriculum, I have illustrated the absence of debate on political hegemonic technological constructions of music education. The contradictory discourses music educators must negotiate have been revealed as well as the need for a questioning of the connection of *technological musical literacy* to commodifying communities in the global context. 'Arabesque' is a metaphor for negotiating the contradictions of essentializing modernist political moves embodied in the recent New Zealand music curriculum.

To reiterate, technologies of music as they are now enframed, are both technical and political. Collective memory involves a politics of knowledge, no less a politics of musical knowledge. The colonisation of memory by the reception of music, music's dependence on memory, memory's deeply social nature, and the fact that listening is an essential part of musicianship, suggests that whatever controls memory affects musicianship. The sites of construction of community in the musical organisation of collective memory therefore require interrogation for ideological purposes. Bearing in mind the seductions and promises of the 'cybermedia corporate complex' (Wertheim & Wertheim, 2003, p. 978) and the way in which it may be used to conceal its own part in circumscribing democratic capabilities, ontological questions concerning technology's role in the ordering and construction of musicality as a site of identity need to be asked. 'Being musical' and the protection of musicality become critical issues for music education. Music education that includes an *aesthetics of difference* (Mansfield, 2000) may bring musicality—*being musical* into unconcealment.

Acknowledgements

I would like to acknowledge David Lines for his thoughtful comments on the earlier drafts of this paper.

Parts of this paper are similar to a paper that will appear in ACCESS, Volume 22 (1 & 2), 2003 Critical Perspectives on Communication, Cultural and Policy Studies, Centre for Communication Research Auckland University of Technology.

Notes

1. Zillar Eisenstein (2001) insists that cyberdiscourse creates an imaginary picture that is must be seen as only partial and incomplete. 'Eightyfour percent of computer users are found in North America and Northern Europe. ... Fully two thirds of the world's population have never made a phone call!' (p. 73). Let us hope that artists and musicians are granted the right to produce work 'that does not entirely yield itself up to the sound bite culture' (Bickers, 2003, p. 343) and have it heard and played.
2. We see here, in fact, the role of music educator as cultural theorist.

References

Brown, M. (2002) The Real Cost of ICT in Schools: Beyond the digital horizon, Paper presented at the New Zealand Association of Research in Education Conference, Palmerston North, 5–8 December, 2002.

Barkin, E. & Hamessley, L. (1999) *Audible Traces* (Zurich, Carciofoli Berlagshaus).

Binas, S. (2001) Sampling the Didjeridoo, in: A. Gebesmair & A. Smidits (eds) *Global Repertoires: Popular Music Within and Beyond the Transnational Music Industry* (Aldershot Burlington USA Singapore Sydney, Ashgate), pp. 47–56.

Eisenstein, Z. (2001) *Global Obscenities: Patriarchy, capitalism and the lure of cyberfantasy* (New York, New York University Press).

Engels-Schwarzpaul, A. C. (2001) *Myth Symbol and Ornament and the Loss of Meaning in Transition*. Ph.D. Dissertation, University of Auckland, New Zealand.

Fitzsimmons, P., Peters, M. & Roberts, P. (1999) Economics and the Education Policy Process in New Zealand, *New Zealand Journal of Education Studies*, 34:1, pp. 35–44.

Gebesmair, A. & Smudits, A. (eds) (2001) *Global Repertoires: Popular music within and beyond the transnational music industry* (Aldershot, Burlington, USA, Ashgate).

Grierson, E. (2001) Political Framing of the Arts in Education, *ACCESS: Critical perspectives on cultural policy studies in education*, 20:1, pp. 35–47.

Grierson, E. (2000) *The Politics Of Knowledge: A poststructuralist approach to visual arts education in tertiary sites*, Ph.D. Dissertation, (Auckland, University of Auckland).

Grierson, E. (2002) *Humanising Globalisation: A search for visible space*. Paper presented at the Global Ethics and Civil Society Second Annual Conference of the Global Studies Association, Roehampton University of Surrey United Kingdom, July 22nd–24th 2002.

Grierson, E. (2003) *Globalisation, Cultural Nation and Truth Claims*. Paper presented at the 'Between Empires: Communication, Globalisation and Identity' Centre for Communication Research Conference, Auckland University of Technology, Auckland, New Zealand, February 2003.

Grierson, E. & Mansfield, J. (2003) *The Arts in the New Zealand Curriculum: Critical perspectives from Aotearoa* (Palmerston North, Dunmore Press).

Haraway, D. (1991) A Cyborg Manifesto: Science, technology and socialist feminism in the late twentieth century, in: *Simians, Cyborgs and Women: The reinvention of nature* (New York, Routledge), pp. 149–181. http://www/stanford.edu/dept/HPSHaraway/CyborgManifesto.html

Hernandez, D. P. (2001) Race, Ethnicity and the Production of Latino Popular Music, in: A. Gebesmair & A. Smudits (eds) *Global Repertoires* (Aldershot Burlington USA, Ashgate), pp. 57–72.

Heidegger, M. (1993) The Question Concerning Technology, in: D. F. Krell (1993) (ed.) *Basic Writings Martin Heidegger* (London, Routledge), pp. 311–341.

Heidegger, M. (1993a) The Origin of the Work of Art, in: D. F. Krell (1993) (ed.) *Basic Writings Martin Heidegger* (London, Routledge), pp. 139–212.

Kennedy, P. & Roudometof, V. (2002) *Communities Across Borders: New immigrants and transnational cultures* (London, Routledge).

Kögler, H. H. (1996) *The Power of Dialogue: Critical hermeneutics after Gadamer and Foucault*. trans. Paul Hendrikson (Cambridge, Massachusetts, MIT Press).

Krell, D. F. (ed.) (1993) *Basic Writings Martin Heidegger* (London, Routledge).

Lines, D. (2001) The First Musical Space: Articulating the music of the moment, *ACCESS: Critical perspectives on cultural and policy studies in education*, 20:1, pp. 82–89.

Lines, D. (2003) Text and Context in Music: Where music dwells, in: E. Grierson & J. Mansfield (2003) (eds) *The Arts in Education: Critical perspectives from Aotearoa New Zealand* (Palmerston Nth, Dunmore Press), pp. 161–179.

Lyotard, J. F. (1984) *The Postmodern Condition: A report on knowledge*, trans. G. Bennington & B. Masusumi (Minneapolis, University of Minnesota Press), (originally published in France as *La Condition postmoderne: rapport sur le savoir*, c1979 by Les Edition de Minuit).

Lunenfeld, P. (1996) Theorizing in Realtime Hyperaesthetics for the Technoculture, *Afterimage*, Jan–Feb 1996, 23:4, p. 16.3 http://web4.infotrac.galegroup.com/itw/infomark/2/448/26355291w4/purl=rc2_EIAM_1

Mansfield, J. E. (2000) *The Arts in the New Zealand Curriculum From Policy to Practice*, Ph.D. Dissertation, (Auckland, The University of Auckland).

Mansfield, J. (2003) Beyond the 'Beauty Full' Classroom: The arts curriculum and teacher education in the postmodern context, in: E. Grierson & J. Mansfield (eds) *The Arts in Education: Critical perspectives from Aotearoa New Zealand.* (Palmerston Nth: Dunmore Press).

Mansfield, J. E. (2003) *The Musical Subject, Technoculture and Curriculum in the Postmodern Condition*, Paper presented at the 'Between Empires: Communication, globalisation and identity' conference, Auckland University of Technology, February, 2003.

Martin, B. (2002) *Avant Rock: Experimental music from the Beatles to Bjork* (Chicago and La Salle, Illinois, Open Court).

Marshall, J. (2000) Technology, Education and Indigenous Peoples: The case of Maori, *EducationalPhilosophy and Theory*, 32:1, pp. 121–131.

Ministry of Education (1995) *Technology in the New Zealand Curriculum* (Wellington, Learning Media).

Ministry of Education (2000) *The Arts in the New Zealand Curriculum* (Wellington, Learning Media).

Ministry of Education (2002) *Digital Horizons: Learning through ICT–a strategy for schools* (Wellington, Leaning Media).

Mitchell, W. J. T. (1986) *Iconology, Image, Text* (Chicago, The University of Chicago Press).

Mowitt, J. (1987) The Sound of Music in the Era of Electronic Reproducibility, in: R. Leppert & S. McClary (eds), *The Politics of Composition, Performance and Reception* (London and New York, University of Cambridge Press).

Naughton, C. (2001) A Critical Examination of Cultural Context in Relation to Music Teacher Training, *ACCESS: Critical perspectives on cultural and policy studies in education*, 20:1, pp. 71–81.

Olssen, M. (1990) Idealist Impulses and Structural Imperatives of Education Policy Proposals, in: J. Codd, R. Harker & R. Nash (eds) *Political Issues in New Zealand Education* (Palmerston North, Dunmore Press), pp. 150–165.

Olssen, M. (1996) In Defence of Welfare State and Publicly Provided Education: A New Zealand perspective, *Journal of Education Policy*, 11:3, pp. 337–362.

Pearse, H. (1992) Beyond Paradigms: Art education theory and practice in a post-paradigmic world. *Studies in Art Education*, 33:4, pp. 244–252.

Peters, M. (1995) Educational Reform and the Politics of Curriculum in New Zealand, in: S. D. Carter & M. H. O'Neill (eds) *International Perspectives on Educational Reform and Policy Implementation* (London, Falmer Press), pp. 52–68.

Peters, M. (1996) *Poststructuralism, Politics and Education* (Westport USA, Bergin and Garvey).

Peters, M. & Lankshear, C. (2000) Curriculum in the Postmodern Condition, *ACCESS: Critical perspectives on cultural and policy studies in education*, 20:1, pp. 10–23.

Peters, M. (2003) Foreword: What Does it Mean to be Critical in Arts Education Today?, in: E. Grierson & J. E. Mansfield (2003) *The Arts in New Zealand Education: Critical perspectives from Aotearoa* (Palmerston North, Dunmore Press).

Rubin, A. (1999) Forum: Composing women, in: E. Barkin & L. Hamessley *Audible Traces* (Zurich, Carciofoli Verlagshaus), pp. 1–25.

Sandoval, C. (1999) New Sciences: Cyborg feminism and the methodology of the oppressed, in: J. Wolmark (ed.), *Cybersexualities: A reader of feminist theory, cyborgs and cyberspace* (Edinburgh, Edinburgh University Press), pp. 247–263.

Scaletti, C. (1999) Forum: Composing women, in: E. Barkin & L. Hamessley (eds), *Audible Traces* (Zurich, Carciofoli Verlagshaus), pp. 1–25.

Solie, R. (1993) *Musicology and Difference: Gender and sexuality in musical scholarship* (London and Los Angeles, University of California Press).

Stock, J. (1994) Concepts of World Music and their Integration within Secondary Music Education, *International Journal of Music Education*, 23, pp. 3–16.

Walker, R. (1996) Music Praxis Freed from Colonialism: A new praxis, *International Society for Music Education*, 2:2, pp. 2–15.

Wertheim, C. & Wertheim, M. (2003) Book Reviews, in: *Signs: Journal of women in culture and society*, 28:3 (Spring), pp. 975–978.

Wolmark, J. (1999) *Cybersexualities: A reader on feminist theory, cyborgs and cyberspace* (Edinburgh, Edinburgh University Press).

Whitley, S. (2000) *Women and Popular Music: Sexuality identity and subjectivity* (London and New York, Routledge).

Zuidervaart, L. (1991) *Adorno's Aesthetic Theory* (Cambridge, MIT Press).

[illegible] B. (2002) [illegible] Santa [illegible] Press.

Marshall, [illegible] (2000) Technology, Standards and Indigenous Peoples [illegible] *Language [illegible]* [illegible] 253–[illegible].

Ministry of Education (1998) [illegible] Wellington: Learning Media.

Ministry of Education (2007) *The New Zealand Curriculum*. Wellington: Learning Media.

[illegible] Wellington: Learning Media.

Mitchell, W. [illegible] University of Chicago [illegible]

[illegible] Cambridge [illegible]

[illegible] Press.

Olsen, M. [illegible] (2003) [illegible] [illegible] Dunedin [illegible] *Pacific Journal* [illegible]

[illegible] *Culture Review* [illegible]

[illegible] New Zealand [illegible]

[illegible] Press.

[illegible] *North* [illegible] Press.

[illegible] (1998) [illegible] *Transactions* [illegible]

Sanders, [illegible] (1994) [illegible] New Zealand [illegible]

[illegible]

[illegible] (2005) [illegible]

[illegible] University of California [illegible]

[illegible] *World* [illegible] Cambridge [illegible]

[illegible]

Walker, [illegible] *Journal of Visual Culture* [illegible] New Zealand [illegible]

[illegible] Edinburgh University Press.

[illegible] (2000) [illegible] New York: Routledge.

[illegible]

Index